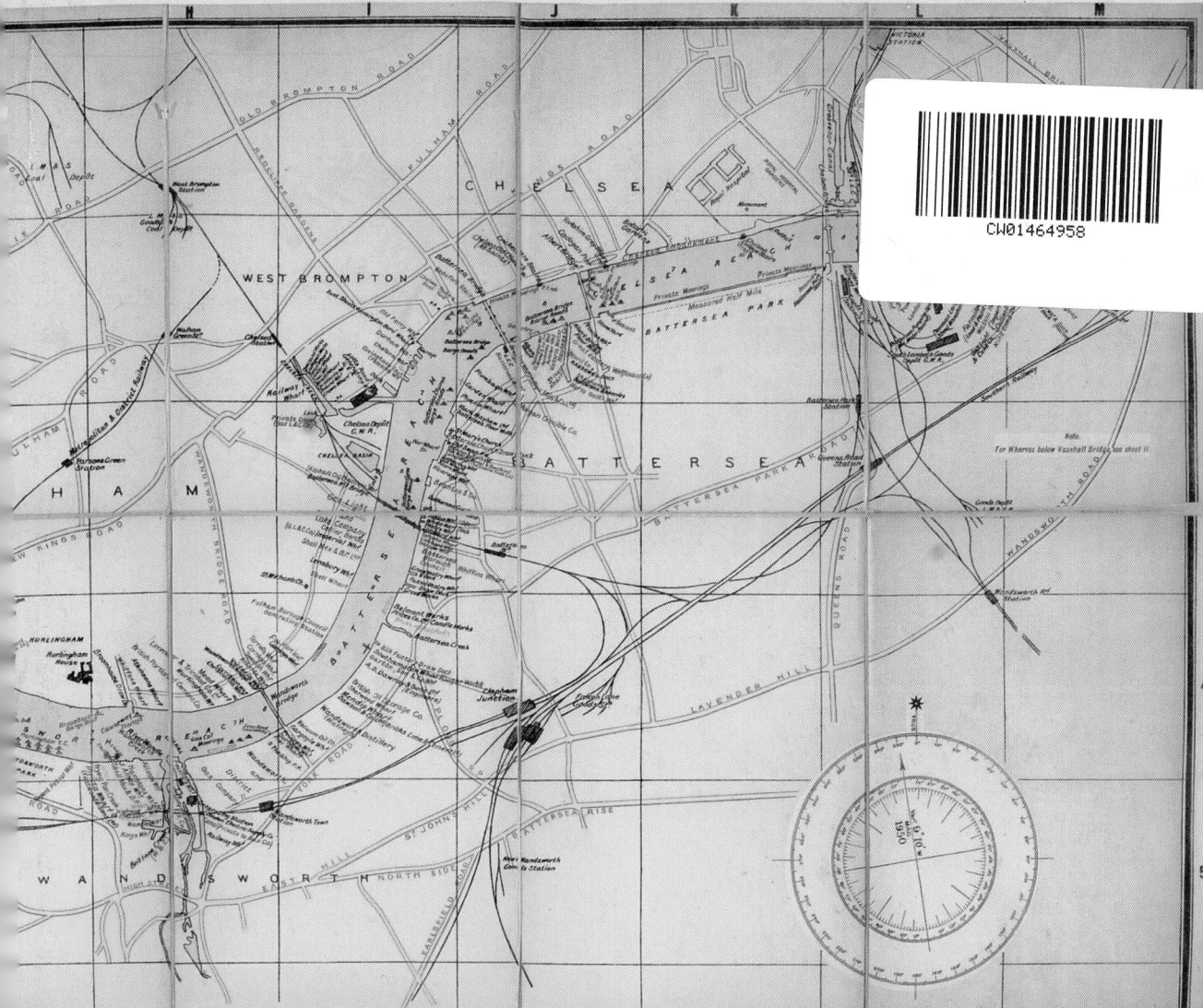

SHEET I.

MES WHARF CHART
ERS, MOORINGS, ETC.
ALL BRIDGE & TEDDINGTON LOCK.

PUBLISHED BY

AURIE, NORIE & WILSON, LTD

5, HACKNEY ROAD, LONDON, E. 2.

Soundings in Feet.

Sheet 2.   Vauxhall to Barking.
Sheet 3.   Barking to Hole Haven.

One Statute Mile

| | 1 | 2 | 3 | 4 | 1 Mile |

Note. For Wharves below Vauxhall Bridge, see sheet II.

NOTES ON RIVER BYE-LAWS.

Steam launches under way at night exhibit white light 4 feet above hull visible from right ahead to 2 points abaft each beam. A red light on port side and a green light on starboard side visible from right ahead to 2 points abaft respective beam. These lights to be visible for at least one mile.

Vessels aground in fairway off any draw dock above Richmond Lock shall at night exhibit a white light visible all round horizon for 1 mile.

All vessels used to mark obstructions or wrecks shall exhibit where best may be seen by day a green flag and two green balls or shapes placed horizontally 6 to 12 feet apart; by night, two green lamps in same place as balls or shapes. Vessels engaged in under-water work may also exhibit these signals.

Speed to be moderate during fog, mist, snow.

Steam vessel to keep clear of sailing vessel.

Steam vessel navigating river should keep to that side of mid-channel which lies on her starboard hand.

Steam vessel crossing river to give way to up or down river traffic.

Steam vessels plying as ferries keep clear of up or down traffic.

Steam vessel navigating against tide when approaching points in river wait before vessel navigating with tide is round.

Overtaking vessel always keep clear of overtaken vessel.

When one vessel is directed by Bye-laws to keep out of way of another, the other should keep her course and speed.

When a vessel is directed by Bye-laws to keep out of way of another, she must go slow, stop or astern if necessary.

Proper look-out always to be kept.   Master is responsible.

Navigable part of channel above Richmond Lock shall always be kept clear for traffic.   No vessel may stop so as to impede the traffic.   No ryepack or punt pole may be left fixed in any part of the river.

Master of every vessel sunk must inform Harbour Master and give notice of her position.

Master of every vessel which has lost her anchor must give notice thereof and position to Harbour Master.

No anchor in use as mooring to be outside line of mooring.

Every vessel navigating or lying in river shall carry her anchor in position which is not dangerous to any other vessel.

Engines of steam vessel moored to buoy, post, dolphin, jetty or other place must not be worked so as to damage that which she is moored to. (This applies to foreshore, as well.)

Master of every steam vessel navigating river must be on bridge or paddle box when under way in river.   No one but crew or pilot are allowed on bridge.

No cargo, rubbish, etc., must be allowed to fall in the river.

Vessels to obtain permission before mooring to piers.

All vessels must be navigated singly except those towed by steam vessels.

No tow of vessels being towed above London Bridge shall exceed 400 feet.

Vessels towed by steam vessels navigating river above Chelsea Bridge may be placed in a single line, but shall not be more than 2 abreast (except vessels not exceeding 14' 9" in width, which may be placed 3 abreast), not more than to such, vessels may be towed at same time, nor distance between any two vessels towed not to exceed 50'.

Vessels must be navigated with minimum of wash.   During periods of exceptional high tides, when the danger of damage being caused to riverside premises, 2 Green lights or 2 Green Flags will be shown at (1) Cadogan Pier (2) Putney Pier (3) Kew Harbour Office. (4) Richmond Lock.

No vessel moored to, or placed in front of, towing path so as to cause obstruction to navigation or use of towing path.

Vessels navigating through Bridges against tide should give way to those navigating with the tide.

Harbour Master and his officers to be obeyed and not obstructed.

Houseboats and launches to remain in positions as defined by the Port Authority.

No person to use obscene language or be intoxicated.

No material to be removed from river banks, weirs or towing paths.

No vessel to enter Richmond Lock unless there is sufficient water to float her and carry her through.

No vessel to enter Richmond Lock with sail up.

Every vessel entering Richmond Lock shall immediately pass ropes or chains ashore for making her fast.

Persons to refrain from damaging banks, etc., with poles and boat-hooks.

No person to touch the gear at Richmond Lock and Weir.

Vessels at regattas and other public occasions to observe the directions of the Officer of the Port Authority.

Steam vessel includes every vessel propelled by machinery.

Attention is drawn to Bye-laws concerning explosives and petroleum, and also the "O.C. in Navigable Waters Act," 1922, in which regulations concerning the transfer of oil to and from a vessel, and the escape of oil from any vessel or any place on shore are plainly described.

DEPTH OF WATER & HEADWAY AT VARIOUS BRIDGES (Centre Arch).

	DEPTH		Width of Centre Arch	L.W. Springs HEADWAY (Centre Arch)		DEPTH
	25' 5"		149' 7"		39' 7"	5' 2"
	26' 3"		174' 0"		39' 9"	6' 5"
	26' 2"		332' 5"		39' 10"	6' 5"
	25' 5"		384' 0"		37' 2"	5' 11"
	25' 4"		163' 0"		37' 6"	6' 0"
	24' 5"		137' 3"		39' 3"	5' 4"
	24' 0"		124' 0"		36' 6"	5' 2"
	21' 10"		144' 0"		38' 7"	3' 5"
	21' 4"		144' 0"		36' 0"	3' 0"
	26' 0"		400' 0"		30' 6"	2' 10"
	21' 8"		120' 0"		34' 6"	4' 9"
	20' 10"		150'		36' 0"	5' 0"
	21' 1"		102' 0"		33' 11"	4' 11"
	20' 10"		133' 0"		33' 4"	4' 11"
	18' 0"		66' 0"			
	8' 6"		99' 6"			
	8' 0"		103' 0"			
	6' 0"		60' 0"			

UNTO THE
TIDEWAY BORN

Christopher Dodd

Published by The Company of Watermen and Lightermen
© Company of Watermen and Lightermen 2015
Text © Christopher Dodd
ISBN: 978-0-9559501-2-4

AUTHOR'S NOTE

Unto the Tideway Born would not have reached the maternity ward without the enormous contribution made by freemen of the Company of Watermen and Lightermen of the River Thames.

The book is designed to supplement the copious volumes about London's great river and to compliment the year-by-year history of five centuries of struggle and achievement already published by the Company by giving voice to the people who work the river. It is dedicated to those who have lived by tides, quays and docks, to those who have handled oars, ropes and cargoes in wherries, barges, tugs and passenger steamers. And to those who still do.

To this end, masters of the Company in office and members of its library and heritage committee under the chairmanship of both Dr Iain Reid and Richard Springford made valuable contributions to shaping the book during its gestation.

Among those who must be singled out are Julian Ebsworth who found incredible images from inside and outside the Watermen's Hall's collection. Professor Alan Lee Williams, John Allen and Richard Goddard set me straight on content and Chris Martin did sterling copy editing. Colin Middlemiss, the Clerk, and Susan Fenwick, the Administrator, cheerfully plundered the archives and kept everything on course.

The following offered advice and expertise on all matters Tideway and Doggett's, with apologies to those whom I have inadvertently left out:

John Barrett, Duncan Clegg, Bob Crouch, Kenny Dwan, Tony Farnham, Simon Goodey, David Gordon, Martin Hackett, Andrew Howard, Tim Keech, Simon McCarthy, Paul Mainds, Scott Neicho, Chas Newens, John Potter, Bobby Prentice Sr., Bobby Prentice Jr., Carol Ratcliffe, John Redmond, Jeremy Randall, Brian Richardson, Richard G. Turk, George Saunders, Tony Smith, Christopher Sprague and Sandra Watts.

I would also like to thank the curators at the River & Rowing Museum – Eloise Chapman, Suzie Tilbury and Aaron Jaffer – for their assistance.

SOURCES

The main sources for *Unto the Tideway Born* are five volumes on the origin and development of the Company from 1514 to 1920 by Henry Humpherus and Jon Temple. Arthur Herman's history of the British navy, To Rule the Waves, was immensely helpful. The origin and story of Doggett's Coat and Badge is to be found in Theodore Cook and Guy Nickalls's Thomas Doggett Deceased, and Robert Cottrell's Thomas Doggett Coat & Badge. Main sources on docklands and the port are Chris Ellmers and Alex Werner's Dockland Life and Nigel Watson's history of the PLA, A Century of Service. For an overall view of the glamour of the Thames and its place in history, try David Starkey and Susan Doran's Royal River and Simon Schama's Landscape and Memory.

These and many more books are listed in the bibliography.

Christopher Dodd, River & Rowing Museum, March 2015

Book design by Steve Hayes
Printed and bound by Lamport Gilbert Ltd, Reading, Berkshire RG2 0TB

Cover: The South East Prospect of Westminster Bridge 1759 (Watermen's Hall Collection)

CONTENTS

PART 1
WATERMEN'S WORLD

1

ALL THE TIDEWAY'S
A STAGE

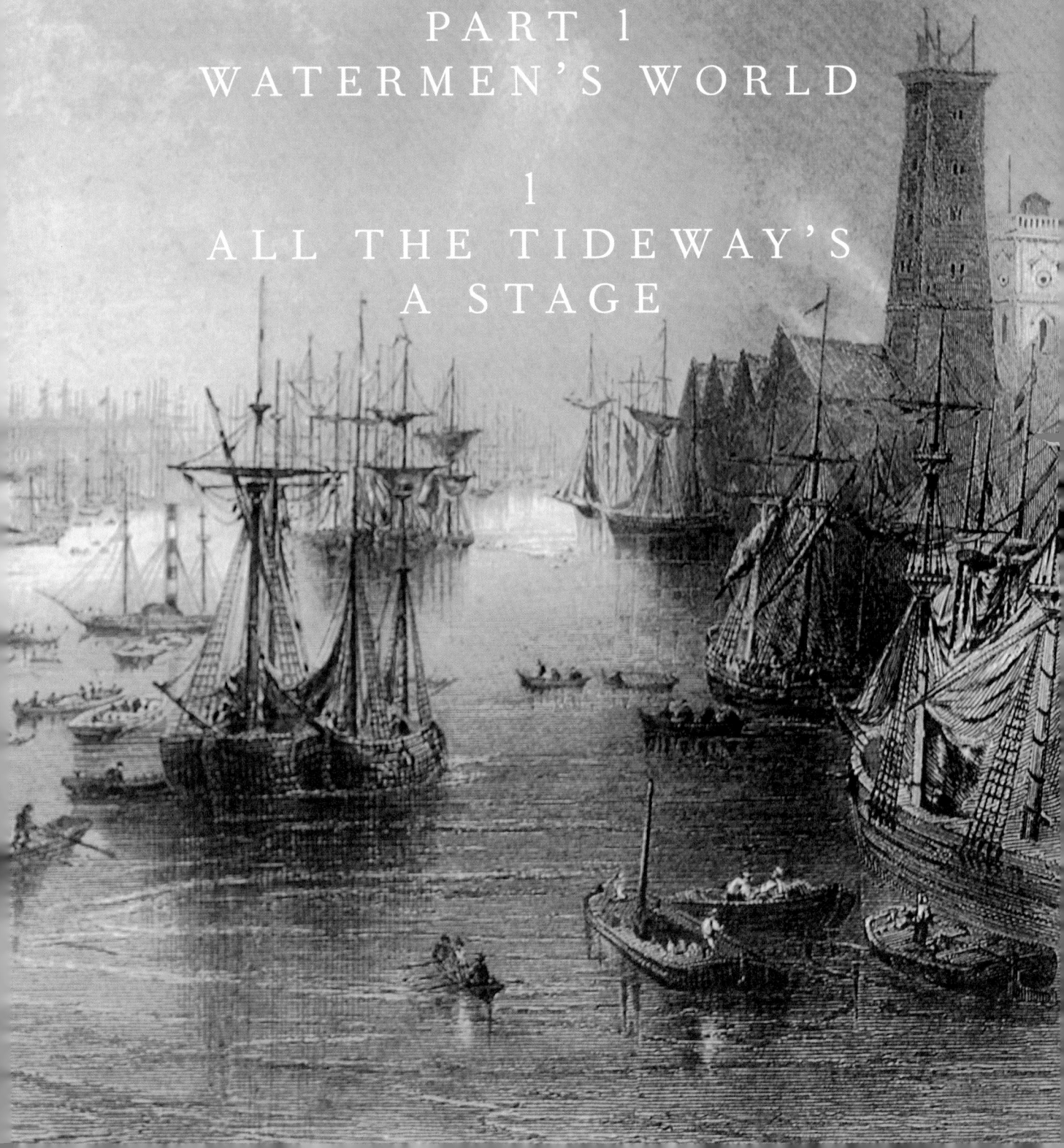

The watermen's story begins at the Nore, in time immemorial. The entrance to the Thames is a broad inlet from the North Sea, its horizon stretching from North Foreland in Kent to the coast of Essex, or even Suffolk at Orfordness. It contracts but slowly to the shape of the river that woos the mariner to a hidden city — a city that began forging its personality in Roman times.

Joseph Conrad, writing as the nineteenth century turned to the twentieth, imagines the mystery that a commander of a Roman galley would feel as he directed his prow westward around the brow of the Nore. Imagine it he might, because as far as we know the Romans did not approach this sceptred isle by this route. But traders and adventurers over the centuries have surely experienced what Conrad's Roman did not on entering the Thamesis. The estuary is without noble features, grandeur of aspect or smiling geniality. But it is spacious, inviting and hospitable. An air of mysteriousness lingers about it. On a summer's day, anyway. Romance and mystery derive from the absence of sight or sound of human labour until the navigator has slipped through twenty-five miles of sands and spits, inlets and tributaries, channels and swirling currents between mudbank and marsh.

In Conrad's own day the Nore is marked by a red lightship, the channels are buoyed, the shores are embanked, the ships are docked, and the wilderness of the estuary is less extensive than the past of his imagination. In our day ships are larger but fewer, marinas replace the quays of commerce, and the detritus of wars and shifting patterns of trade and industry leave their marks on the still welcoming mouth of the Thames – the spooky stork-like Maunsell forts from the Second World War, the rotting superstructure of the doomed liberty ship *Richard Montgomery*, still with 1500 tons of explosive in her hold. But Conrad's feeling for the estuary and its expectant course to what was then the world's greatest port and what remains a city of Olympic proportions is valid today.

Our story is of the men who work the tidal river. Our starting point is the sixteenth century, on a high tide at sunset when the sailor coming in from the sea rounds a bend to arrive before an imposing red-brick palace fronting onto the river on the southern shore, set below green parkland rising to a fringe of trees. Wherries and barges weave passages around the royal steps and the creek beyond. Greenwich Palace serves as a great gate house to a twisting Grand Canal of hustle and bustle like nowhere else on earth. Soon we pass the hulk factory of Henry VIII's naval dockyard at Deptford, in full flow. Along this artery the chronology of the city and the watermen who man it is buffeted by cross currents of history on the tide's ebb and flow.

The story of London, Westminster and Southwark is a struggle of stakeholders on a god-given tideway. Royal households centred on the palace at Westminster were prominent among these in Tudor and Stuart times. Royal families maintained separate households and moved between each other's houses by horse, cart and litter. But chief among conveyances was the barge, for the Thames is the lubricant of the royal fiefdom, linking Greenwich to Hampton Court via the Tower — five-star guest house for monarchs and their guests, but dungeon of doom for unfortunates admitted through the Traitors' Gate — Whitehall, Westminster, Kew, Richmond and beyond Hampton

Previous page: The Port of London 1842 (Reginald Francis Print Collection)

to Windsor. On the way, too, are grand edifices erected by bishops and nobility, such as Somerset House and the piles fronting the river along the Strand that links London, the centre of wealth, with Westminster, the centre of power.

The main obstacle to royal progress up or downstream is London Bridge, the only crossing point before Kingston-upon-Thames, 25 miles upstream towards Hampton Court and first referred to as a crossing point in the twelfth or thirteenth century. London Bridge links London with Southwark and the road to the Cinque Ports and the south coast. Horseback or Shanks's pony were the only means of getting around on bad and often dangerous roads. Conveying people and goods on the river was not only essential, but increased in importance as trade, shipping, naval activity and population grew. Hundreds, thousands, of small boats plied the tidal river on a daily basis, unregulated.

The bridge's narrow arches define the turning point for sizeable ships. Thus the centre of waterborne trade is below the bridge in what became known as the Pool of London, where roads of moored vessels disgorge or heave aboard wares from four corners of the kingdom and beyond. Barges fuss around them to lighten their loads beneath a forest of masts and spars. Wherries are everywhere, ship-to-shoring mariners and ferrying people up, down and across the Thames. The royal highway hereabouts is where the mayor and aldermen of the City of London hold sway. Behind the quays and warehouses piled with barrels and sacks, alleys lead to crowded streets of stalls and taverns, of factories and shops, of shippers and brokers, of bear pits and theatres. Those who use the river are keen to control it, while those who work it regard it as their own.

Our sailor's ship has reached the end of its voyage. He collects his pay and takes a wherry to Billingsgate below the bridge or Three Cranes stairs above it and makes for the Old Swan to drink ale and find his feet. Once done, his search by foot or wherry for bed, board, bawd and bard enables him to glimpse other parts of the canvas. On the north shore London never rests, whether below the bridge by the Pool or upstream toward the religious houses and the exit of the Fleet to the Thames at Blackfriars. On the opposite side, Southwark harbours whores, sleaze and satire behind shoreline. Upstream, fields fringe the water's edge on the southern bank at Lambeth, while on the north shore Somerset House and the palaces of Whitehall and Westminster step down from gardens and terraces to their landing stairs. They turn their backs to the land, their fronts to the river. The river is the main, massive thoroughfare. It is London's Grand Canal, and wherries are its gondolas.

Like Venice's Grand Canal, the river is more than a highway. The rivalry between royal progressions and mayoral processions turns it into a theatre of the spectacular. Monarchs' flamboyances are countered by the puffing chests of the city's livery companies, rowed about on ever grander and larger gilded barges. Cardinals and chancellors, merchants and aldermen pay calls by barge, powered by their own retained liveried watermen. The arrival of a new queen or the occasion of a coronation is turned into theatrical extravaganza that brings fame and profit to the dramatists of Tudor England. At the drop of a bag of coin they lay on enormous pageants — sea battles against infidels, firework displays to light up the town, floating street theatre to stun the populace.

All this requires manning the oars, shifting the scenery, building the floats, setting the stage and gilding the lily. The entertainment business created work for men in boats just as did manning rich men's barges, over and above the regular business of servicing ships at anchor and ferrying the population upstream and down. And being pressed, usually against one's will, into the navy.

So our sailor is swallowed up into the midst of the practice addressed by Henry VIII in his statute of 1514: 'It had been a laudable custome and usage tyme out of mind to use the river in barge or whery bote'. The king has heard the prevailing low opinion of watermen and their practices and clearly thinks it is time to bring order to fares and follies practised between Greenwich and Richmond. There was sufficient concern for Parliament to pass an Act governing fares for passengers and their fardells—little bundles of carry-on hand luggage — between tidal Thames and Medway. The Act, the first attempt to

1514 Act of Parliament

The fixing of the Rates or Fares of Watermen by Antient Act of Parliament is in yᵉ Power of the Lord Mayor and Court of Aldermen by whom they were last set forth September 7, 1671, and are as follows :—

	Oars. s. d.	Sculls. s. d.
Over the water directly	o 4	o 2
From London Bridge to Westminster Stairs or from any one of the Stairs to another between the Bridge and Westminster Stairs	o 6	o 3
From any of yᵉ Stairs above Bridge and below Pauls Wharf to Lambeth and Vaux Hall	I o	o 6
From Pauls Wharf, Black Fryers, Dorset or Temple Stairs, etc. to Lambeth and Vaux Hall	o 8	o 4
From White Hall to Lambeth or Vaux Hall	o 6	o 3

Note yᵉ Fares are yᵉ same on either side yᵉ river.

1671 Fare Table (from Thomas Doggett Deceased)

regulate watermen, wherrymen and bargemen, attempted to deal fairness to intrepid passengers, but failed to put in place any method of enforcing its pieties.

Enforcement was achieved by King Philip of Spain and Queen Mary forty-one years later. Their statute 'touching Watermen and Bargemen upon the River Thames' in 1555 sets about the watermen in no uncertain terms. 'There have divers and many misfortunes and mischances happened… to a great number of the King and Queen's subjects, as well as to nobility…'

Passengers have encountered rude, ignorant and unskilled watermen, boys of small age and little skill who 'do for the most part of their time use dicing and carding, and other unlawful games, to the great and evil example of such like, and against the commonwealth of this realm.' Even when these evil and ignorant persons have been pressed into service with the navy they 'convey themselves into the country, and other secret places' upon discharge and practise their robberies and felonies as before. 'Oftimes the said evil persons do repair again to their former trade of rowing' even though they may lack the time to obtain sufficient knowledge of their occupation. They receive their majesties' loving subjects aboard their boats and convey them from place to place 'whereby divers have been robbed and spoiled of their goods, and also drowned.' It is lamentable, say the monarchs, that people be daily put in fear of their lives.

The preamble identifies a further problem: 'the most part of the wherries and boats… being made so little and small in portion, and so straight and narrow in the bottom… so shallow and tickle, that thereby great peril and danger of drowning hath many times ensued, and daily is like to ensue, unless some speedy remedy be herein had and provided.'

Was this simply a question of poor boat building, a desire for cheaper boats, or a quest for lighter and speedier craft to get the passenger to his destination quicker and satisfy the racing challenges that are bound to arise on the river?

To deal with the evils outlined, the King and Queen's majesties, the Lords spiritual and temporal and the Commons in Parliament assembled enacted that eight persons 'most wise, discreet, and the best sort of watermen, being householders, and occupying as watermen upon the said river, between Gravesend and Windsor' be appointed to oversee watermen and their activities.

This enactment is, in effect, the birth of the Company. The overseers, or 'rulers', were to be appointed initially by the mayor and court of aldermen of London. Their powers were spelt out: after the said first day of March 1555 they would maintain good order and obedience amongst wherrymen and watermen upon the Thames betwixt Gravesend and Windsor 'according to the meaning of the Act'.

The Act also gives birth to apprenticeship. In a two-man boat at least one waterman must have exercised rowing on the Thames for at least two years. A qualified man must have the evidence in writing from the rulers or run the risk of up to a month in the clink. Further, from the feast of Pentecost next spring, no single man, 'not keeping a household and not retained, shall use or exercise to row between Gravesend and Windsor… unless he be *prentice* or in service retained with a master, by a whole year at least.' The Lord Mayor and the JPs of adjoining counties were empowered to prosecute offenders referred by the rulers.

Boat construction is now regulated. Any wherry or boat for carrying people that is not at least 22ft in length and 4ft 6in broad at midships or that is too insubstantial to 'carry two persons on one side tight' or 'carried insufficient quantity, scantling or thickness of board as heretofore used shall be forfeited', the proceeds going half to the Queen and half to the royal courts to be set aside against claims.

The Act spells out two weeks' gaol and a year and a day's rowing ban for any waterman who 'willingly, voluntarily and obstinately withdraw, hide, convey him or themselves into secret places and out corners' when the navy's press gangs were in action.

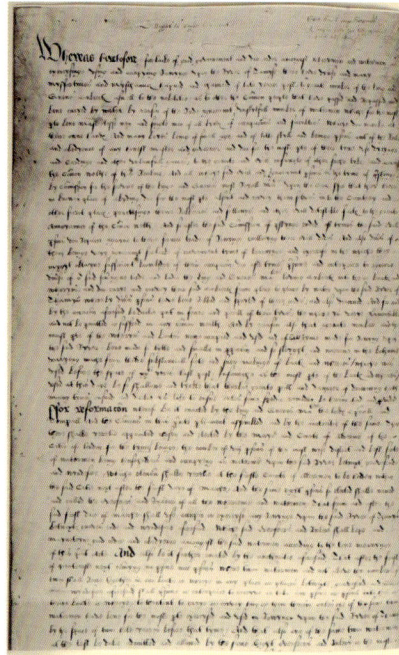

1555 Act of Parliament

In pursuance of the above, the rulers are charged with creating a register of qualified watermen and of inspecting new boats before they are launched.

The Lord Mayor and aldermen are given discretionary powers to limit, set and assess the price of fares paid to authorised watermen between Gravesend and Windsor, with heavy fines for over-chargers. The table of fares must be displayed at the Guildhall, Westminster Hall 'and elsewhere'. It is another four years before the fare structure comes into use.

Western barges — the vessels that conveyed goods inland along the Thames valley to Henley and Oxford — are required to take single persons on a retainer of at least one year.

Thus began the rule of the rulers of the Company of Watermen of the River Thames. Four years after the Act, the fare tables were duly published. Complaints against the rulers and offences committed were under jurisdiction of the Lord Mayor and aldermen of the City of London and the justices of the peace of the shires bordering the river, with powers to fine rulers found negligent. It did not take long for the condemnation of watermen's moral code and dastardly habits to mellow, because in 1558 the Commons resolved 'that the watermen of the Thamyse shall have moryers, hakbutts and shot', though in defence of what is not clear.

Perhaps it was to safeguard nobility in passage and pageantry. For if all the Tideway's a stage, then watermen are its ushers, stagehands and technicians, mixing skill with hard labour at the oars, their eyes and ears skimmed close to the surface.

View of Greenwich and the Thames looking upstream 1795 (Reginald Francis Print Collection)

View of London from Greenwich Park 1799 (Reginald Francis Print Collection)

IAMES,

Of that Name THE FIRST,

And I. Monarch of the whole Iland of GREAT BRITAINE, &c.

WEre all the flatt'ry of the world in me,
Great King of hearts & Arts, great Britaines
Yet all that flattery could not flatter thee: (King
Or adde to thy renowne the smallest thing,
My Muse (with truth and freedome) dares to sing,
Thou wert a Monarch lou'd of God and Men.
Tw' famous Kingdomes thou to one didst bring,
And gau'it lost Britaines name her name agen.
Thou causedst Doctors with their learned pen,
The sacred Bible newly to translate.
Thy wisdome found the damned powder'd Den,
That hell had hatcht, to overthrow thy state.
And all the world thy Motto must allow,
The peace-makers are blest; and so art thou.

Anno Dom. 1602, March 24, Thursday.

Iames the first of that name, King of England, Scotland, France & Ireland (the first King that was crowned to England since the Norman Conquest) at the age of 36 yeeres, 9 moneths, and 5 daies, hee was crowned at Westminster (with his wife Queene Anne) by the hands of Iohn Whitgift, Archbishop of Canterbury. There was a conspiracy to surprise the King and enforce him to grant a tolleration of Religion, but the plot was discovered, and the offenders were some executed, & some others (by the Kings Clemency) banished, and imprisoned, with good competency of meanes allowed them. This King was a King of Peace, and withall victorious; for he had more then his predecessor King Henry the 7th, (who vnited the houses of Lancaster and Yorke.) But King Iames (most happy) vnited kingdomes, vniting England and Scotland into one glorious Monarchy, by the name and stile of Great Britaine. Anno 1605, November 5, the powder-plot perdition was; but by the mercy of the Almighty (and a token deliuerance of a Letter, and the deepe wisedome of the King,) the horrid Treason was discouered, preuented, and the Traitours confounded in their owne wicked deuice. King Iames was so renowned, that Germany, Poland, Sweaueland, Russia, France, Spaine, Holland, Zeaeland, the Arch-Duke of Austria, the estate or Seigniory of Venice: The great Duke of Florence, all these Princes and Potentates did send their Ambassadors into England, to hold Amity and Leauge with King Iames. Amongst Kings he was the adorned mirrour of Learning, the Patterne and Patrone of all pietie, such a sweet and well composed mixture of Iustice and mercy was innated in his Royall brest: that mercy and truth did meet, kisse and combine together, all the time of his most auspicious reigne: like a second Sallomon in his gouernment was blest with peace and plenty, so that he might iustly be stiled, (vnder God) The Peace-maker of Christendome, and the louing father and preseruer of his owne people, Realmes and Dominions: his life was generally beloued, and his death as much lamented, which was the 27 of March, being Sunday, there being but 2 daies difference to be obserued betwixt the accompt of the beginning and ending of his reigne; for he began the 24 of March 1602, and ended the 27 of March 1625. Two Tuesdaies were fortunate to him, for on a Tuesday the 5 of August 1602, he escaped a dangerous conspiracy of the Earle Gowrie, and on Tuesday the 5 of Nouember, 1605, he (with all that could be called his) was preserued from that Grandmaster piece of Satan, the Powder Treason, and as on Saturday the 8 of May, 1603, he was receiued with ioy into London, so on Saturday the 8 of May 1625, he was with griefe buried at Westminster.

CHARLES,

Of that Name The First,

And II. *Monarch* of the whole Iland
of GREAT BRITAINE.

KING of ENGLAND, SCOTLAND,
FRANCE and IRELAND, Gods immediate VICEGERENT, Su-
preame HEAD, &c.

Illustrious Off-spring of most glorious Stems,
Our happy hope, our Royall CHARLES the great,
Successiue Heyre to foure Rich Diadems,
With gifts of Grace, and Learning high repleat.
For thee th'Almighties ayd I doe intreat,
To guide and prosper thy proceedings still,
That long thou maist suruiue a Prince compleat,
To guard the good, and to subuert the ill.
And when (by Gods determin'd boundlesse will)
Thy mortall part shall made immortall be,
Then let thy liuing Fame the world full fill,
In blessed famous memory of thee,
    And all true *Britaines* pray to God aboue,
    To match thy life and fortune with their loue.

STEWARTE
CHARLES   MARIE

Anagramma.

Christ Arme vs Euer AT AL,

Though feinds and men, to hurt vs should endeaur,
(Against their force) AT AL, CHRIST ARME VS
                                    (EVER.

Anno. Dom. 1625. March 27. Sunday.

The vniuersall Soueraigne, Swayer of Kings and
kingdomes, hauing (in mercy) taken our Peacefull
Iames (from this vale of strife) to his peace euer-
lasting, our Royall CHARLES is the vndoubted heire of
his blessed Fathers Crowne and vertues, was crown'd
...by the hands of the Right Reue-
rend father in God, Iohn Williams, the now present Lord Bishop of Lincolne and Deane of Westminster. He is Charles (the first of that name) and
second Monarch of great Britaine, he is Gods Immediate Vicegerent, and God is his Immediate Soueraigne, he is Defender of the True, Ancient, Apo-
stolicall and Christian Faith; and that faith is his
shield against all his bodily and ghostly enemies: in
the first yeere of his reigne, he married with the Illustrious and vertuous Princesse Henrietta Maria, daughter to that admyred Mirrour and Mars of
martiallists Henry the 4th the French King (last
of that name) vpon the 22 day of Iune 1625, shee
safely arriued at Douer in Kent, where the King
stay'd till her comming, and to both their ioyes, and the
ioy of this kingdome he enioyed, and enioyes her. This
Noble Prince was borne the 19th of Nouember,
Ao 1600. he was second and youngest Sonne to King
Iames the 6 of Scotland, and first of that name of
England. (Our last dread Soueraigne) In the yeere
1623, he went into Spaine priuately, and (by Gods
gracious assistance) came backe safely from thence
the 26 of October, in the same yeere, whose safe re-
turne, all true hearted Britaines did and doe esteeme
a most infinite and happy blessing: his clemency, pie-
ty, pitty is manifest, his Royall and Princely en-
dowments are ample, his fame and Magnificence is
ouer all; The graces and cardinall vertues haue
taken vp their habitations in his Heroick and Mag-
nanimous brest. Long may hee with his gracious
Queene reigne ouer these his Dominions, to the glo-

John Taylor, waterman and Water Poet, published an Apologie for Watermen in a work entitled The Nipping or Snipping of Abuses in about 1614. It is dedicated to the masters and assistants of the Company of Watermen. It begins "And this I know, and therefore doth maintaine…"

Such imputations, and such daily wrongs

Are laid on watermen – by envious tong's;

To clear the which, if I should silent be,

'Twere basenesse and stupidity in me.

Nor doe I purpose now with inke and pen,

To write of them, as they are watermen;

But this I speake, defending their vocation

From slander's false and idle imputation.

Yet should I onely of the men but speake,

I could the top of envies coxcombe breake;

For I would have all men to understand

A waterman's a man, by sea or land;

And on the land and sea can service do

To serve his King, as well as other too.

He'll guard his country, both on seas and shore,

An what (a God's name) can a man do more?

Like double men, they well can play indeed

The soldiers and the saylors, for a need,

If they did yeerely use to scoure the maine,

As erst they did, in wars 'twixt us and Spaine,

I then to speak would boldly seeme to dare,

Previous page: Pages from the complete works of John Taylor

One sailer with two soldiers should compare.

But now sweet peace their skill at sea so duls,

That many are more fit to use their sculs

Then for the sea, for why? The want of use

Is art's confusion, and best skil's abuse.

And not to be too partiall in my words,

I think no company more knaves affords;

And this must be the reason, because farre

Above all companies their numbers are;

And where the multitude of men most is,

By consequence there must be most amisse,

And sure of honest men it hath as many

As any other company hath any.

Though not of wealth they have superfluous store,

Content's a kingdome, and they seek no more,

Of mercers, grocers, drapers, men shall finde

Men that to loose behaviour are inclinde;

Of goldsmiths, silkmen, clothworkers, and skinners,

When they are at the best, they all are sinners,

And drunken rascalls are of every trade,

should I name all, I o'er the bootes should wade;

If watermen be only knaves alone,

Let all that's faultless cast at them a stone.

Some may reply to my apologie,

How they in plying are unmannerly;

And one from tother hale, and pull, and teare,

And raile, and brawle, and curse, and ban, and swear;

In this I'l not defend them with excuses,

I alwaies did and doe hate those abuses.

The honest use of this true trade I sing,

And not th'abuses that from thence do spring.

And sure no company had laws more strict

Than watermen, which weekely they inflict

Upon offenders, who are made pay duely,

Then fined, or prison'd, 'cause they plide unruly.

They keepe no shops, nor sell deceitfull wares,

But like to pilgrims, travell for their fares;

And they must aske the question where they go,

If men will goe by water, yea or no?

Which being spoke aright, the fault's not such

But any tradesman (sure) will doe as much.

The mercer, as you passe along the way,

Will aske you what d'e lack? Come neer I pray.

The draper, whose warme ware doth clad the back,

Will be so bold as aske ye what d'e lack?

The goldsmith, with his silver and his gold,

To aske ye what d'e lack? He will be bold.

This being granted, as none can deny,

Most trades, as well as watermen, doe ply;

If in their plying they do chance to jarre,

They doe but like the lawyers at the barre,

Who plead as if they meant by th'ears to fall,

And when the court doth rise, to friendship fall.

So watermen, that for a fare contends,

The fare once gone, the watermen are friends.

And this I know, and therefore doth maintaine,

That he that truly labours and takes paine,

May with a better conscience sleepe in bed,

Then he that is with ill-got thousands sped.

So well I like it, and such love I owe,

Unto it, that I'll fall again to rowe;

'Twill keepe my health from falling to decay,

get money, and chase idlenesse away.

I'm sure it for antiquity hath stood,

Since the world's drowning universall flood,

And howsoever now it rise or fall,

The boate in Noah's deluge carried all.

And though our wits be like our purses, bare,

With any company we'll make compare

To write a verse, provided that they be

No better skil'd in scholership than wee,

And then come one, come thousands, nay, come all,

And for a wager we'll to versing fall.

20

TO THE NOBILITY, GEN
AND COMMVNALTY, WHO
INHABITANTS, OR WEL-WILLERS T
THE WELFARE OF THE CITIE OF Salisbv
ry, AND COVNTY OF Wiltshire.

Right Honourable,

WOrshipfull, *and louing Country-men, I ha
my Booke and Voyage, The VVorst, o
which I euer vndertooke & finished, and it
pleasures, to make it which you please ; 7
toyle, trauaile, and danger, as yet I neuer h
or a more difficult passage, which the en
course will truly testifie ; yet all those perils past, I shall acco
sures, if my infallible Reasons may moue or perswade you to
Riuer, and make it Nauigable from the Sea to your Citie ;
part touched what the profit and Commodities of it will be vnto
haue briefly shewed the Inconueniences which you haue throug
of it : I haue also declared, that the maine intent or scope of m
vnto you with a VVherry, was, to see what lets or Impedimen
hinderances vnto so good and beneficiall a worke. All wh
(according to my simple Suruey, and weake Capacity) set dow
with the merrinesse of my most Hazardous Sea-progresse, I b
dicate to your Noble, Worshipfull, and worthy Acceptance
knowledging my selfe and my Labour in your seruices to be
in all dutie,*

IOHN TAYL

A DISCOVERY BY SEA,
FROM London TO
SALISBVRY.

AS our accounts in Almanacks agree,
The yeere cal'd sixteene hundred twenty three:
That Iulyes twenty eight, two houres past dinner,
We with our *Wherry*, and fiue men within her,
Along the christall Thames did cut and curry,
Betwixt the Counties, Middlesex and Surry:
Whilst thousãds gaz'd, we past the bridge with wõ-
Where fooles & wise men goe aboue & vnder.(der,
We thus our Voyage brauely did begin
Downe by S. *Katherines*, where the Priest fell in,
By *Wapping*, where as hang'd drownd *Pirats* dye;
('Or else such * *Rats*, I thinke as would eate *Pie*.)
And passing further, I at first obseru'd,
That * *Cuckolds-Hauen* was but badly seru'd:
For there old *Time* had such confusion wrought,
That of that Ancient place remained nought.
No monumentall memorable Horne,
Or Tree, or Post, which hath those Trophees borne,
Was left, whereby Posterity may know
Where their forefathers Crests did grow, or show.
Which put into a maze my muzing Muse,
Both at the worlds neglect, and times abuse,
That that stout Pillar, to Obliuions pit
should fall, whereon *Plus vltra* might be writ,
That such a marke of Reuerend note should lye
Forgot, and hid, in blacke obscurity:
Especially when men of euery sort
Of countries, Cities, warlike Campes or Court,
Vnto that *Tree* are plaintiffs or defendants,
Whose * loues, or feares, are fellowes or attendants :
Of all estates, this *Hauen* hath some partakers
By lot, some Cuckolds, and some Cuckold-makers.
And can they all so much forgetfull be
Vnto that Ancient, and Renowned *Tree*,
That hath so many ages stood Erected,
And by such store of Patrons beene protected,
And now ingloriously to lye vnseene,
As if it were not, or had neuer beene?

Is Lechery wax'd scarce, is Bawdry scant,
Is there of Whores, or Cuckolds any want?
Are Whore-masters decai'd, are all Bawds dead ?
Are Panders, Pimps, and Apple-squires, all fled ?
No surely, for the Surgeons can declare
That *Venus* warres, more hot thent *Marses* are.
Why then, for shame this worthy *Port* mainetaine,
Let's haue our *Tree*, and Hornes set vp againe :
That Passengers may shew obedience to it,
In putting off their Hats, and homage doe it.
Let not the *Cornucopiaes* of our land,
Vnsightly and vnseene neglected stand :
I know it were in vaine for me to call,
That you should rayse some famous Hospitall,
Some Free-schoole or some Almshouse for the pore,
That might increase good deeds, &ope heau'ns dore.
'Tis no taxation great, or no collection
Which I doe speake of, for This great erection :
For if it were, mens goodnesses, I know,
Would proue exceeding barren, dull, and slow :
A Post and Hornes, will build it firme and stable,
Which charge to beare, there's many a begger able :
The place is Ancient, of Respect most famous,
The want of due regard to it, doth shame vs,
For *Cuckolds Hauen*, my request is still,
And so I leaue the Reader to his will.
But holla Muse, no longer be offended,
'Tis worthily Repair'd, and brauely mended,
For which great meritorious worke, my pen
Shall giue the glory vnto *Greenwitch* men.
It was their onely cost, they were the Actors
Without the helpe of other Benefactors,
For which my pen their prayses here adornes,
As they haue beautifi'd the Hau'n with Hornes.
From thence to *Detford* we amaine were driuen,
Whereas an Anker vnto me was giuen :
With parting pintes, and quarts for our farewell;
We tooke our leaues, and so to *Greenwitch* fell.
There shaking hands, adiews, and drinkings store,
We tooke our Ship againe, and left the shore.
Then downe to *Erith*, 'gainst the tyde we went,
Next *London*, greatest Maior towne in *Kent*

* Any *Rat* that eates *Pye*, is a *Pyrat*. * When I past downe
the Riuer, there was not any Post or Horne there, but since
it is most worthily Repaired. * All estates or degrees doe
either loue or feare this Hauen.

O.

Pages from the
complete works of
John Taylor

3

POMP AND CIRCUMSTANCE

More than five hundred examples of pageantry and processions are mentioned in the Company history from Magna Carta in 1215, to which King John travelled by water, to the late Victorian period when other conveyances had long replaced plying the oars to get about the metropolis. They range from meet and greet expeditions for kings, queens, ambassadors and potentates, celebrations for embarkation and homecoming of naval expeditions, Lord Mayor's processions and royal coronations, weddings and funerals.

Henry VIII's quest for a legitimate male heir brought a potent conflict between politics and religion to a combustible head in the middle of the sixteenth century. A waterman toiling at oars on a regular basis would have experienced some remarkable changes. His fares between Greenwich with its maritime affairs, London with its mayor and corporation, Southwark with its low life and Westminster with its court and parliament would have been full of gossip, confidences, intelligence and speculation. If his working life had spanned the middle of the sixteenth century he would witness plenty of pageantry, mystery and fun, and he would retire in a very different world from the one he had known as a teenager learning the ropes.

Royalty and the government certainly made the most of the waterway, both to maintain their own position and in the service of foreign affairs. In 1520, for example, French nobles were taken by water from Greenwich to the City and to the royal palace at Richmond after Henry VIII and Francis I's bonding exercise at the Field of the Cloth of Gold. When Charles V, the emperor of Germany, arrived at Gravesend in 1522, he and his host were conveyed upriver from Gravesend by thirty barges. In 1527 schoolboys of St Paul's were taken down river in six boats to perform a mystery play at the Old Palace in Greenwich, probably to entertain visiting ambassadors. In 1553 the Duke of Northumberland's unsuccessful attempt to put Lady Jane Grey on the throne began with a water procession from his mansion to her thrown within the Tower.

> 'A squadron of fifty superbly gilt barges, some decorated with banners and streamers, some with cloth of gold and arras... others with innumerable silken pennons, to which were attached small silver bells, making a goodly noise and a goodly sight as they waved in the wind... Each barge was escorted by a light galley, termed a foist or wafter, manageable either by oar or sail... attached to its companion by a stout silken tow-line. The Lady Jane Grey embarked in a magnificent barge... its sides were hung with metal escutcheons... and its decks covered with the richest silks and tissues... In the galleys, besides the rowers... and the men-at-arms, whose tall pikes, steel caps, and polished corsets flashed in the sunbeams, sat bands of minstrels, provided with sackbuts, shawms, cornets, rebecs, &c.'

In 1557, during the reign of Mary and Philip of Spain, Princess Elizabeth visited her half sister at Richmond, taking the Queen's barge from Somerset Place. The barge was richly hung with garlands, 'covered with a canopy of green sarsenet, wrought with branches of eglantine on embroidery, and powdered with blossoms of gold.' She was accompanied by Sir Thomas Pope and four ladies of her chamber, with six boats in attendance for her

Previous page: The Palace of Whitehall – Charles II and his Consort witnessing the Lord Mayor's procession to Westminster 29 Oct 1683 (Reginald Francis Print Collection)

retinue who were 'habited in russet damask and blue embroidered satin, lapelled and spangled in silver, with bonnets of cloth of silver, plumed with green feathers.' After a sumptuous banquet the party returned to Somerset Place by the same method.

Tragedy occasionally occurred, as in 1568 when Thomas Appletree accidentally discharged his piece on the royal barge. The bullet ran through both arms of a Queen's waterman. Elizabeth, the queen in question, pardoned Appletree.

Something significant for watermen happened in 1565 when Guylliam Boonen of Holland presented Queen Elizabeth with a coach that was a considerable improvement on the 1550s chariot used for the coronation of Mary. Thus was born the first big threat to watermen's livelihood, but it would be a long time in gestation.

We can presume that spectaculars and waterborne affairs of city and state were only the tip of the iceberg as far as business and messing about in boats are concerned. There were plenty of treats and diversions for those who lived by the river and those who worked it. Tiltings, tournaments, frost fairs and other amusements were frequent. In 1253 there was a riot at a game of quintain, which can be described loosely as water jousting. A shield was fixed on a pole in midstream. A man standing in a boat had to break his lance on the shield while avoiding a pitching overboard. Another version required wherries with two oarsmen armed with staves to row head on at each other, the object being to duck your opponent. Unscheduled events included escort of dissidents to the Tower and escapes therefrom, incursions into the Thames by enemy ships, and occurrences such as Edward Osborne's spectacular leap from London Bridge to save the life of his master's daughter in 1536.

From time to time, natural events caused commotion and enlivened the tapestry of Thames life. In 1240 eleven whales were cast ashore, one travelling as far upstream as Mortlake. In 1457 two whales were caught off Erith, together with a swordfish. In 1626 a waterspout appeared on the river. In 1642, a time of political turmoil and disputes over remuneration of watermen and seamen, the newspaper *Marine Mercury* reported the strange appearance of a man-fish in the river, carrying a musket in one hand and a petition in the other, attested by six sailors who saw and talked with him. The same paper also reported a story that, one suspects, again got in the way of the facts: 'A perfect mermaid was by the last great wind driven ashore near Greenwich, with her comb in one hand and her looking-glass in the other. A most fair and beautiful woman.'

The number of barges kept by the nobility increased significantly in Henry VIII's reign, and the Company history's account of Cardinal Wolsey's habits illustrates the lifestyle of the well endowed. Wolsey lived by the river in his grand York House, once the abode of the Archbishop of York and later renamed Whitehall. There he kept a retinue of watermen and several boats for his personal use. His habit was to resort to the court at Greenwich every Sunday aboard his own barge from his own stairs with his own yeomen. He landed again at the Three Cranes stairs, from whence 'he rode upon his mule, with his crosses, his pillers, his hat, and the broad seal carried before him on horseback, through Thames Street until he came to Billingsgate, and there took his barge again,' and so rowed to Greenwich. This diversion was to avoid passing under the narrow arches of London Bridge on the rushing water of a falling tide at the mercy of the watermen who specialised in shooting it.

The joys of riding the surf with the bridge shooters was described by Henry's librarian, John Leland:

> *Yet here we may not longer stay,*
> *But shoot the bridge and dart away,*
> *Though with resistless fall, the tide*
> *Is dashing on the bulwarks' side;*
> *And roaring torrents drown my song*
> *As o'er the surge I drift along.*

Shooting London Bridge was not for the faint hearted, and there were times and tides when it was prudent to do as Wolsey did and pass it on foot — just as there were occasions when crossing directly by boat from one bank to the other was quicker than battling one's way on foot through the crowds and carts on the bridge roadway.

In 1613 John Taylor, waterman and self-styled Water Poet, described the public rejoicings at the proposed marriage of Frederick, the Elector Palatine, with James I's daughter Elizabeth. He described the pair as 'the two peerlesse paragons of Christindome' and recorded Saturday 13 February's goings on thus:

> 'The representation of a sea fight consisted of sixteen ships, sixteen gallies, and six friggots; the ships were manned by Christians, and the gallies by Turks; all rigged and trimmed, well manned, and furnished with great ordnance and musquettiers. Bounds from Temple stairs to Lambeth stairs were marked out using lighters, hoys and other boats numbering about two hundred and fifty, set out in a half moon shape from the southern shore so that boats could pass between the London bank and the lighters. The Turkish galleys lying at anchor off Westminster… and supposed to belong to a barbarian's castle, the Venetian argosy and its convoy set off from the Temple, and driving up with the wind and tide to

Queen Catherine's procession up the Thames 23 August 1662
(© National Maritime Museum, Greenwich, London)

York house, where four gallies met and encountered with them, when upon a suddaine there was an exchange of small shot and great ordnance Etc; and on a beacon being fired by the Turks, giving notice of the coming of the Christian fleet, a general attack took place, which lasted three hours, command was then given that the retreat should be sounded on both sides.'

Five hundred watermen and a thousand musketeers took part. The royal party saw the whole thing from the steps of Whitehall. Fireworks 'of a very splendid description' took place to round off the night.

Soon after Charles I came to the throne in 1625 there was a splendid pageant when his new bride Henrietta Maria, daughter of Henry IV of France, crossed the Channel. Charles greeted her at Dover and accompanied her by sea to Gravesend on 14 June, where they transferred to barges and were conveyed through London Bridge to Whitehall. Ships and forts discharged ordnance as the procession progressed, particularly heartily from the Tower. Thousands of boats accompanied the barges through the bridge and thousands stood in wherries, houses, ships, lighters and barges on each side of the shore. The royal couple stood behind the windows of their barge, open despite a vehement shower, and 'she put out her hand and shaked it to them, and all the people shouting amain'. Two hundred people on board a ship leaning against Tower wharf rushed to one side to get a view and overthrew it into the Thames.

Lord Mayors were not to be outdone in the pageantry stakes. Thomas Heywood left this account of the procession of 1638 on the ascent to office of the Rt. Hon. Sir Maurice Abbott, a draper and merchant trading from Turkey to Muscovy:

The first show by water is presented by Proteus, in a beautiful sea chariot, for the better ornament decored with divers marine nymphs and sea goddesses, &c; he sitteth or rideth upon a moving tortois, which is reckoned amongst the amphibiae, one of those creatures that live in two elements, alluding to the trading of the present Lord Mayor.'

Draper and stapler Sir John Jolles's procession in 1615 included a goodly argosy, or Venetian-style merchant ship, rowed by a number of comely eunuchs. The golden fleece was also represented, together with Medea and eight royal virtues. Sir George Bollis's 1617 pageant included islands, Indian chariots, castles of fame and ships. Henry Garway's in 1639 had 'a person representing the ancient river Nilus, mounted on a sea chariot, and seated on a silver scallop, accompanied by marine nymphs and goddesses… drawn by two crocodiles.' This was the last mayor's procession until 1655, owing to political upheaval. In 1663 the poet John Tatham recorded Sir Anthony Bateman's procession from Three Cranes wharf to Westminster as accompanied by drums, trumpets, hoboys, streamers, banners and ordnance discharged from Bankside.

On 23 August 1662 there occurred the 'most magnificent triumph that ever floated on the Thames to welcome Charles II's new queen, Catherine of Braganza, to London. Their majesties were conveyed from Hampton Court to Whitehall in an antique shaped barge with a canopy of cloth of gold shaped as a cupola supported by corinthian pillars and wreathed in flowers and garlands. A thousand boats were on the river. The barges of the Lord Mayor and the livery companies met the royal party at Chelsea and led them for the rest of the way. A rendition of "the watermen's song" greeted them at Whitehall.

Fireworks on the Thames near Whitehall on 15 May 1749 to celebrate the signing of the Treaty of Aix-la-Chapelle, for which occasion Handel composed his Music for the Royal Fireworks (Bridgeman Images)

The pageantry surrounding Braganza was a watershed in the river's relationship with the capital. Everyday transport was increasingly undertaken in improved carriages on improved roads. For the monarchy, barges were henceforth for ceremony only. It was forty years since a coach works had been established in London, and stables and coach houses were being added to palaces. Furthermore, the palaces themselves were turning their backs on the Thames as proprietors remodelled them to front the street instead of the river. The shape of things to come was evident in 1711 when the Lord Mayor took to a coach instead of horseback to get about in the City.

John Taylor, the Water Poet, campaigned against the evil of the carriage in a pamphlet for his fellow watermen back in 1623:

'The first coach was a strange monster, it amazed both horse and man. Some said it was a great crab-shell brought out of China; some thought it was one of the pagan temples, in which the cannibals adored the devil… Since Phaeton broke his neck, never land hath endured more trouble than ours, by the continued rumbling of these upstart four-wheeled tortoises. When comes leather so dear? By reason or against it of the multitude of coaches which consume all the best hides in the kingdom; when many honest shoemakers are undone, and many poor Christians go barefoot at Christmas. Yet a coach or carouch is a mere engine of pride, which no one can deny to be one of the seven deadly sins.'

The South East Prospect of Westminster Bridge 1759 (Watermen's Hall Collection)

A good example of another kind of entertainment occurred in the winter of 1684, when a severe freeze-up lasted from the beginning of December to February. Frosts were generally bad news for watermen and for the port. Ships became icebound and work scarce, while a different, impromptu economy thrived until the thaw. The historian Maitland described the frost of 1684 as congealing the river to the degree that another city was erected upon it. Streets lined with fair booths appeared. Evelyn noted in his diary that coaches plied from Westminster to Temple. Large boats were fitted with tilts – like an awning - for passengers and were pulled as sleds by horses or watermen. People slid on skates and sledges, walked the river from Horseferry to Lambeth, while Hackney carriages travelled on ice from Temple to Southwark. There were ox roasts, bull baiting, and the King Charles took part in a fox hunt on the river. There was great distress among watermen, their families and apprentices, and rejoicing reflected in 'The Thames encased, or, the Watermen's Song upon the Thaw':

Come, ye merry men all

Of Watermen's hall,

Let's hoist out our boats and caressing;

The Thames it does melt,

And the coald is scarce felt,

Not an icicle is now to be seen.

An accurate View (*drawn & etched by J.T.Smith, Engraver of the ANTIQUITIES of* London & Westminster) *from the House of* W.Tunnard,Esq. *on the Bankside*
Greenwich to Whitehall; *comprehending not only the Vessels attending & the various other objects incide*
First Barge, covered with black cloth. The Standard, borne by Capt. Sir Fra. Laforey Bt. Supported by Lieut.s Barker and Antram:
The Guidon, borne by Capt.Baynton (in the absence of Capt.Durham) supported by 2 Lieut.s Rouge croix and Bluemantle,
prisuivants. — Second Barge, cover'd with black Cloth: Heralds of Arms, bearing the Surcoat, Target & Sword Helm and
Crest & the Gauntlet & Spurs of the deceased: The Banner of the deceased, as K.B. borne by Capt.Rotheram supp. by 2 Lieut.s
The great Banner with the augmentations, borne by Capt.Moorsom, supported by Lieut.s Keys & Tucker. — Third Barge, cov.
with black Velvet, black plumes, &c. Capt.Yule, Atkinson (Master of the Victory) Capt.Williams, Lieut.s Brown & Porches.
The BODY. Norrey, K. of Arms (in the absence of Clarenceux, indisposed) Union Flag: Attendants on the Body, while

Dear is the Triumph, whe
"Though Victory crownd r
"He was ever the defender o
"mind; and continued his love

London, Feb.r 15th 1806, published according to

Admiral Nelson's funeral on 8 January 1806 (Watermen's Hall Collection)

...oining the Scite of Shakspeare's Theatre. — on Wednesday the 8th January, 1806; when the remains of the great ADMIRAL LORD NELSON were brought from ...to that Procession; but also the principal Buildings,&c between the Monument & Saint Pauls, inclusive.

me breath must tell — ...yet the Hero fell! "

e Citizens, both in body &
...vards his countrymen, all his life":
                    Maccabees.
...f Parliament, by J.T. Smith, N.º 36, Newman Street.

at Greenwich: Fourth Barge, cov. with blk Cloth: Chief Mourner Sir Peter Parker, Bt Adm. of the Fleet, supp. by Admi Viscount Hood & Adm. Lord Radstock: 6 assistant Mourners, viz Adm. Caldwell, Curtis, Bligh, Pole, Nugent & Hamilton: 4 Supp. rs of the Pall, viz. Vice Adm. Whitshed & Taylor, Adm. Orde (in the absence of Vice Adm. Savage) & Rear Adm. Eliab Harvey: 6 Supp. rs of the Canopy, viz. Rear Adm. Drury, Douglas, Wells, Coffin, Aylmer & Donett. Train Bearer to the Chief Mourner Hon. Henry Blackwood: Windsor Herald, acting for Norroy K. of Arms: The Banner of Emblems borne by Capt. Hardy, supported by Lieut ts King & Bligh: His Majesty's Barge. The Lords Commissioners of the Admiralty, their Barge, & immediately after the City State Barge (the Rt Hon. James Shaw, Lord Mayor) followed by the Barges of several of the Companies of the City of London.   The Engraver is signally obliged to Francis Townsend Esq. Windsor Herald. F.A.S. for his liberal communications

In 1700 the lightermen, the men who 'lightened' laden ships in the river and conveyed their cargo to quayside in lighters, joined the Watermen's Company, having previously been members of the Woodmongers' Company. The coming century saw another development that would eventually knock a huge hole in the watermen's boat. A wooden bridge was constructed at Putney in 1729, devastating the working lives of waterman based there. Although still a considerable distance from the city, the new bridge, combined with greatly improved condition of roads for miles outside the capital, was a precursor of what was to come. London Bridge continued as the only crossing in the city until Westminster Bridge opened in 1750. The mayor and corporation perceived Westminster as a threat to the City and built Blackfriars Bridge on their western boundary in 1769. Compensation was paid for loss of trade, but by the end of the century the wherrymen's trade was under serious threat, and not merely in the centre. One attraction of bridging the river was to access roads to Dover and the Channel ports which affected the shipping trade from Gravesend round the Kent coast.

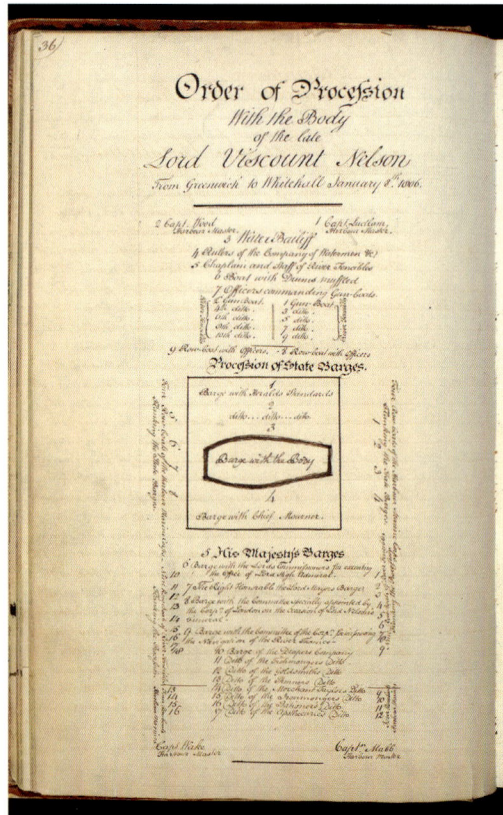

Order of procession to accompany Viscount Nelson's body from Greenwich to Whitehall, 8 January 1806 (Drapers' Company)

Meanwhile, odd and spectacular occurences continued. The capture of a 40ft whale at Gravesend in 1718 caused great excitement. In 1749 a porpoise was pursued upstream by nearly one hundred watermen before it was shot above London Bridge. It is said that a whale landed at Greenland Dock in 1762 was visited by 50,000 people. In 1783 a 21ft two-toed cachalot was caught above London Bridge. Fishermen who dragged a sickly shark into their boat off Poplar in 1787 found it to contain a silver watch, metal chain, cornelian seal and pieces of gold fringe. The watch was traced by its maker to a gent who had given it to his son who had drowned off Falmouth in the English Channel. It was presumed that the shark's digestion could not cope with metals, leading to its sickness.

On 15 May 1749, the Privy Gardens and the river were lit up by the Duke of Richmond's pyrotechnic spectacular for the Duke of Modena. Two hundred water mines, two hundred air balloons, two hundred fire trees, five thousand war rockets, five thousand sky rockets, a hundred fire showers, twenty suns and a hundred stars formed the grand illumination for hundreds in boats on the river.

In 1768, those lucky enough to be about on 30 August would have seen a curious present for George III being paddled up to Richmond by thirty men. It was a *mohr punkee* or peacock boat brought from India, deriving its name from the figure of the bird on its prow. Eighty feet long, the peacock plumage flowed in painted depiction all along its sides. The stern terminated in a richly gilt fish's head, an emblem of India's royalty. A pavilion of crimson velvet covered the widest part of the boat.

Frost fair on Thames 1814 (Reginald Francis Print Collection)

April Fool's Day in 1785 saw the launch of an 'aquatic balloon' that was sunk in the river above Westminster Bridge. The inventor was inside, breathing through a tube fixed at its top. It floated to Lambeth stairs before the submariner signalled for help and the watermen in attendance rescued him from his waterlogged experiment. This was not the first attempt to create a submarine. The Dutchman Cornelius Drebbel was much more successful 150 years before when he adapted a 1578 design by William Bourne to build a submersible for the Royal Navy. Drebbel's final version in 1624 had six oars and carried up to sixteen persons. It was demonstrated as capable of remaining submerged for up to three hours. It was rowed from Westminster to Greenwich and back at a depth of 12 to 15 feet, and King James himself was taken for a test dive beneath the Thames, but Drebbel's sub failed to convince the navy of its value for combat. Mark Edwards built a replica in 2002 for the BBC programme Building the Impossible. It was tested successfully at Dorney Lake but was barred from the Thames.

Other entertainments in the eighteenth century included the sailor and waterman's apprentice who slid down a rope from the gallery of the Monument to the Three Tuns Tavern in Gracechurch Street in 1732. In1765 a waterman named Carr laid wager that he and his dog would leap from the centre arch of Westminster Bridge and land at Lambeth within a minute of each other. Carr jumped off and the dog followed, 'but not knowing the bet, and fearing his master would be drowned, laid hold of him by the neck and dragged him ashore to the no small diversion of the spectators on the bridge and in the boats.'

In July 1766 a man crossed the river from Somerset stairs on a butcher's tray for a wager, using his hands to propel himself. It was said that seventy boats bore witness and £1,400 in bets rode on the result. Later that month Dobins, a waterman, swam on his back from Westminster Bridge to Putney in 1 hour 26 minutes, 19 minutes short of 1 hour 45 minutes allowed.

Among entertainments of a different kind were thrills like the execution of the notorious pirate named Williams at Execution Dock in 1735, after which he was hanged in chains at Bugsby's Hole, near Blackwall. Thomas Round was hung, drawn and quartered in1743 for high treason, 'conveyed from Newgate on a hurdle by four horses covered with ribbons to Execution Dock; one of the sheriff's officers carried a silver oar before him, the naval emblem representing the jurisdiction of London for trying and executing offenders against Admiralty laws. Jack Ketch rode on the hurdle, dressed in a white frock, a knife and steel by his side, and a drawn scymeter in his hand; the culprit's body after execution was drawn and quartered.' Elizabeth Herring came to a frazzled end after killing her waterman husband. On 13th September 1773 she was tied to a stake and burned to death, watched by 20,000 people, some of whom were trodden to death in the crush.

There are recorded instances of 'common scolds' being on the receiving end of duckings. In 1745 the woman who kept the Queen's Head alehouse in Kingston, Surrey, was ordered by the court to be placed in a chair and ducked under Kingston Bridge, witnessed by more than two thousand people. Sometimes gossips were paraded through town wearing a brank, also known as a scold's bit or a gossip's bridge. The bridle enclosed the head and was fastened behind by a padlock, while a small piece of iron held the offender's tongue.

Entertainment could take a bad turn, as did a firework display at Westminster Bridge in 1792 when two west country barges that were lashed together ran against one of the lighters where incendiaries were being let off. The lighter's anchor dragged and the barges drifted against a pier of the bridge. Three small boats tethered to the lighter sank, one of them dashed to pieces, and nine people lost their lives in the melée.

Despite carriages and new bridges, the great Tideway was thriving as port and pageant-way as the century came to an end. It served ever-growing tonnage and an ever-growing navy. The Lord Mayor commissioned a new gondola or state barge in 1807 that was able to pass through all locks to Oxford. She was of English oak, 85ft in length and 13ft 8in broad at the widest point, propelled by eighteen oars and decorated in gilt. She cost £2,579. The Royal barge designed by William Kent and built by John

Hall at his yard opposite Whitehall for Prince Frederick in 1732 was used regularly by monarchs until 1849, when its last royal appearance was to convey Prince Albert to open the Coal Exchange.

On 2 July 1818 Mr Usher, *grimacier* or clown of the Coburgh Theatre, sailed 'in a machine like a washing tub' drawn by four geese attached by a pole from Southwark bridge at 12.30 through four bridges, arriving at Cumberland gardens at 2.30. The geese were sometimes tractable, sometimes restive, and the adventure, in answer to a wager, was followed by many in boats and witnessed by many from bridges. Usher offered to return through the centre arch of London Bridge for 100 guineas, but nobody would accept his challenge. His adventure is a reminder of the long established mutual dependence between watermen and the theatre world that survives today in the guise of Doggett's Coat and Badge race founded by the actor-manager Thomas Doggett in 1715.

In 1815 a Bill got up to allow bathing in the river failed. Bathing was banned from Blackwall to Battersea. This probably encouraged the man who leapt from the centre arch of London Bridge at 4 a.m. one summer night in 1840 and swam to Greenwich in an hour and a half for a wager. It was said that he showed no sign of exhaustion when he stepped ashore. In November that same year Samuel Scott, an American, took a flying leap from topgallant yard of a brig off Rotherhithe and entertained the concourse for an hour. His acrobatics included running from one end of the yard to the other and hanging himself in a slip noose. Scott claimed to have jumped off the falls of Niagara and the cliffs of Port Isaac in Cornwall. But next year he was hoist by his own petard. He challenged a hundred guineas that he would run from Drury Lane to Waterloo Bridge, leap into the water, and return within the hour each day for a week. On 11 January thousands of spectators gathered on the bridge in sight of the temporary scaffold erected above the second arch. Scott mounted the tower and swung by his head and then his feet before placing his head in a rope. The rope became fixed and strangled him. He was cut down too late, his friends believing that the tragedy was part of his act.

Events of an entirely different kind brought boats, majesty and dignity to the river. In 1806 the body of Admiral Horatio Nelson lay at Greenwich for three days, attracting 20,000 mourners a day. He was then conveyed by water to the Admiralty in a procession of boats carrying the two harbour masters and their water bailiffs, the Company of Watermen and Lightermen's shallop with rulers and clerk, the chief officers of the river fencibles, boats with muffled drums, ten gun boats proceeding in pairs, nine state barges rowed by Greenwich pensioners draped in black, Admiralty officials and heralds of arms bearing the insignia of the deceased. A barge contained the body and was rowed by sixteen seamen from the *Victory*. It was covered in black velvet and adorned with plumes of black feathers, the body covered with a sheet and pall of velvet and six escutcheons. Eighteen row boats of the river fencibles accompanied this part of the procession. Eight livery company barges followed – Drapers, Fishmongers, Goldsmiths, Skinners, Merchant Taylors, Ironmongers, Stationers and Apothecaries. Then came the Lord Mayor's barge and one containing the flag of the *Victory*. Minute guns were fired as the procession passed the Tower, and three hours after leaving Greenwich, the procession arrived at Whitehall stairs. Nelson's bier passed between barges which had formed two lines as the band played the Dead March from Saul and other dirgeful strains. Gun boats fired minute guns throughout, and a tremendous hailstorm occurred at disembarkation.

A few days later, on 9 January, Nelson's remains were processed to St. Paul's Cathedral and interred. Watermen who had served the admiral donned black coats and joined the procession. The whole proceedings, at public expense, was judged the 'most magnificent spectacle of a religious character ever witnessed in this country' — only to be matched by Winston Churchill's departure a century and a half later.

By mid-nineteenth century, the great commercial street that was the Thames remained a Grand Canal of pageantry. By then, however, carriages, roads and bridges were the least of the watermen's worries. Steam engines, railways and enclosures in the form of docks were making an impact on the great Tideway and adding to their woes.

Cranes dipped in salute at Churchill's funeral 30 January 1965 (Getty Images)

Queen Elizabeth II and the Duke of Edinburgh on the royal barge at the Diamond Jubilee pageant on 3 June 2012, attended by Her Majesty's Bargemaster and Past Master of the Company, Paul Ludwig (left), and Past Master Robert Prentice (right) (Corbis Images)

The Thames Jubilee Pageant by Lynda Minter (River & Rowing Museum)

OF the nine Worthies was this Worthy one,
Denmarke, and *Norway*, did obey his Throne:
In twelue set Battels he the *Saxons* beat,
Great, and to make his Victories more great,
The Faithlesse *Sarazens* he ouercame,
And made them honour high *Iehouah's* Name.
The Noble order of the *Table round*,
At *Winchester*, his first inuention found.
Whilst he beyond Sea fought to win Renowne,
His Nephew *Mordred* did vsurpe his Crowne,
But he return'd, and *Mordred* did confound,
And in the fight great *Arthur* got a wound,
That prou'd so mortall, that immortally
It made him liue, although it made him dye.
Full sixteene yeeres the Diadem he wore,
And euery day gaind Honour more and more.

Arthur the great was buried at Glastenbury.

96. *Constantine, the fourth.* 542.
97. *Aurelius Conanus.* 545.

COnstantine was by King *Aurelius* kil'd:
Aurelius (*Brittaine*) thirty three yeeres held,
Seuen Kingdomes heere at once the *Saxons* held,
And slaughter launc'd, when proud ambition sweld.

This Constantine *was kinsman to King* Arthur, *and was slaine by* Conanus. Constantine *was a wicked Prince, and slaine in battell by his kinsman* Conanus, *when he had reigned neere 3. yeeres. Of the tyme of this* Aurelius Conanus *his reigne, there is much variation in Histories.*

this Land, namely, Kent, South-Saxons, West-Saxons, East-Saxons, Northumberland, Mercia, and East-Angles: which diuision continued more then 600. yeeres, before it was all vnited into one Monarchy, the names of the Kings, & times of their reignes, and limits of their Kingdomes, are hereunder expressed.

1 KEnt was only a kingdome which had 17 Kings, namely, 1 *Hengist*, 2 *Eth*, 3 *Octa*, 4 *Ymerick*, 5 *Ethelbert*, who was the first Christian King of *Kent*, hee was an ayde and helper of *Sebert*, King of the *East-Saxons*, in the famous and memorable buildings of St. Pauls Church in *London*, and Saint Peters at *Westminster*. 6 *Eabald*, 7 *Ercombert*, 8 *Egbert*, 9 *Lother*, 10 *Edrick*, 11 *Withred*, 12 *Egbert*, 13 *Edelbert*, 14 *Alick*, 15 *Ethilbert*, 16 *Cuthred*, 17 *Baldred*. These Kings reigned in *Kent* 372. yeeres, from the yeere of Grace 455. till the yeere 827.

2 The kingdome of the South-Saxons contained the Counties of *Sussex* and *Surrie*, it continued from the yeere 488. vntill the yeere 601. being 113 yeeres: they had three Kings, namely, 1 *Ella*, 2 *Cissa*, 3 *Ethelwolfe* a Christian King, 4 *Berthrum*, 5 *Authum*.

3 The West-Saxons kingdome, whose beginning was in the yeer 519. and ended, Anno. 166. lasted 561 yeeres, hauing 17 Kings, namely, 1 *Cherdick*, 2 *Kenrick*, 3 *Chequilin*, 4 *Cealick*, 5 *Chelwold*, 6 *Kingils*, a Christian, 7 *Kenwald*, 8 *Eskwin*, 9 *Kentwin*, 10 *Ceadwald*, 11 *Inas*, 12 *Ethelarc*, 13 *Cuthred*, 14 *Sigebert*, 15 *Kenwolfe*, 16 *Brightrik*, 17 *Egbert*, : These Kings had vnder their gouernments, the Counties of Cornewall, Deuonshire, Somersetshire, Wiltshire, Hampshire and Barkshire.

4 The East-Saxons reigned 281 yeeres, beginning Anno. 527. and ending in the yeere 827. Their bounds were Essex and Middle-Sex, and their Kings were in number 14, namely, 1 *Erchenwin*, 2 *Sledda*, 3 *Seba*

King of Kent, in the building of the Churches of Saint *Paul* and Saint *Peter* aforesaid. 4 *Seward*, 5 *Sigebert*, 6 *Sigibert*, 7 *Swithelme*, 8 *Sighere*, 9 *Sebba*, 10 *Sigherd*, 11 *Seofrid*, 12 *Offa*, 13 *Selred*, 14 *Suthred*.

5 *Northumberland* was sometimes diuided into two kingdomes. It contained the Counties of *Yorkshire, Durham, Lancashire, Westmerland, Cumberland* and *Northumberland*: this Kingdome beganne in the yeere of our Lord, 547. and expired in 926. continuing 379. yeeres vnder 23 Kings, whose names were, 1 *Ella*, 2 *Adda*, 3 *Theodwald*, 4 *Frethulfe*, 5 *Theodrick*, 6 *Ethelrick*, 7 *Ethel*... ...wald, 10 *Oswy*, 11 *Egfrid*, 12 *Alfrid*, 13 *Osred*, 14 *Kenred*, 15 ... 18 *Osvvolfe*, 19 *Ethwald*, 20 *Alured*, 21 *Ethelred*, 22 *Alswald*, 23 *Osred*. Amongst these, *Edwin* was their first Christian King.

6 The East Angles vnder 15 seuerall Kings, continued 353 yeeres, beginning in *Anno*, 575. and ended in 914. their Territories were *Suffolke, Norfolk, Cambridgeshire* and the Ile of *Ely*, their Kings names were, 1 *Uffa*, 2 *Titulus*, 3 *Redwald* their first Christian King, 4 *Erpenvold*, 5 *Sigebert*, 6 *Egrik*, 7 *Anna*, 8 *Ethelbert*, 9 *Ethwald*, 10 *Aldwolfe*, 11 *Aswald*, 12 *Beorn*, 13 *Ethelred*, 14 *Ethelbert*, 15 *Edmund*.

7 The seuenth Kingdome were the Mercians, who had 20 Kings and 17 shires vnder their command: their Kings were, 1 *Creda*, 2 *Wibba*, 3 *Cheorle*, 4 *Penda*, 5 *Peada* their first Christian King, 6 *Wolfere*, 7 *Ethelred*, 8 *Kenred*, 9 *Chelred*, 10 *Ethelbald*, 11 *Offa*, 12 *Egfrid*, 13 *Kenwolfe*, 14 *Kenelme*, 15 *Chelwolfe*, 16 *Bernulfe*, 17 *Ludecan*, 18 *Whitlafe*, 19 *Bertwolfe*, 20 *Burdred*. Their bounds and dominions were 17 Counties, as of Northampton, Leister, Darby, Lincolne, Huntington, Rutland, Notingham, Cheshire, Oxfordshire, Staffordshire, Worcestershire, Glostershire, Shropshire, Warwickeshire, Bedfordshire, Buckinghamshire, and Hartfordshire.

4
HONEST JOHN,
POET AND PAMPHLETEER

98 *Vortiporus.* 578.   99 *Malgo.* 581.

THis *Vortipore* from good Kings did decline,
Kept his wiues Daughter as his Concubine:
And *Malgo* put his Wife to bloudy slaughter,
To liue in Incest with his brothers Daughter.

Albanact his sonne beganne, the Monke, Mellitus, Iustus ...preached... reigned 4 yeeres. Malgo, his raigne was short and wicked.

100. *Careticus.* 586.

GErmundus hither out of *Ireland* came,
And with the *Saxons* ioyn'd with sword and ...
The King to *Wales* did flye, his life to saue,
Whereas he chang'd his Kingdome for a Graue.

He reigned 3 yeeres: and now the Saxons had all England, the Brittaines and their Kings being expulsed and chased to the West sides of the Riuers Seauerne, and Dee.

Cadwane. 613.

THis *Cadwan* did the *Saxon* force withstand,
Of *Ethelfrodus* of *Northumberland*:
And made him to entreate and sue for peace:
Raign'd two and twenty yeeres, then did decease.

John Taylor was a waterman who became famous as a writer, satirist and pamphleteer as a result of his adventures and his tireless campaigns for the rights of the men who manned oars on the Thames. Typical was his slim volume attacking the carriage trade in 1623 in which the 'Water Poet', as he became known (likely at his own instigation), alleged that 'never land hath endured more trouble than ours, by the continued rumbling of these upstart four-wheeled tortoises'. Coaches were, indeed, the first serious threat to the livelihood of watermen, and Taylor puts it thus:

> Carroches, coaches, jades and Flanders mares,
>
> Do rob us of our shares, our wares, our fares;
>
> Against the ground we stand and knock our heeles,
>
> Whilst all our profit runs away on wheelees.
>
> …
>
> Then watermen at sea had service still,
>
> And those that stay'd at home had worke at will:
>
> Then upstart hel-cart coaches were to seek,
>
> A man could scarce see twenty in a weeke;
>
> But now I thinke a man may dayly see
>
> More than the wherrys on the Thames can be.

Years later, in 1636, watermen organised a collection for Taylor to defray the £34 he spent over eighteen months to secure the 1635 proclamation on coaches. He recovered £19:4s.

Taylor was born in Gloucester in 1578, took an apprenticeship with a waterman, and in 1596 was either pressed into the fleet or volunteered for the navy. He served aboard the *Rainbow* under the Earl of Essex and saw action at the taking of Cadiz. He is said to have made sixteen voyages with the navy. He was also appointed a royal waterman, and in 1608 became 'collector of wines' for the Lieutenant of the Tower, a post that lasted for fourteen years. When he moved on, he published a work entitled Farewell to Tower Bottles, the story of Richard II's gift to the Tower of two black leather bottles or lombards from every ship that brought wine into the Thames. Unsurprisingly, this decree led to dispute and some black bottle marketing, and Taylor sometimes was required to paddle a difficult course.

Previous page: Pages from the complete works of John Taylor

The warders knows, each bottleman (but I)

Had always a crack'd crown, or black eye,

Oft beaten like a dog, with a scratch'd face,

Turn'd empty, beaten back with vile disgrace.

And now and then be tumbled over board,

And tho' these mischiefs I have kept me fro',

No other bottleman could e'er do so;

'Tis known you have been stabb'd, thrown in the Thames,

and he that fil'd you, beaten with exclaims.

Nevertheless, working for Sir William Ward, Lieutenant of the Tower, had its rewards:

I was a waterman twice four year long year,

And lived in a contented happy state,

Then turned the whirling wheel of fickle fate

From water unto wine: Sir William Wade

Did freely and for nothing turn my trade.

Ten years almost the place I did retain,

And glean's great Bacchus' blood from France and Spain.

Taylor lived on Bankside and fostered his literary interests by conversing with actors, playwrights and poets who frequented Southwark. He was witty, polite and conversed easily with the high and the low, but his pen soon got him into trouble. His first work, published in 1612, is entitled 'The Sculler: Rowing from Tiber to Thames with a hotch-potch or gallimawfry of Sonnets, Satyres, and Epigrams, Etc'. The volume contains some firebrand stuff, the dedication setting the tone: 'To the whole kennell of AntiChrists hounds, Priests, friers, monks, and Jesuits, mastiffs, mongrells, Islands, Spanniells, blood-hounds, bobtailetike, or foysting-hound: the Sculler sends greeting.'

Curse, exorcize, with beads, with booke, & bell

Poluted shauelings: rage and doe your worst:

Use conjurations till your bellies burst,

With many a Nigromanticke mumbling spell,

I feare you not, nor all your friends that fell

With Lucifer: ye damned dogs that durst

Devise that thundring treason most accurst,

Whose like before was never hatchd in hell:

Halfe men, halfe devils, who never dreamd of good,

To you from faire and sweetly sliding Thames,

A popomasticke Sculler war proclaimes,

As to the suckers of imperiall blood.

An Anti-Jesuit Sculler with his pen,

Defies your Babell Beast, and all his den.

The Sculler makes derisive comments about fellow writers, one being Tom Coryate, the royal jester, with whom he sparked a pamphlet war. Taylor also attacked William Fenner, and a trial of wit was arranged between Taylor and Fenner on the stage of the Hope on Bankside. When Fenner did not show, the audience pelted and abused Taylor. Next year the pamphleteer retaliated in verse in 'Taylor's Revenge; or, the rhymer William Fenner, firk'd, ferrited, and finelf fettcht over the coales, Etc. Printed at Rotterdam, at the sign of the Blue Bitch, in Dog lane'.

Taylor became a prolific writer of books and pamphlets, amassing around 140 during his lifetime, plus broadsheets, birthday odes and funeral elegies. Many of his books were published by selling advanced subscriptions. By 1613 he was campaigning against playhouses seeking licences to operate in London and Middlesex on the grounds that such a development endangered watermen's livelihood. He petitioned on the matter vigorously on behalf of the Company and published a lengthy pamphlet, *The True Cause of the Watermen's Suit Concerning Players*, setting out the watermen's plight of being drastically reduced in number by navy service and then bled of Bankside's theatre trade. Despite support from the likes of Francis Bacon, the King ignored the protestations.

In 1642 Taylor's writings publicised the attempt by members of the Company to democratize its leadership by campaigning for the right to put forward candidates for the annual election of rulers.

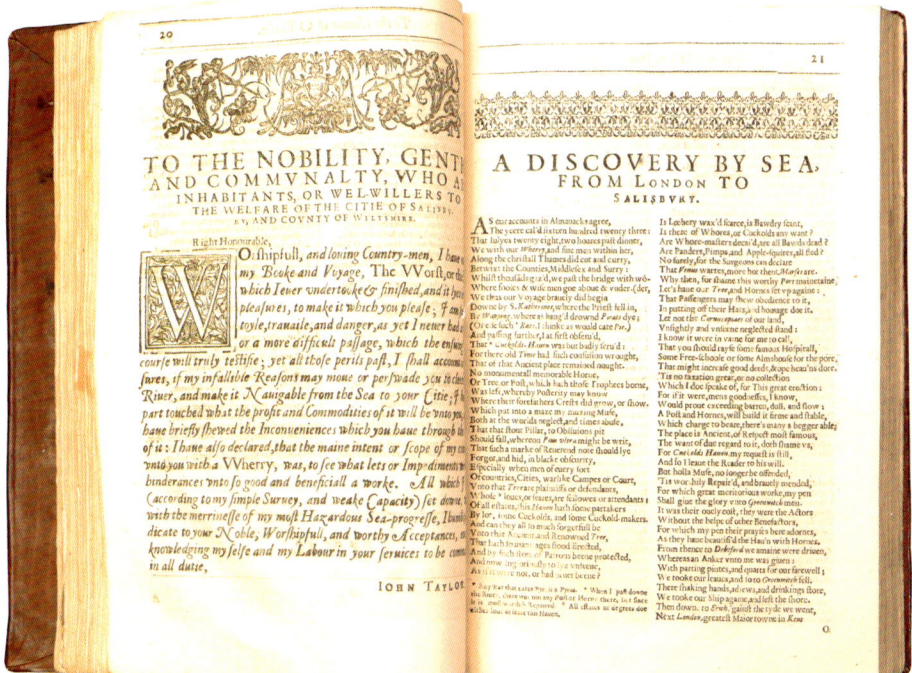

Pages from the complete works of John Taylor

He made a series of voyages and reported on the diversions and wonders of his travels. He voyaged from London to Hamburg in 1617, and in 1618 walked from London to Edinburgh with no money about him, living on alms and the land. In 1620 he took a paper boat from London to Queenborough in Kent, using two stockfish tied to canes as oars (so it is said). In 1623 he undertook two adventures, one to York with Job Pennel, another royal waterman, and one to Salisbury by wherry. In 1641 he was still voyaging, sculling from London via Oxford to his birth place, Gloucester via Shrewsbury, Bristol, Bath, Monmouth and Hereford, and nine years later made a round trip by boat from London to Harwich, Ipswich, Norwich, King's Lynn and Cambridge.

Taylor's verses reflect state and city occasions. During the plague in 1626 he followed the court to Oxford and associated himself with Oriel, using books and dictionaries in the college library and signing his work 'John Taylor, of Oriel College, Oxford'. He kept a victualling house in Oxford and wrote anti-Roundhead propaganda. When he returned to London he worked as a waterman, based at Whitehall stairs:

Let trencher poets scrape for their base vails,

I'll take an oar in hand when writing fails;

And 'twixt the boat and pen I make no doubt

But I shall shift to pick a living out.

One of Taylor's literary achievments was to write the first recorded palindrome: 'Lewd did I live, & evil I did dwel.' He continued to publish books in Oxford until the 1640s, but was never really admitted into the first rank of writers of his time. From 1649 until his death in 1653 he kept a pub in Phoenix Alley, Long Acre, which became known as the Poet's Head on account of its sign, a self-portrait of the landlord.

There's many a King's head hang'd up for a sign,

And many a Saint's head too — then why not mine?

He was buried on the southern side of St Martin in the Fields, an area known as the watermen's burial ground.

Here lies the Water Poet, honest John,

Who rowed on the stream of Helicon;

Where, having many rocks and dangers past,

He at the haven of heaven arrived at last.

Portrait of John Taylor, the Water Poet (1580-1653) by unattributed artist, possibly a relative, also named John Taylor (Watermen's Hall Collection)

ry,
tone
ment
varre·

Remaining
the defence
and munic-
tion·

	Gonnes of Brasse		Gonnes of yron		Gonnpowder	
	Bd Cannons	ij	porte pecys	ij	Serpentyn	
	Culveryns	iiij	& Slynge	ij	powder in	x
	Saker	j	ffowlers	ij	barrells	
			Basses	vij	ffyne corne	xviij
			Tope pece	j	powder	
			hawle shott pecys	xij		
			handgonnes			
	Summa iij		complet	xij		
			Summa xlij			

☩ℎℯ · Anne · Gallante · Tunnes · iiij C·

5

THE NAVY LARK

The English navy's manpower was sustained by press gangs as it began its long voyage to become the world's greatest sea power. The ability of the monarch to requisition ships and crew them by entrapped men enabled the navy to spread its tentacles up all the creeks of known seas and uncharted waters.

When Henry III mounted an expedition against rebels in Gascony in 1253, he requisitioned all vessels on the Thames for troop carrying duties. Fourteen years later, when the Gascon fleet was laid up before the Tower, foreign traders were licensed to convey merchandise to and from London. Vessels from France, Spain, Flanders, Brabant and Germany were required to pay £75:6s:10d for a half year. Duties on imported wool and leather were used for erecting a landing place built on piles at Westminster.

King Henry VIII
by unknown artist
oil on panel,
1590s-1620
(National Portrait
Gallery, London)

In March 1355, Edward III fitted out a fleet on the south bank at Rotherhithe and sailed for France on 10 July. He manned his ships by impressing watermen and others to serve. Thus began the practices of requisitioning ships and men. A succession of monarchs would indulge in them for nearly five hundred years.

By the eighteenth century, impressment in the alleys and dark streets along the banks of the London river was a regular occurrence. The Watermen's Company history records impressments for upwards of 100 times from 1555, the year when the rulers of the Company began to regulate watermen, until the revision of naval practice that took place after the Napoleonic wars — a period of roughly 300 years. Wars and speculative expeditions were never far away. Throughout this period the Royal Navy grew into a formidable force, and thus the key element in the spread of British power and influence. The navy also transformed from a life of brutal buccaneering, piracy and war making to a model for peacekeeping, something that it continues on a modest scale in the twenty-first century. Impressment was the umbilical cord between the navy's meritocracy and the men who worked the River Thames, and for 300 years it had a profound effect on their lives.

From Roman times the Thames was a strategic river. Occasionally, foreign adventurers rubbed in its importance. In 1216 French ships reached London Bridge. In 1264 Cinque Port ships blockaded the Thames and Eleanor of Provence was repelled at London Bridge by the mayor's forces. The Thames was a moat against invaders from the south or the east as well as a two-way artery for people and goods between the estuary and inland. Every age entertains a struggle between the more and the less fortunate of the river's stakeholders. In the sixteenth century the main

Previous page: *Anne Gallante* – Roll of the Galleys of Henry VIII; 1546 (Bridgeman Images)

contenders ranged along the Thames are the monarch, Parliament, corporate bodies and the mayor and corporation of London. Their fortunes were sustained by their ability to raise revenue and support from merchants, gilds, landowners, religious institutions and other interested parties, particularly those concerned with key industries such as wool, coal and buccaneering on the high seas.

He who controlled foreign trade, either by treaty or privateering, amassed wealth and power, and the navy was a vital element in this process. Henry VII struck a blow for the monarchy in 1488 when he spent £14,000 on the *Great Harry*, the first purpose-designed military vessel. This was the mother ship of the Royal Navy. Until this time there was no national naval establishment. Vessels, men and boys were furnished to the state by different seaports, free of charge, for fifteen days in each year. Crews were victualled and paid by the king if detained for longer. The mayor and corporation and London's livery companies were also required to provide and clothe men. In 1489 the mayor was given jurisdiction over the tidal river with powers over such matters as unlawful fishing nets.

London and Thames commercial activities exist because of each other, and they grew by the century. It was not only goods and wealth that ebbed and flowed in abundance between the country and the continents. The struggle for power and the thirst for intelligence processed up and down with the tides —and no doubt reached the ears of toilers at the oars and others who were not intended to be party.

Wherrymen were well placed to witness comings and goings and great state occasions. In 1544, for example, Henry embarked for Calais to do battle with Francis I of France by taking a barge in two stages from Westminster to Gravesend, from where he continued on horseback to Dover. Two years later, after the peace of Guysnes and Arde, thirteen French galleys visited the Thames with dignitaries and six hundred horsemen on board. They disembarked at the Tower wharf, where was shot a "terrible peel of ordnance".

In 1547 Henry was succeeded by Edward, his son by his third wife, Jane Seymour. Aged nine, Edward VI was paraded by water from the Tower to Westminster for his coronation. Edward's reign was marked by publication of the first navy list. This revealed a fleet of twenty ships, fifteen galleasses, ten pinnaces and thirteen row barges, totalling 12,450 tons and manned by 8,546 seamen. The young king witnessed Lord Clinton being installed as Admiral of England at Deptford and wrote an account in his diary of the sham battle laid on for the occasion, which included capture of a 'fort made upon a great lighter' on the Thames — an early, if not the first, reference to a 'lighter'. At around this time, Paul Hentzner, a visitor to London, observed that the river abounds with swans, 'agreeable to the fleets that meet them in their course'. Everywhere, he said, were nets to catch salmon and shad.

In 1515 the first English double-decker, the 1,000 ton *Harry Grace à Dieu*, was launched from the dockyard at Woolwich. Known as the *Great Harry*, she was larger than her contemporary, the *Mary Rose*, and one of the first ships to be fitted with gun ports. But like the *Mary Rose*, she was top heavy. She saw little action but was the vessel that conveyed Henry to his meeting with Francis I at the Field of the Cloth of Gold. In the previous year came the first mention of Trinity Corporation, located at Deptford Creek, which was also a navy station. In this century a breed of adventurers from Devon and Cornwall emerged, men who challenged the global system forged by Spain and Portugal after Christopher Columbus found his way to America, when the unknown world had been divided between Spain and Portugal by papal bull in 1494. The likes of John Hawkins, Francis Drake, Richard Grenville and Walter Raleigh set about destabilising the trade routes. Their escapades in the Caribbean and the West Indies — capturing or looting galleons of cargoes of gold, silver, pearls, sugar, hides, and in Hawkins's case, profitable slave

Sir Richard Grenville
after Unknown artist
oil on canvas, 17th
century (1571)
(National Portrait
Gallery, London)

trading — not only made them rich, but convinced them that the key to prosperity and dominance over other countries was sea power.

Sir Francis Drake
after an engraving
attributed to
Jodocus Hondius
oil on panel, circa 1583
(National Portrait
Gallery, London)

Meanwhile, Henry VIII created a Navy Board, and when his daughter Elizabeth came to the throne in 1558, things were in better shape than they ever had been. The inventory listed 21 naval ships in service, with a further ten in reserve but beyond use. Another 45 merchantmen suitable for conversion in time of war were available, a force adequate to secure the English Channel if not to take on the Spanish empire.

After a disastrous episode in Spanish waters in 1568, John Hawkins assembled a private navy in Plymouth consisting of 16 ships with 400 cannon and 1,500 men that became the core of England's first fighting fleet. Hawkins in effect fathered the Royal Navy. He also became a double agent and was instrumental in foiling the Ridolfi plot in

Sir John Hawkins by Magdalena de Passe, by Willem de Passe line engraving, published 1620 (National Portrait Gallery, London)

which the Spanish tried to put Mary, Queen of Scots, on the English throne. Hawkins and his fellow West Country buccaneers came together to defeat the Spanish Armada in 1588, albeit aided by luck and favourable winds.

In January 1577 Hawkins succeeded his father-in-law, Benjamin Gonson, as treasurer to the Navy Board, enabling him to take things to the next level. Hawkins could review most of his new empire on a downstream passage by rowboat from his office at Tower Hill. Such a voyage would pass Henry's Deptford ship building docks, naval activity at Greenwich and the ordnance depots at Woolwich, Gravesend and Tilbury where sea and land forces assembled in time of war, and Chatham dockyard in the River Medway. The dockyard at Chatham was protected by sentinel forts at Upnor and Sheerness, and served as the navy's main anchorage for 150 years. Ships at Chatham were stripped of rigging, masts, sails and spars while shipwrights and dockyard workers painted, cleaned, repaired and replaced faulty planks and cleared the hulls of vermin.

During Hawkins's first year, two galleons to a new design were nearing completion— the *Revenge and Scout*—sister ships to *Dreadnought* that had been completed in 1573. The Dreadnought class were longer in the keel relative to their beam than predecessors, 'the head of a cod and the tail of a mackerel' in the words of their builders. They carried heavy guns, and size gave way to speed, manoeuvrability and firepower. Building from plans and drawings was introduced so that construction could be carried out in the absence of the naval architect. Hawkins

Sir Walter Raleigh by Nicholas Hilliard watercolour on vellum, circa 1585 (National Portrait Gallery, London)

built the first true dry dock at Deptford, giving the English navy the edge of being able to carry out below-waterline work routinely.

Hawkins also took advantage of the English discovery of cast iron for manufacturing cannon. Cast iron was inferior to the bronze, but cheaper. Bronze was preferred for culverins, the heaviest guns produced in the royal foundry at Houndsditch, but cast iron demi-culverins could smash a wooden ship to smithereens at 400 yards. The Revenge had 46 guns of which 22 were heavy, and they could be wheeled round the deck. Contrast this with the *Mary Rose* — the ship that turned over outside Portsmouth in 1545. *Mary Rose* carried nearly a hundred guns, but only six were heavy ordnance. *Revenge* had four times the firepower but half the guns of the *Mary Rose*.

Royal dockyard at Deptford 1773 (Watermen's Hall Collection)

Hawkins was also concerned for the welfare of the men. Too often sailors were regarded as dogs and treated as such. Pay was often delayed or not forthcoming at all. Sailors found an effective method of claiming their disputed deserts, though. They would take down or 'strike' the sails, hence the term still applied to withdrawing labour. Hawkins doubled the monthly pay for seamen from 5 shillings in Henry's day to 10 shillings in 1585.

Hawkins's progression from slave trader to the pinnacle of service to the state was exonerated when William Wynter, the master of ordnance, accused him of administrative malfeasance. An investigation ordered by Elizabeth found that he built a navy second to none while running his office without undue corruption — two remarkable feats. His light ships were faster, carried more shot and gunpowder and were more heavily armed than any rivals. They could also be made ready faster. Ironically, the experts brought in by the investigators included Hawkins's fellow seafaring chancers—Drake, Frobisher and Raleigh.

Impressment was a key ingredient of Hawkins's navy. In 1578 impressment took place to meet the threat from Spain, and ships were stationed in the river, a chain was installed across it and beacons were erected to give warning of enemy approaches. In 1588 a writer quoted in the Company history states that the royal navy consisted of 28 sail, augmented by more than 70 vessels armed and manned by the City, nobility and livery companies, augmented by ships from other ports, and 'most of the Thames watermen readily joined in the service'. When the Spanish Armada came, there were 181 ships and 17,472 sailors to repulse it, and the fleet brought together Hawkins who was in the Caribbean, Drake who was in Panama and Frobisher who was in Newfoundland.

The defeat of the Armada changed the world order, although Philip II and the Spanish empire were not yet dead. The English patrols in the Azores failed to stop Spanish treasure convoys until 1595. The Cornish ports of Mousehole, Newlyn and Penzance were burned by Spanish forces in 1594, and in 1599, the year after Philip's death, rumours of invasion led to 30,000 militiamen being amassed at Tilbury.

Meanwhile, British seamen continued their tradition of buccaneering, backed by a navy that could blockade the Spanish Main and keep the high seas open at the same time. Two hundred and thirty-five privateers sailed from English ports in the two years after the armada to prey on unarmed international shipping from the Channel to Cadiz, with some ranging as far afield as the West Indies. Sir Walter Raleigh and Sir Richard Leveson wreaked havoc in the Mediterranean. Watermen were impressed for Drake's expedition to conquer Portugal in 1589, and for Frobisher's expedition against Spain in 1592. In 1598 one estimate claims 40,000 watermen on the Company rolls, of whom 8,000 of a possible 20,000 eligible for employment were in the service of the fleet. A new generation of naval adventurers was taking over as the heroic age of Elizabethan statesmen and seamen faded. The Queen's advisors Leicester and Walsingham died in 1588 and 1590 respectively. By the turn of the century Frobisher and Grenville had been killed in action, and Hawkins and Drake were dead.

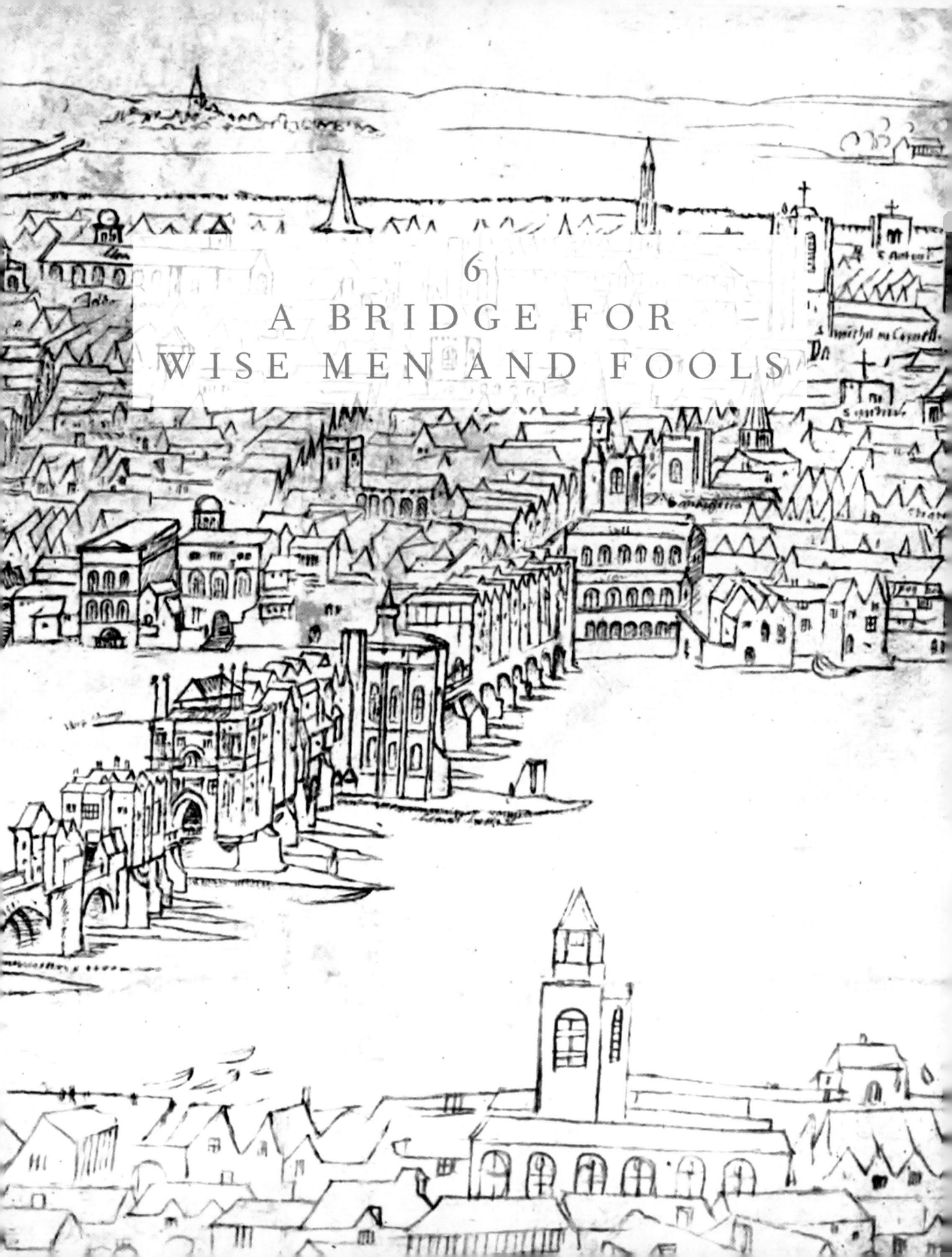

6

A BRIDGE FOR
WISE MEN AND FOOLS

London Bridge marks both the watermen's beginning and end. Two thousand years ago its site was a marsh, the first point beyond the estuary where it was possibly to cross the sprawling river. Romans and Danes and Saxons lighted on the strategic significance of this place. About AD50 the Romans erected a military pontoon bridge here, at 51° North and 0.5° West, and built a trading settlement close by which they called Londinium. They followed that with a piled bridge that met its end at the hands of Queen Boudicca, but the Romans returned to build another wooden bridge and a town of stone.

The Saxons viewed the Thames as a border between Mercia and Wessex. There are references to 'London' bridges and their destruction by Vikings in 1014, by storm in 1091 and by fire in 1136. In 1163 Peter de Colechurch was appointed warden of the bridge, and thirteen years later work began on a stone structure. What started in the reign of Henry II was finished in 1209 when King John was on the throne. The bridge had nineteen arches and a drawbridge with a defensive gatehouse at the southern end. Houses and shops up to seven stories high were erected along both sides of the roadway.

The arches were narrow. Waterwheels in the two northern arches powered water pumps and in the two southern arches turned grain mills, thus hampering flow and navigation at both ends of the bridge. The piers were protected by boat-shaped wooden 'starlings' that further hindered navigation. The difference between water

A west view of London Bridge showing the chasms occasioned by the burning of the temporary bridge, by which it was rendered impassable 1758 (Reginald Francis Print Collection)

Previous page: Excerpt from Wyngaerdes's Panorama of London c1544

London Bridge in the time of Charles I (Reginald Francis Print Collection)

levels above and below the bridge could be as much as six feet (two metres), a barrier that held up the tide. Thus shooting the bridge in either direction was hazardous when the tide ran. The bridge was for 'wise men to pass over and for fools to pass under'. A special breed of watermen known as the bridge shooters arose, prepared to take on the rushing waters. But accidents there were many.

Crossing over the bridge was often as frustrating as passing under it. The roadway which linked the parish of St Magnus on the north side with that of St Olave on the south was 26 feet wide but reduced by up to 14 feet by the two hundred buildings and places of business along the way. Congestion was often extreme – it could take an hour to cross to the other side. Thus watermen plying the stairs on either bank up and down stream of the bridge provided a highly competitive service for those on foot, as well as a direct link to a choice of places to alight.

The significance of London Bridge is that, for centuries, it was the only passage over the Thames until Kingston was reached, some 25 miles upstream. There had been a crossing there since Saxon times. This distance was shortened to eleven miles when Putney and Fulham were joined in 1729. Bridge building first threatened watermen's livings at Putney, although London Bridge remained the boundary between 'upriver' and 'downriver', the kernel of transport for London and the core of crossing points well into the twentieth century.

7

WALKING ON COALS,
SCULLING UNDER FIRE

The main thrust of this story has been a tale of man-made solutions to the demands of moving people and goods on a fickle waterscape. But climatic elements beyond control of man also play their part. Frost, flood, fog and fire fuel the flow of the Thames, and the elements bring brimstone on the lives of its people. Ice closes the river down, while fire scorches it with loss. The compilers of the Company history record a significant fire among warehouses and wharfs every two or three years, many of them tragic for lives as well as economy. But nothing really compared with the great fire of 1666 that raged for four days and took out a swathe of four hundred streets from Holborn to the Tower.

Samuel Pepys, the secretary of the navy board, rose at 3 o'clock in the morning on Sunday 2 September in Seething Lane when a servant roused him to tell of the fire she had seen in the direction of Billingsgate. He walked to the Tower and climbed to a high place from where he could see houses ablaze at the end of London Bridge. Three hundred burned that night. He came across the Lieutenant of the Tower, who told him it started in the King's baker Faryner's shop in Pudding Lane, ten doors from Thames Street, and spread along Fish Street by the bridge. Pepys walked to the waterside and took a boat up through the bridge, seeing houses burning as far as the Old Swan - 'evry body endeavouring to remove their goods, and flinging into the river, or bringing them into lighters that lay off,' he wrote in his diary. 'Poor people staying in their houses as long as till the very fire touched them, and then running into boats, or clambering from one pair of stairs by the waterside to another.'

It was a shocking scene. The long drought in the previous weeks had left everything combustible, even the stone of churches. The poor pigeons, Pepys noted, 'hovered about the windows and balconys, till they burned their wings, and fell down.'

He progressed upstream to Whitehall, where he told the King that he must command houses to be pulled down, and the King bade him to go and find Sir Thomas Bludworth, the mayor, to tell him that more soldiers were available.

In the streets there were carts and human backs everywhere, loaded with goods. Pepys found the mayor in Canning Street 'like a man spent, with a handkercher about his neck.'

'Lord, what can I do?' asks Bludworth. 'People will not obey me. I have been pulling down houses; but the fire overtakes us faster than we can do it.' He needed no more soldiers, he said. He must go and refresh himself, having been up all night.

The diarist set off for home by foot, observing that there was no means of quenching the fire. The warehouses in Thames Street were full of pitch and tar, oil, wines and brandy. At 12 noon he enjoyed an extra good dinner with his household, afterwards walking through the City where the streets were full of carts and people running over one another, removing stuff out of Canning Street into Lombard Street. He reached Paul's Wharf and took to the water again, being rowed above and below the bridge to see the fire that had spread in both directions since the morning.

The scene on the river was similar to that in the streets: 'River full of lighters and boats taking in goods, and goods swimming in the water.' Riverside dwellers were flinging their

Previous page: The Great Fire of London 1666 (Bridgeman Images)

goods and furniture into boats and barges, or into the river itself. Bankside was covered with loaded craft until tents and other places could be organised for reception of property. Pepys saw a boat bearing a pair of virginalls – a type of spinet. Charles and the Duke of York were now hither and thither aboard the king's barge, exerting others to check the progress of the flames. The navy man accompanied them to Queenhithe, where there were good hopes of stopping the fire at Three Cranes above the bridge and Botolph's Wharf below. But the wind carried it further into the City.

Watermen's Hall 1647 (Watermen's Hall Collection)

The Company history does not offer any enlightenment on whether men manning wherries made merry with fares or ran a humanitarian rescue service, but given the emphasis on moving possessions, the former seems more likely. Concern for the Hall is recorded, though. 'It is worthy of observation that when Watermen's Hall was discovered to be on fire, King Charles, who was stated to be on the roof of one of the houses, in one of the narrow alleys leading to Three Cranes, in the Vintry, was so stirred by the sight that he made fresh efforts to check the progress of the conflagration, by ordering more houses to be demolished.'

Pepys went upriver to Whitehall again where he met his wife in St. James's Park, and they walked back to the boat, 'and there upon the water again, and to the fire up and down, it still encreasing, and the wind great. So near the fire as we could for smoke; and all over the Thames, with one's faces in the wind, you were almost burned with a shower of fire-drops.'

Flakes of fire ignited more houses, and the fire moved faster than the demolition squads who were trying desperately to create chasms that flames could not leap.

Pepys and his party repaired to an ale-house on Bankside across the Thames from Three Cranes, and stayed until almost dark, 'and saw the fire grow, and as it grew darker, appeared more and more, and in corners and upon steeples, and between churches and houses, as far as we could see up the hill of the City, in a most horrid malicious bloody flame, not like the fine flame of an ordinary fire. One entire arch of fire from this to the other side of the bridge, and in a bow up the hill for an arch of above a mile long: it made me weep to see it. The churches, houses, and all on fire, and flaming at once; and a horrid noise the flames made, and the cracking houses at their ruine.' And so home, he writes, with a sad heart.

Later that night the Pepyses began to pack their own goods, carrying much to the garden in the moonlight, and carting money and iron chests to the cellar. At 4am on Monday

morning Samuel, in his nightgown, accompanied his money and plate by cart to a friend's at Bethnal Green, through streets full of runners and riders. Later that day he took his goods over Tower Hill to a lighter moored above Tower Dock, ready to transport them downriver. On Tuesday he got the lighter away, observing that the fire was moving into Tower Street where houses near Trinity House and the Dolphin tavern were being blown up. The sky was on fire at night; flames had reached Old Bailey, Fleet Street, St Paul's and Cheapside. That night Pepys slept in his office, and on Wednesday the fire was nearing his house in Seething Lane. He sent his wife Elizabeth away and arranged to carry his hoard of £2,350 by Proundy's boat to Woolwich.

Great Fire of London 1666 (Southwark Local History Library)

'But Lord!' Pepys wrote, 'What a sad sight it was by moone-light to see the whole City almost on fire, that you might see it plain at Woolwich, as if you were by it. There, when I come [to the dockyard], I find the gates shut, but no guard kept at all; which troubled me, because of discourse now begun, that there is a plot in it, and that the French had done it.'

He managed to get the gates open and lock up his gold, and went back to town, where to his relief neither his office nor home was on fire: 'I find that by blowing up of houses… there is a good stop given to it… it having only burned the dyall of Barking Church [All Hallows by the Tower], and part of the porch, and was there quenched. I up to the top of Barking steeple, and there saw the saddest sight of desolation that I ever saw; everywhere great fires, oyle-cellars, and brimstone, and other things burning. I became afraid to stay there long, and therefore down again as fast as I could.' He walked – 'our feet ready to burn, walking on coals' – to the Exchange and into Moorfields and then home via Cheapside and Newgate market, all burned. Moorfields was full of 'poor wretches carrying their goods'. Always concerned with people, was Pepys. He set watchmen to guard his office and went home for the night.

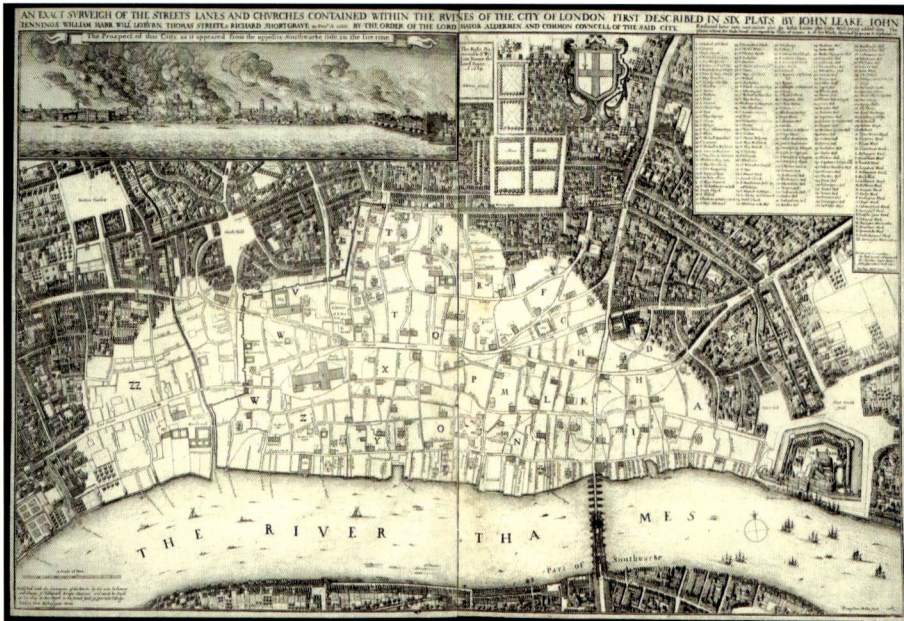

Map, completed in 1677, shows the remains of the city after the Great Fire
(© The British Library Board, Maps.Crace.Port.1.50.)

Next morning, 6 September, he was up again at 5am. Fire broke out at Bishopsgate, giving grounds to people, 'and me too,' to think there is some kind of plot in this; on the day before there had been rumours of the French and Dutch 'being risen'. But the fire was quickly extinguished, together with the rumour. Pepys took a boat to Southwark and from there across to Westminster, searching in vain for a place to buy a shirt or a pair of gloves. He found that the Exchequer's coffers had been put aboard vessels and taken to Nonesuch House, near Epsom. He went to the Swan to be trimmed, walked around Whitehall 'but

Original apprentice bindings register book 1656-1665, only known Company artefact to survive the Great Fire of London

saw nobody', and then returned home. He joined a large and merry company for fried breast of mutton at Sir R. Ford's. There was rejoicing among the ashes that the flames had died and the sky was no longer red or wreathed in smoke.

The Great Fire consumed Waterman's Hall and all the Company's records, leaving only a registry book recording binding of apprentices from 15 June 1656 to 28 June 1665. The Guildhall, Trinity House, Custom House, 52 halls and 86 churches, including St Paul's, were destroyed. In addition 13,200 houses were either burned or reduced to rubble to prevent fire spreading. As John Dryden put it:

A key of fire ran all along the shore,

And lighten'd all the river with a blaze;

The waken'd tides began again to roar,

And wond'ring fish in shining water gaze.

8
THE POWER OF SAIL

The seventeenth century reinforced Francis Drake's observation that the wealth of both Indies was in great part an accessory to the command of the seas. The navy dominated English life, and was influential in Parliament's victory in the English Civil War. Naval power became an irrevocable part of English national identity. Thirty trading companies were formed in the fifty years up to 1630. Some of them, like the Providence Island Company for trade with an island off Nicaragua, included privateers as well as trade in the specification. The first levy for the navy applicable to inland towns in addition to ports was introduced in 1634, and regular patrols round the British Isles began in the same year. England became a key player in the Atlantic economy. The idea that a permanent naval base within striking distance of the Spanish Caribbean was desirable soon took root. Places such as Boston, Plymouth, Jamestown and Roanoke were there for the choosing from the hundred and fifty North American colonial settlements.

It was not all plain sailing or one-sided. The 1604 peace with Spain negotiated by the theologian and scholarly King James a year after he succeeded Elizabeth resulted in the navy going to pot for a while. There was a low point of naval history in 1625 when a disastrous attack on Cadiz took place. The Providence Island Company failed. The Dutch, fellow protestants and former protégés, embraced the century after their release from the yoke of Spanish domination. In an embarrassing move in 1639, the Dutch trapped and destroyed the Spanish fleet off the Goodwin Sands while the English navy looked on, powerless to prevent fisticuffs in its own neutral waters.

By 1625 there were about forty thousand seamen involved in naval service. The Navy Board built ships and fitted them out while the Admiralty commissioned captains and officers whose job it was to find crews. A Royal Navy officer corps and a career structure for regularly employed seamen were still in the future. Thus in the seventeenth century the navy was still concerned with ships rather than men — hence the importance of the press gangs in times of trouble.

Seamen's pay rose to 15 shillings per month in 1626. A ship's company was organised into two shifts or watches named starboard (after the right or steer board side of the ship) and larboard (after the left side used for loading goods in port, hence 'port' side). Each shift worked on deck for three four-hour stretches in twenty-four hours, varied by two two-hour 'dog watches' between four to six and six to eight in the evening so that sailors did not keep the same watch each day. Deck work was under the captain, lieutenant and sailing and navigation masters. Warrant officers—sailors authorized by the Admiralty for supervisory duties—organised other activities. There was a bosun in charge of sails and rigging, a master gunner in charge of cannon, a quartermaster in charge of ammunition, a purser in charge of victuals and a trumpeter to blow orders and ship-to-ship communications. One effect of the navy levy of 1634 was the permanent deployment of surgeons and chaplains on board ships, and what came to be known as 'tarpaulin' officers — professional officers with experience, often drawn from lower ranks.

During the republican years under Oliver Cromwell, customs and excise duties were harnessed to support the navy, and the demands on it rendered armed merchantmen

Previous page: View of Greenwich Hospital 1798 (Reginald Francis Print Collection)

no longer suitable for complex operations in the Channel, Irish Sea, North Africa or the coast of Portugal. The strength was 45 ships in 1647, 72 by 1650 and more than 130 by 1654, when monthly pay for sailors had reached 24 shillings. The fleet included 100-gun, 80-gun and 60-gun classes as well as new smaller but faster 'frigates' of Spanish design. Long-distance merchantmen continued to go armed but were no longer called into navy service.

Meanwhile, there remained plenty of wild west in the Caribbean, where the navy drove the Spanish out of Jamaica in 1655, leaving Port Royal to be adopted as a base for English pirates. In 1688 Henry Morgan's dozen ships captured the assembly point for Spain's bullion flotillas, the fort at Portobello in Panama, and exacted a massive ransom from the governor.

Despite a new Anglo-Spanish treaty in 1670 in which Britain agreed to rein in its privateers, Morgan and Thomas Modyford, Jamaica's governor, attacked Panama City itself in 1671 with 2,000 men and 38 ships. The governor of Panama torched his own city, and little bullion was found. Modyford wound up in the Tower, but Morgan turned gamekeeper through his aristocratic connections and was sent back to Jamaica

Samuel Pepys by John Hayls 1666 (National Portrait Gallery, London)

to clean up the buccaneering business and create a safe Caribbean fortress for the navy. The navy was, indeed, beginning to trade buccaneering for policing.

When Samuel Pepys became clerk for the Navy Board in 1660, the year that Charles II returned from exile to restore the monarchy, he began a programme of reform that would ensure that the navy would remain second to none. As an able administrator, Pepys left his mark despite the failure of his Stuart patrons' foreign policy, and despite being accused of Papal and Jacobean sympathies. A landlubber himself, he set about learning everything he could about navigation, tide tables, backstaffs and telescopes, ship construction, spars and rigging, qualities of wood and methods of making ropes. In summer he would walk to Deptford or Woolwich in the early morning or take a boat to Chatham to hobnob with designers and observe shipwrights at work.

When he retired as secretary of the Admiralty in 1688 after James II fled the country, Pepys had supervised the construction of ten new one-class ships of 80 guns and twenty 'third raters', meeting uniform standards of tonnage and design and equipped with iron cannon instead of brass, no matter in which yard they were built. A million oak trees were planted for future shipbuilding. Examinations were introduced for the rank of lieutenant, trainees being termed 'midshipmen'. This move compelled aristocrats who joined the navy to go to sea to gain experience while enabling tarpaulins to rise from the ranks. Unemployed flag officers were put on half pay, thus creating a professional naval reserve. A royal observatory was built at Greenwich for the study of astronomy and navigation under Jonas Moore. Pepys's contemporary diarist, John Evelyn, was in charge of sick and wounded sailors and prisoners of war, and the idea of a seamen's hospital took root. It opened at Greenwich Palace in 1696.

A petition to the monarch in 1668 resulted in a direction to the Company to restore the rights of apprentices who found that their masters had died while they were on naval service during the Dutch war. Another problem faced by watermen was impressments for land duties. They were exempted from such in 1672, but James II impressed watermen for army service in 1688, to a chorus of complaints.

In 1679 the rulers of the Company contributed to a fund to secure release of several hundred sailors, many of whom were watermen, imprisoned by the Dey of Algiers.

Pepys almost lost his place in history during the Popish Plot hysteria when he was falsely accused of Catholic sympathies, but he emerged as first secretary for the affairs of the Admiralty in 1684 after a period of political turmoil that saw the emergence of the first Whigs under Lord Shaftesbury and the first Tories under the Earl of Danby. This office gave him control over both Admiralty and Navy Board, and he also became president of the Royal Academy in the same year. He retired when James went into exile after William and Mary united Dutch and English interests in the Glorious Revolution of 1688.

In 1689 William squared up to Louis XIV of France and his acolyte, James, in a conflict which lasted for twenty years and required the navy to patrol the Channel, escort convoys in the Atlantic and the Mediterranean, and support land operations in Ireland and on the Continent. In short, year-round service on several fronts, facing a well-organised French navy that had faster and better-armed ships. Things went off on the wrong foot, with British sailors refusing to join ships because they had not been paid. The French defeated the Dutch and English fleets off Beachy Head and briefly had the run of the Channel, but could not maintain their foothold in Torbay, while their army in Ireland under James's command was defeated at the Battle of the Boyne.

In 1692 Louis launched an invasion from the Cherbourg peninsular, but his fleet was outgunned and burned off Barfleur and La Hougue by Admiral Russell's Anglo-Dutch squadrons, marking the point when Britannia took command of the waves. Russell had written down his fighting and navigation instructions and perfected the line ahead formation that was to serve the navy through the American war of independence almost a century later. Ground was broken for the seamen's hospital in Greenwich in gratitude. The navy now fronted every maritime technical, scientific and medical development. In 1693 the first coastal survey of Britain was carried out, and at the turn of the century experiments were under way for a new way to steer ships — the wheel. A keen observer of navy practice at this time was Czar Peter the Great of Russia, who in 1698 spent several months studying shipbuilding at the royal dockyard at Deptford. He was a skilled sailor and oarsman, taking to the river with Sir Anthony Deane, commissioner of the navy. He and his cronies boozed in a tavern in Great Tower Street that changed its name to 'Czar of Muskovy'.

The French, however, were not finished yet. They turned to a systematic campaign of privateering from their Atlantic ports and wreaked havoc on English and Dutch merchant shipping, taking more than four thousand prizes. The Royal Navy bottled up the French in the Mediterranean but could not contain them elsewhere. In the peace treaty of 1696 Louis was blunted but not beaten.

Soon after the century turned came the War of the Spanish Succession that lasted for nearly twelve years. The extraordinary requirements of the navy for watermen and apprentices brought pressure on the mayor and alderman to change the rules of engagement. The committee appointed to hear the Company's objections and report to the mayor's court recommended that, for the duration of the present war only, the seven years of freedom that a freeman must serve before taking on an apprentice be reduced to four. It also suggested that a freeman be able to bind a second apprentice when his first had served four years, instead of waiting until the first apprentice was within three months of qualifying for his freedom. The mayor's court decreed that this should take effect on 23 January 1694, but no record of proceedings to alter the byelaws accordingly remains. The Company history surmises that the rulers objected and therefore did nothing, instead trying to obtain further parliamentary powers in the ensuing session.

Peter the Great of Russia by Bernard Vogel; after Jan Kupecký mezzotint, published 1737 (National Portrait Gallery, London)

An impressment for that year's summer expedition revealed that thousands of bound apprentices never took up their freedom in order to avoid the draft. The rulers apparently prepared a Bill to go before Parliament that promised to make un-free watermen liable for impressment. It also promised a master chosen by the Company court to hold a casting vote over the eight elected rulers, which proposition did not come to pass until 1827. It proposed a school for training youth in the art of navigation. It promised to empower the company to suppress [sic] all such as profane the Sabbath while on the water. It empowered auditors to prevent embezzlement. But it never became law.

The rulers were between a rock and a hard place over impressment in 1694, caught between the demands of the order of 23 January to make more apprentices eligible for the navy and complaints about unskilled, under age and unbound boys being caught by the press gangs. Meanwhile, protected watermen were being recruited to the navy, and it seemed that only the old and maimed watermen and boys were left alone for

Greenwich Hospital 1826 (Reginald Francis Print Collection)

Greenwich Hospital 1835 (Reginald Francis Print Collection)

the public service. On 4 July an order forbade under-eighteens to be apprenticed unless they were sons of watermen, in which case the limit was set at sixteen years.

Impressment continued every year from 1703 to 1713, when the Treaty of Utrecht was signed. There was trouble in 1705 when the zealous Lieutenant Church of *HMS Tilbury*, recruiting for the relief of Gibraltar, impressed nine of the twenty-eight older watermen operating Sunday ferries on 11 March in that year. This alarmed others who were selected to operate Sunday ferries because they had large families to support. Many consequently disappeared and left the public to cross the river as best they could. An appeal for redress to the Lord High Admiral fell on deaf ears, so the rulers petitioned the Queen in council. In May the Queen referred the matter back to the Lord High Admiral, who again justified the impressment and retaining of men. The rulers again appealed to the Queen, pointing out that the Sunday ferrymen were exempt from impressment by act of parliament. The petition also addressed the argument that the navy's requirement for watermen was falling short by pointing out that warships now remained in commission round the year instead of paying off their crews in the autumn; that the bounty was such that watermen liable for impressment often joined up of their free will; further, that watermen who had not enlisted did so once the Company received a warrant for impressment in order to avoid it. Captains and lieutenants were impressing watermen willy-nilly, ignorant of exemptions issued by the Company for infirmity, age or number of children to support. Many hundreds of watermen were also protected by essential work for the office of ordnance, Custom House, the navy, the victualing office, or the Admiralty itself. Since the beginning of the war more than three thousand watermen had volunteered for the navy. The under-manning of Sunday ferries caused overloading above the legal limit of eight passengers per boat. The outcome of this petition is not recorded.

In 1707 protection from impressments was extended to firemen. The Act said that watermen belonging to each fire insurance office within the cities of London and Westminster, not exceeding thirty for each office, shall be free from being impressed or serving as marines or soldiers. Sunday ferrymen, however, were taken again in the next year. An Act of Parliament on fire protection reinforced protection for firemen in 1774. 'And whereas the several offices for insuring houses against loss by fire retain in their several services, and give coats, badges, and other rewards unto watermen for their service and assistance, in and towards the extinguishing of fire,' it stated, 'and who are to be always ready when wanted, and are provided with various sorts of poles, hooks, hatchets, and several other instruments and things,' said watermen shall not be compelled to go to sea. The Act noted that fire-fighting watermen were found to venture much further, and to have the skill and experience to give greater help, than other persons.

9

DOGGETT MAKES
HIS DAY

Before the Great Fire that destroyed it, the Old Swan in Upper Thames Street was a regular haunt of the chief secretary to the Admiralty and diary keeper, Samuel Pepys. One of the attractions of the Swan and the nearby 'wine-shade' that survived the fire was their proximity to London Bridge and the flow of traffic passing over and under it. Imbibers enjoyed the hourly tidal wave of passing humanity, and customers of the wine house could drink their 'genuine old port and sherry, drawn from casks,' and view the bridge shooters and boat races.

Here was the crossroads of the City, where the purveyors of bread and circuses met and posted their bills of fare. Thousands traversed between Middlesex and Surrey on the bridge, while watermen at nearby stairs had a never ending queue of customers wishing, in the words of an unknown poet, to 'lightning flog it, up the Thames as swiftly jog it' for Westminster, Gravesend, Greenwich or Lambeth and all stairs in between. The bridge was a barrier and therefore a transport hub. At times of strong tides, many chose to disembark upstream or downstream of it and take another wherry after passing it on terra firma, while the more adventurous would throw in their lot with the specialist bridge shooters.

John Evelyn spelt out the danger in his diary on 19 January 1649: 'I returned home passing an extraordinary danger of being drowned by our wherries falling foul in the night on another vessel then at anchor, shooting the bridge at three quarters ebb, for which His mercy God Almighty be praised.'

John Taylor, the water poet, estimated boldly that forty thousand watermen plied their trade from Richmond to Gravesend by 1600, and one of the busiest places on the London river was right here near the Old Swan and the Old Swan Stairs, where wherries nudged their noses onto the beach at low tide or pushed into the steps at high, and the watermen touted for custom and haggled for passengers. There were about forty stairs between the bridge and the Horseferry at Westminster on the north side, and a similar number below the bridge to Limehouse. A few yards upstream from Old Swan were Cold Harbour stairs and then Three Cranes, while opposite were stairs at Pepper Dock, St. Saviour's Dock and St. Mary Ovaries. Below the bridge on the north side was Billingsgate, centre of the fish trade, Sabb's Stairs and then Custom House, and on the south side Tooley Street, Battle Bridge and Pickle Herring.

The bustle brought constant struggle for a living among the wherrymen. Their charges were first regulated by parliament in the sixteenth century, and the latest revision was in 1770, examples being 6d. in oars or 3d. for a sculler from all stairs between London and Westminster; 2s. in oars or 4d. per head in company for London to Putney; 4s. 6d. in oars or 9d with company from London to Gravesend.

There were other specialists beside the bridge shooters. John Reeves, who died in 1730, plied at Essex stairs and charged anglers two shillings a day to fish the river for plentiful roach, dace, perch, plaice, smelts, flounders, salmon, shad, eels, gudgeon and dabs. His regular customers clubbed together to buy him a waterman's coat and a silver badge that sported an impress of himself with an angler in his boat. They gave him a new coat each year. Tackle and bait shops in the vicinity of the bridge illustrated

Previous page: The first winner of Doggett's Coat and Badge by Peter Monamy 1681-1749 (Watermen's Hall Collection)

the importance of fish until the river became poisoned by pollution in the mid 1800s. On 7 June 1749, for example, there were two great draughts of salmon caught, thirty-five in one and twenty-two in the other.

Watermen had always been prone to frost and plague, the first depriving them of water and therefore trade, and the second closing down places of entertainment for months at a time. Theatres, bear pits and pleasure gardens satisfied a huge demand for entertainment for nobs and mobs alike, and theatre companies and their audiences were dependent on wherries to fill their galleries and pits. Theatrical and low life was concentrated in Southwark on the south bank before it made inroads on the north side, when its growth offset any falling off in waterborne trade.

The career of Edward Alleyne, famous for his leading roles in Christopher Marlowe's plays, demonstrates the extent of the entertainment industry in the late sixteenth century. Alleyne joined his father-in-law Philip Henslowe in profitable promotions of

John (Jack) Broughton, winner of Doggett's in 1730. Broughton boxed under the Duke of Cumberland's patronage and was champion of England from 1734 to 1750. His 1743 code for boxing earned him the soubriquet 'father of English boxing' (Watermen's Hall Collection)

playhouses, bear pits and brothels, building a fortune that would endow Dulwich College. Among their enterprises were the Rose theatre on Bankside, the Fortune theatre on Finsbury Fields and the Paris Garden on the south approach of what is now Blackfriars Bridge. Here Alleyne and Henslowe put on plays and jointly held the office of Master of the King's Games, for which they kept mastiffs, bandoggs, bears and other creatures. The *Morning Chronicle* described three of Alleyne's favourite dogs fighting a lion at the Tower in the presence of James I.

Alleyne's empire stood astride the London River, and entertainment was stock-in-trade for watermen. Theatre thrived, particularly after 1660 when women began to appear on the stage. Pepys and Evelyn and the pioneers of journalism, Joseph Addison and Richard Steele, had the opportunity to see actors of the calibre of Barton Booth and his dancer wife Hester Santlow, Thomas Betterton, Anne Bracegirdle, Nance Oldfield, Spranger Barry, Hannah Pritchard and David Garrick. Bartholomew Fair's booths were in full voice each year as a testing ground for talent. Drury Lane and the Queen's Theatre were leading producers of comedy and drama. The Yorkshire-born William Congreve was making waves in comedy and play writing, his mentor John Dryden in criticism and all things Reformation, and his friend Jonathan Swift in satire and political pamphleteering.

Document dated 1715 bearing the signature of Thomas Doggett (The Garrick Club)

Doggett's entries for 1852

FINISH OF THE RACE FOR DOGGETT'S COAT AND BADGE.
From the original by Rowlandson in the British Museum.

Finish of the race for Doggett's Coat and Badge by Thomas Rowlandson 1756-1827 (Watermen's Hall Collection)

Divine providence perhaps had a hand in the abeyance of plague during the most active period of William Shakespeare's work from 1594 to 1603, after which theatres were more closed than open for seven years. Plague, and sometimes war, closed theatres at least three times in each of the sixteenth and seventeenth centuries, causing watermen to petition for their re-opening. What turned out to be the last serious outbreak of bubonic plague took place in 1665, in all probability incinerated by the Great Fire in 1666. It is evident, therefore, that thespians and watermen were mutually dependent, although already river trade was threatened by the advent of sedan chairs and Hackney carriages. The former were restricted to two hundred and the latter to eight hundred in 1710, but the writing was in the wake.

One of Drury Lane's managers carved a name for himself in Congreve's comedies, a Dubliner by the name of Thomas Doggett. His was not a name that sprang to mind as readily as some of those mentioned above in the taverns and eating places, but his biographer Theodore Cook says that he possessed the rare combination of Celtic wit and Saxon business qualities. He was a good actor, a good manager, and made a good living. He was also a committed Whig, and when the Hanoverians arrived on the British throne in 1714 on the death of Queen Anne, Doggett did something that would draw far more attention of many more people than ever applauded his efforts or his very presence on the stage. On 1 August 1715 he offered a prize of a coat and badge for the winner of a sculling race from the Old Swan at London Bridge to the White Swan in Chelsea. Furthermore, he specified that the race, restricted to six watermen in their first year of freedom from apprenticeship, should be held in perpetuity— and made provision in his will to try and ensure that it was. The prize was a coat of orange red to match that of the King's watermen, and a silver badge depicting Liberty, the horse of the House of Hanover.

Doggett, who like Pepys was an habitué of the Swan, announced his prize on the night before it was due by posting a notice at London Bridge, while a playbill distributed at Drury Lane Theatre said that the start could be seen from the Old Swan at 4 p.m. Thus began a revered and enduring sporting event.

Doggett's match was not the earliest. Pepys wrote in his diary for 18 May 1661: 'Was fain to stand upon one of the piers about the bridge… I found the Thames full of boats and galleys and upon inquiry found there was a wager to be run this morning. So spying of Payne in a gally, I went in to him, and there staid, thinking to have gone to Chelsy with them. But upon the start the wager boats fell foul of one another, till at last one of them gives over, pretending foul play, and so the other row away alone and all our sport lost.'

1808 Doggett's Badge won by George Newell of Battle Bridge

This reference to a course from the bridge to Chelsea comes more than fifty years before Doggett's, and perhaps indicates that this was already a customary match course. The attraction of such events went much deeper than excitement of following the race. For the participants, a prize was deadly serious in that it gave its winner prowess, status and sometimes the tools for the business of plying for hire. Ned Warde's *London Spy* gave a flavour of a passenger's lot in 1703:

'A Jolly Grizzle Pated Charon handed us into his wherry, strips off his short skirted doublet whereon was a badge to show whose fool he was, then fixes his stretcher, bids us trim the boat and away he rowed us, but we had not swum above the length of a West Country barge before a scoundrel crew of Lambeth gardeners attacked us with such a volley of fancy nonsense that it made my eyes stare, my head ake, my tongue run and my ears tingle.' This was followed, said the scribe, by a torrent of unquoted lurid language.

Wherry men were required to serve an apprenticeship and were the first public servants to wear a livery. A special coat or a gleaming silver badge weighing about twelve ounces depicting, in the case of Doggett's, the Hanoverian horse of liberty, would stand out in the throng at the plying place. The winner of a wherry would be set up with the essential vehicle to last his working lifetime. Charles Dibdin illustrated the point in his ballad opera, The Watermen on the First of August, first performed at the Haymarket in 1774. In it Tom Tug wins Doggett's and the heart of his mistress who watches from the window of an inn.

And did you not hear of a jolly young waterman,

Who at Blackfriars Bridge used for to ply?

He feathered his oars with such skill and dexterity,

Winning each heart, and delighting each eye;

He looked so neat , and he row'd so steadily

The maidens all flock'd to his boat so readily,

And he eyed the young rogues with so charming an air,

That this waterman ne'er was in want of a fare…

So whenever a coat and badge, or better still a prize wherry, was offered, hundreds proffered their names to be drawn out of the hat to contest the six-boat final, six boats abreast being the maximum that the river, crowded with ships, could accommodate.

The six Doggett's contenders who each year struggled with each other to Chelsea against the strongest ebb tide were selected thus by lot for more than 150 years. Luck rather than talent or oarsmanship was therefore the arbiter. Each year there were likely several outstanding scullers who never had a look in, and the qualification rule allowed only one chance.

1850 Doggett's Coat ensemble won by William Henry Campbell of Westminster

Doggett organised his race himself from its inception to his death in 1721, when responsibility was vested in Edward Burt of the Admiralty Office until Doggett's executors paid £300 to the Fishmongers' Company. The company added a further £50, and has carried out the comedian's wishes ever since. In 1751 there was a scheme afoot to raise a subscription for a boat to present to the winner, but nothing came of it. In 1747 Sir William Joliff bequeathed £200 of South Sea stock to the race, the interest to be divided in proportion five eighths and three eighths to the men who arrived at Chelsea second and third. The Fishmongers thus handed out £4:17s: 9d as the second prize and £2:18s: 9d as the third prize in that year. The prizes were increased in about 1820 so that the winner received a guinea in addition to the coat and badge, while the fourth received £1:11s: 6d and the fifth and sixth 1 guinea provided they rowed the distance.

Change came slowly to Doggett's. In 1769 the draw was switched from Watermen's Hall to Fishmongers' because of bad behaviour by watermen. At the same time regulations were laid down to prevent unfair lightening of boats, and lots were introduced for their use, requiring a deposit of half a guinea. This occurred because boats had become a problem. Contestants' response to being required to pull a four-seater passenger wherry for five miles and more against the tide was to reduce the weight as much as possible by stripping the boat of all unnecessary accoutrements. This resulted in the construction of boats suited only for racing, and gave a flying start to a contestant with a light craft, which was regarded as against the spirit of Doggett's.

The imposition of craft approved by Fishmongers' inspection was intended to put an end to this, but the progression towards boats known as 'old fashions' was not entirely about safety. Old fashions were narrow wager boats with flared wooden wings. Guy Nickalls, Theodore Cook's co-author, described them thus: 'the sides of the boat were carried up and out, the boats got narrower and narrower, and the wooden wings, which of course now assumed the form of wooden outriggers, had their interstices filled in with thin cedar planking.' They were thus exceedingly hard to sit. If a wave got on top of the wing it held the boat down on one scull with little chance of recovery, or if a roller hit the boat underneath the wing it could roll the oarsman over. When iron outriggers came along, they were banned until 'best' boats with conventional riggers were allowed from 1907. In 1955 the fishmongers, watermen, tugmen, master lightermen and barge owners funded a set of clinker gigs to be used in the race, replaced in 1964, 1981 and 2005, by now smooth-bottomed standard racing shells.

Interference by chance or design was a problem for the race. In 1807 a re-row was ordered after trouble near Westminster Bridge resulted in all but the winner declining the contest. There was a foul on the first attempt in 1809, and a false start in 1814. In 1817 the boats ran foul of a galliot at Blackfriars, and the race was re-run on another day.

In 1905 a confession was posted at Fishmongers' Hall, signed by the clerk's grandfather, in reference to a race in the 1820s. It said: 'We the undernamed, James Cole and William Mount of St Catherine's Stairs, watermen, and James Reid, of Blackfriars, waterman, with others in a cutter, did wilfully and riotously obstruct two of the wagermen rowing for the said Prize by intentionally running athwart near Old Swan Stairs and stopping their boats with a boathook, whereby they were impeded in contending for the Prize; and in such act one of the wagermen was struck with the boathook and the whole were obliged to be started a second time.'

In 1824 George Fogo won Doggett's. The *Morning Chronicle* reported that 'the whole six rowed without their shirts, and the shooting of the muscle along the upper part of the arm, at each stroke, was as fine an anatomical spectacle as can well be conceived, while the scapula behind kept admirable line to the play of the arm.'

In 1826 the win by *Boet* was attributed by the same newspaper to his being piloted by Bob Brocking who was in a cutter a little astern. The reporter commented: 'This may be good tactics along the coast of Milbank, but in other parts of the world, the vessel intended to pilot, would in all human probability have gone a little ahead.' The newspaper also noted a race for a prize wherry given by the amateurs of Blackfriars on the next day, the Tower wherry contest on the day after that, and a match for a supper given by the timber merchant Mr. Lett of Lambeth 'as an encouragement to industry' on the day after that.

In 1843 the *Era* reported: 'The [Doggett's] match will be re-rowed in consequence of Fry, who was just breaking away from Scott, having been fouled, and almost run over by a boat filled with dastardly fellows who had evidently some interest in the result. The umpire accordingly fired for the boats to return, as under the circumstances it would not be considered a match.'

The unsatisfactory practice of drawing lots to determine who should take part lasted until the second half of the nineteenth century. Any number of men in their first year of freedom could put their names down to take part, but only the first six to be drawn were assigned a place in the race. Drawing lots was contentious, but there were ways of getting round it. A report in 1862 said, 'For some years past the Fishmongers' Company has allowed any one of the six chosen men, desirous of not competing, to dispose of his lot to one of the other participants, of whom plenty may be found ready to purchase a chance, and accordingly this year James Worrledge of Hungerford sold his lot to John Bartlett of Horselydown, who contended in his place.'

Two years later W. Wentworth and J. Bury disposed of their chances to David Coombes, son of the former world champion Robert, and James Groves respectively, both of Horselydown. Coombes, having bought a chance and being qualified to row for the Horselydown, travelled from Dublin expressly to row. The betting just before the start was 2 to 1 on Frank Kilsby, 5 to 2 against Coombes and 8 to 1 against any other. The *Lotus, Rifleman* and *Stork* steamers accompanied the race. Mr. Dards, barge master to the Fishmongers', umpired for the twenty-fourth time on the fifty-eighth occasion that he had attended Doggett's. The race started at 1.25 p.m., and Coombes and Kilsby soon left the others. Passing Southwark Bridge, Kilsby had a slight lead but eased up, and Coombes went ahead with some assistance from his cutter which sent considerable wash Kilsby's way. Wittington, Groves, Darby and Doo were out of sight and contention at Lambeth Suspension Bridge. At Vauxhall Bridge Coombes was ten lengths clear. It was a 'dead noser' along Battersea Reach, where the scullers encountered strong wind and rough water through Chelsea New Bridge. Coombes hung on to the advantage and won by 55 seconds. He was rowing in the celebrated *Antigallican* built by G. Salter and 'coached up' the course by George Sinclair of Thames Bank in an eight-oared cutter steered by Tom Coombes. Kilsby was

Harry Phelps, bargemaster to the Fishmongers' Company, c1937 (The Phelps Dynasty)

steered up by his brother John in a ten-oar cutter dubbed 'leviathan', steered by Horace Cole of Chelsea.

In 1866 one reporter hinted that Doggett's should be moved to calmer waters: 'We have on former occasions called attention to the absurdity of attempting to bring off a race, with any degree of fairness, between London Bridge and Chelsea, and without zeal for removal of ancient landmarks etc. The Fishmongers' Company should look for "fresh fields and pastures new" higher up the river. The custom of rowing against the tide has gradually become honoured more in the breach than the observance, and the men were started at a quarter past five so that they had a drain of tide with them all the way.' Dollars and 'half-bulls' were the current standard of speculation. Arthur Iles, rowing a Salters' build, was hot favourite and shown up successfully by Jockey Driver. Iles was from Kew, and became the first Doggett's winner from somewhere upstream of Putney.

The 1868 report returned to the misgivings of the draw, reminding readers that aspirants have to take their chance in a lucky-bag before they can enter the lists and that therefore the contest does not confer a championship among participants and is only a partial test of swiftness. It also returned to the theme of moving upriver, pointing out that the steamers at London Bridge render a course clear of impediments impossible. Rough conditions were a good test, but the race was not supposed to be a bumping match with steamers. The six names drawn two weeks before the date of the race were all down river men; that is, they plied their trade below London Bridge. Block was swamped at Pimlico. Alfred Egalton had won coats and badges at Blackfriars in 1865 and 1866 and added Doggett's to his wardrobe by reaching the flag boat in 37 minutes from the start. Egalton was the first to get a red coat, for hitherto the colour specified by Thomas Doggett had been orange. The reason for the change is not known.

The issues surrounding the draw were resolved when an amateur oarsman, Frank Playford of London Rowing Club, suggested two important changes: that the race should take place on the strength of the flood, and that preliminary heats should be held in the days before the race at Putney. Thus a new era of Doggett's with a more proficient entry began in 1873. Heats were held between Hammersmith and Putney a couple of weeks before the race, presumably organised by the club of which Playford was captain.

The other major change in 1873 was that henceforth the race would be rowed with the tide. The days of dragging a heavy boat from London Bridge to Chelsea, sometimes for nearly two hours, were over. Henceforth the average time taken for the distance fell by at least an hour. By chance, the change was marked by the demolition of the Swan for the construction of Chelsea embankment. Cadogan Pier became the finishing post.

Nickalls records that in 1906, the last year in which the old fashioned wager boats were used, the captain of Thames Rowing Club, Robert Henry Forster, kept such a boat in trust for Putney competitors. It was used by Cobb in the race, which was won by E. L. Brewer of Putney after one Dyckhoff was knocked out of his old-fashioned by a roller. He got back in and finished fourth. By now colours were drawn as well as stations, with the white, red, black, green, blue and yellow being drawn on the morning of the race.

The introduction of heats undoubtedly channelled the better scullers into the 'final' of Doggett's, but did not put a stop to impediments to the race. Interference continued, as alluded to in reports of the 1872 and 1874 races. That of 1872 said:

Christopher Anness, Doggett's winner 2011 in his blue Diamond Jubilee winner's Coat and Badge, and Merlin Dwan, Doggett's winner 2012 (Photograph by Susan Fenwick)

'During the last few years some good men have taken part in the contests, which year after year attract vast numbers of spectators, not one twentieth of whom would think of going as far as Putney to witness the meeting of the best oarsmen of the present day. There is evidently a good deal in a name; and some of the proofs of this frequently have very disagreeable results to the parties concerned, as the number of steamboats and row-boats which swarm over the course on such occasions has a tendency to greatly impede, and sometimes altogether destroy the chances of these competitors who happen to be a little astern after the first couple of hundred yards.'

In 1874, well-known upriver names like J. T. Phelps and W. H. Biffen came through the preliminary heats. After the race was won by R. W. Burwood of Wapping, Biffen wrote complaining that he was fouled five times — once by Phelps, once by Short and three times by Curd, the latter knocking a hole in both ends of his boat. Biffen also claimed that he was suffered interference from a barge, a skiff and the umpire's eight that sat in front of him for a mile. His allegation that the regulations were not enforced appears to have fallen on deaf ears, although as we have seen, there were several occasions when the race was re-run, as encouraged by Thomas Doggett's will, following affidavits alleging unfairness.

10
A FARCE ON HIS FACE

Thomas Doggett was by no means the best known actor of his day, but he benefited from a good press. It is said that in his early life he had to 'fight a passage through the rough shambles of life as best he could', an experience no doubt shared by many watermen. He was equal to the fray, and his biographer Theodore Cook afforded him common sense, sturdiness, independence and honourable rectitude in his private life, while describing him as painstaking, industrious, trustworthy and admired by contemporaries such as Steele and Addison in his public life.

Cook supposes that Doggett was born in Dublin about 1650, came to England to seek his fortune, married Mary Owen at Eltham, Kent, when aged about thirty and spent about ten years with travelling companies of actors before returning to London towards the end of the 1680s. Anthony Ashton described him as 'a lively, spract man, of very good sense, but illiterate,' the last of which Cook takes issue with. On another occasion Ashton says Doggett is a lively little man, modest, cheerful and complaisant. 'He sang in company very agreeably and in public very comically. He danced the Cheshire Round full well as Captain George. I travelled with him in his strolling company and found him a man of very good sense… he dressed neat and something fine, in plain cloth coat and brocaded waistcoat.'

Theatre Royal Drury Lane in Doggett's day (George Hoare Theatre Collection)

FRONT of DRURY-LANE THEATRE.

This somewhat contrasts with a description given in the Company's history when he was older, but this passage surely describes Doggett the actor, made up for one of the parts that he made his own:

'He wore an enormous wig with long lappets of hair hanging over his shoulders, which enveloped his head, and on top of it was stuck a small cocked hat, which it would have been a great effort of balancing to retain in its place without the aid of pins; his coat very broad in the tails, reaches below his knees, his waistcoat with flap pockets of large size extend half way down his thighs, his small clothes are tight and buckled at the knees, where they are met by coloured stockings, which rise out of square toed, red heeled, silver buckled shoes; under his left arm he carries a clouded or amber coloured cane, while his right hand is continually titillating his olfactory nerve with snuff from out of a box set with precious stones, while the indispensable rapier hangs at his side.'

Cook has Doggett prefacing his move to Drury Lane with performances at Bartholomew's Fair, where talent was tested to breaking point. The fair had booths for rope dancing and tumbling, stalls baking pies and roasting pigs, and an abundance of mountebanks, pedlars and pickpockets. In 1691 Doggett appeared there in a tragic-comedy, The Royal Voyage or the Irish Expedition, about the defeat of James II and Tyrconnel at the Battle of the Boyne, the outcome of which would have found Doggett's approval. In 1702 Doggett's booth at Hosier Lane End had a new production described as a 'droll'. In 1691 the

Previous page: The Contest for Doggett's Coat and Badge c1850 (Reginald Francis Print Collection)

Likeness by Ying Yang 2009 of the original painting of Thomas Doggett by Thomas Murray at Sherborne Castle (Watermen's Hall Collection)

comedian is at Drury Lane playing Nincompoop in Love for Money and Solon in Marriage-Hater Matched, both by D'Urfey. Friendship with the up-and-coming playwright William Congreve takes Doggett to high critical acclaim. 'If an alderman appears upon the stage, you may be sure it is in order to be cuckolded,' wrote Addison in the Spectator in 1712. 'An husband that is a little grave or elderly, generally meets with the same fate. Knights and baronets, country squires, and justices of the quorum, come up to town for no other purpose. I have seen poor Doggett cuckolded in all these circumstances.'

In the 1690s there was a boom in theatre-going brought about by Peter the Great's domicile in Deptford to study naval architecture. The Russian tsar became a frequent visitor to plays and pubs. During this time Doggett appeared in plays by Cibber, Lord Landsdowne, Vanbrugh, Dilke, Buckingham, Shadwell and Ben Jonson. In 1696 he played Young Hob in the only play he wrote himself, The Country Wake, a comedy at New Theatre in Little Lincoln's Inn Fields. In this the waterman gets a mention:

> *Writing's the fatal Rock on which has split*
> *Many a stout and well-built Man of Wit,*
> *And yet there's not a sculler but shall dare*
> *To venture his week rotten Cockboat there.*

Whether the parts maketh the actor or the comedian maketh the parts, Doggett trod the boards on and off until 1717 when he retired except to perform occasional renderings of his favourite characters - Ben, Fondlewife and Hob. He attracted wide critical acclaim. Steele wrote: 'The craft of a usurer, the absurdity of a rich fool, the awkward roughness of a fellow of half courage, the ungraceful mirth of a creature of half wit, might be for ever put out of countenance by proper parts for Doggett.' Downes wrote: 'Very spectabound, wearing a farce on his face… ' Cibber wrote: 'The most original of all his contemporaries. His manner was his own… he could be extremely ridiculous without stepping into the least impropriety.' John Dryden praised his singing in The Richmond Heiress as 'wonderfully good' and said of Love Triumphant that he had 'the best understanding of any man in the playhouse'. Another: 'The most diligent, most laborious, most useful actor seen upon the stage in a long course of years.'

In truth, though Drury Lane enjoyed twenty years of good management under Wilks, Cibber and Doggett. Wilks's extravagance was balanced by Doggett's caution, and Cibber was the perfect mediator. The triumvirate kept strict payrolls and discharged all debts every Monday, as well as being fine actors who gained the trust of their company members.

There was a pugnacious side to Thomas Doggett as well, perhaps rarely shown in company, but apparent when the great Whig fell out with his former partners Cibber and Wilks over Barton Booth and Tory involvement at the theatre in Drury Lane. Visits to Button's coffee house when Cibber was present were marked by 'indignant snorts and bellicose demeanour of the wronged Irishman in presence of his oppressor', according to Cook. This grumbling argument was sorted when Cibber wrote an anonymous premature obituary notice of his erstwhile friend which led to an ice-breaking session at the coffee house. Suffice it to say that the great benefactor of the coat and badge was a man of principle who not only understood the umbilical cord that theatricals shared with watermen, but stood tenaciously for the rights of his fellow actors.

Pacing the streets had its dangers for Doggett and his fellow citizens, dangers that added to the attraction of travelling by water. Once when venturing forth to witness the race for his own coat and badge, he was making his way through the Friars when, 'intending to take water at Temple Stairs… one of those rake helly fellows that so beset the town, stopped me, and cocking his hat, with arms akimbo, cried Whig or Tory? He did not care a Queen Anne's farthing for my politics, but made it the pretext for a quarrel; I wipped out my hanger in a trice, set my back to the wall, and cried "Hurrah for the King George and long life to him", and yet I had like to have fared scurvily, had I not bethought me, that my own name for the nonce would stand me even in better stead than the king's – so when being surrounded by a host of tatterdemalions, and pronounced a rat that must bleed, I said be it so my masters, and though you fail in the recognition, know that I am Doggett, whereat the varlets laughed; true I escaped with a whole skin, but at the expense of a guinea this is the gist on't – so now to dinner and afterwards to the White Swan, there to drink a cool tankard and shake hands with the winner.'

Doggett died in 1721 and was buried in the churchyard of St John the Baptist in Eltham. The Worshipful Company of Fishmongers to whom his trustees eventually transferred the running of the race, put up a wooden plaque at the church in 1964, briefly mentioning his achievement but concluding: 'He died a pauper'. But his will makes generous bequests to relatives and others, including £30 a year to his female servant and elaborate provisions for the future of his Coat and Badge: £5 for the silver badge, 18 shillings for the scarlet cloth and £1.1s for the tailoring, and 30 shillings to the clerk of the Watermen's Hall, to whom the organisation was entrusted. There is a churchwardens' note that 13 shillings and fourpence had been duly paid for digging his grave. Not such a pauper, then.

An epitaph appeared on a Lambeth window pane on August 1, 1736:

Tom Dogget, the greatest sly drole in his parts
In acting was certain a Master of Arts;
A monument left – no herald is fuller
His praise is sung yearly by many a sculler;
Ten thousand years hence, if this world lasts so long,
Tom Dogget will still be the theme of their song;
When old Noll, with great Lewis, and Baubon are forgot,
And when numberless Kings in oblivion shall rot.

Guylliam Boonen's present of a coach to Queen Elizabeth in 1565 amounted to a ripple on the surface of the Thames that signalled a rapacious predator on the trade of watermen.

Dutchman Boonen's vehicle was a great improvement on the 'chariot of cloth of tissue, drawn by six horses' used for Queen Mary's coronation in 1553. After receiving the gift, Elizabeth had built 'a chariot throne, with foure pillers behind to bear a canopy, with a crowne imperiall on the toppe, and before two lower pillers, whereon stood a lion and a dragon, the supporters of the armes of England.' She used it on occasions such as her process to St. Paul's to give thanks for deliverance of her realm from the Spanish Armada in 1588.

Four of Spades playing card, 1588 (© National Maritime Museum, Greenwich, London)

It is reported that 'divers great ladies, with as great jealousie of the Queene's displeasure, made them coaches, and rid in them up and down the countries, to the great admiration of all beholders.' Little by little, the use of such vehicles spread amongst the nobility and the wealthy. A bill to restrain the excessive and superfluous use of coaches failed in the Lords in 1601. And as coaches increased in number on the streets of London, watermen became fearful of ruin — although the Company history's entry for 1602 mentioned that London's port trade had been increasing annually from 1331 so that customs duties on foreign manufactures had increased by more than five-fold to reach £50,000 per annum, and employment for watermen and bargemen had grown in proportion.

Burgeoning trade also had the effect of increasing the number of carts on the streets, and in 1601 the Lord Mayor complained of the ineffectiveness of the woodmongers' control of traffic in the city. The origin of the woodmongers as fuellers and keepers of wood and coal wharves adjoining the river seems hazy, but they apparently were a body regulated by the corporation that bestowed on them the right of regulating

Previous page: Cabs, wagons, buses and trams - the wheels of ill-fortune for watermen (TfL from the London Transport Museum collection)

'cars and carts'. The Carmen's company, incorporated in Henry VIII's reign, and the governors of Christ's Hospital both had rights in this area. In 1605 the Company of Woodmongers and the Company of Carmen 'appear to have been incorporated by charter', but disputes between them continued.

In 1610 the Watermen's Company notes further encroachment on watermen's livelihood from the use of carriages for entertaining the royal court's VIPs. This was revealed in the expense account of the master of ceremonies, Sir Lewis Lewkener. But in 1624 there was good news for watermen when an act of parliament shifted heavy goods conveyance between Oxford and London from road to river. The act noted that stone from Oxford and coal and other necessities from London was 'now coming at dear rate only by land carriage, whereby roads are becoming exceedingly bad', while the river was navigable from London to Burcot and many miles above Oxford. License was issued for bargemen to haul barges by winches, ropes and engines against the stream westwards on the Thames, and seven miles of navigation was deepened to open access to seven counties. All this created employment for watermen and bargemen.

Entrance to the City via London Bridge (Reginald Francis Print Collection)

As the seventeenth century progressed, however, pressure on water-borne passenger traffic in London increased under the rapid rise of the taxi business. In 1634 a Hackney carriage stand appeared by the maypole in the Strand, near Somerset House. Captain Bailey of the Royal Navy set it up, his livery consisting of four cabs with uniformed drivers. The Company petitioned against it. Next year Hackneys were banned for journeys of less than three miles outside London or Westminster, and in 1652 their numbers were restricted to two hundred for daily plying in the streets. Two years later the maximum number was raised to three hundred and horses to pull them to six hundred within six miles of London and Westminster, and regulation of them was vested in the city corporation.

Alongside horse-drawn vehicles for hire, private carriages burgeoned. This was a tide that the watermen could never stem. In 1660 there was proclamation by Charles II against Hackneys plying for hire on the streets, but before the century was out there was an act for providing for carriages as well as barges for the king's use, and renewal of legislation to provide for navy and ordnance carriage by both land and water.

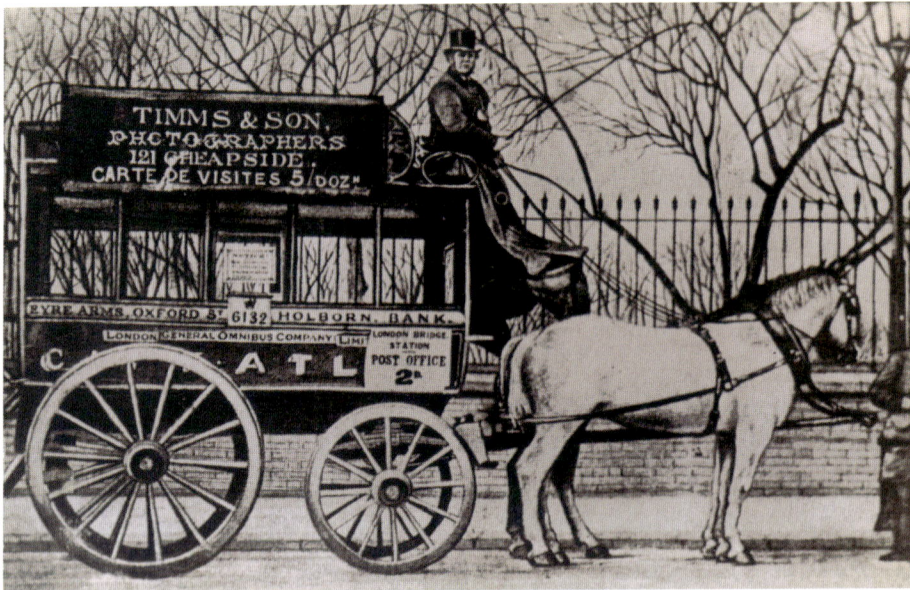

The first bus to cross Holborn Viaduct, which was opened by Queen Victoria, 6 November 1869 – (TfL from the London Transport Museum collection)

In 1710 the number of permitted Hackneys rose to eight hundred, owners paying five shillings a week to put them on the road. By now there were also sedan chairs in the streets, their permitted number reaching three hundred in the next year, their fee being ten shillings per annum. In 1710 also an act provided for a general post office 'for all her majesty's dominions,' although it appears that watermen and bargemen continued to carry letters. In 1711 a new state coach was built for the Lord Mayor. Previously he had rode on horseback to and from the waterside for his annual procession. His coach was replaced in 1757, the same year as a royal state coach came into service.

During the next century the carriage dam burst. Cabriolets or 'cabs' appeared from Paris, painted uniformly in chocolate colour with a side seat for the driver. Gigs and other vehicles soon followed, interfering further with watermen's labour. That was in 1810. In 1829 along came the omnibus. On 4 July Shillibeer's, the '*Yorkshire Stingo*', ran from Paddington to the City, drawn by three beautiful bays. It was shaped like a van with windows along each side and at the end, and could carry up to eighteen passengers. The fare was a shilling, soon to be reduced to six pence.

Far away in the north of England, the Stockton and Darlington Railway opened, four years before the appearance of Shillibeer's omnibus. The waterman was already in mortal combat with the wheel. Soon he would come face to face with the wonder of the age, steam traction. Steam power would impact on road and waterways, and trains would join road vehicles in ringing the death-knell of watermen's work.

Philip
Coale-
at the G
in All-h
Tham

12

COAL, CARTAGE
AND CHAOS

The Port of London has its roots beyond the Roman empire. Tacitus noted that London was packed with merchant ships. Wharfs along the Strand, by the Fleet and at Queenhithe traded in wine, pottery, oil, glassware, bronze and silverware from Gaul, the Rhineland, Italy and Spain. Dealers and shippers brought grain, coal and stone from Kent, Devon and Cornwall; marble from Dorset; lead from Somerset; jet from Yorkshire and pottery from Oxford and Huntingdon. Exports included jet to Rome and English cloth, much in demand in Europe.

The kings Edgar and Aethelred encouraged Easterlings to settle during the second half of the tenth century. These German merchants established trading associations, controlled sea routes and organized the port and the quays. Meanwhile, Danish and Norman kings opened parts of northern Europe to trading opportunities. Markets for imported goods settled at Mark Lane, Mincing Lane, Pudding Lane and Tooley Street. Billingsgate, on the site of the first extensive Roman quay, dealt in fish. In 1225 Henry III decreed that all ships from outside London should unload produce at Queenhithe, the area upstream of London Bridge on the north bank between modern-day Southwark and Blackfriars bridges, so that he could collect dues for passing through the bridge. This was ineffective: shippers defied the ruling, and fish continued to be unloaded at Billingsgate, downstream of the bridge.

Henry VIII turned his attention to safety at sea when he gave a charter to Trinity House to train pilots and place buoys and lights along the coast and in estuaries in 1514. In 1593 Trinity House was granted a monopoly to dredge channels to supply ballast to ships leaving the port. This was an important move in keeping the Thames accessible for shipping.

The monarchy was in competition with other stakeholders in trade. The City established control of all markets within a seven mile radius, including Long Southwark in Borough High Street for imports, livestock and farm produce from Kent, Surrey and Sussex. This market began life on London Bridge but was moved to relieve congestion (arriving at its present site in 1762). In the 1600s the predominant trade in Borough High Street was butchery, accompanied by the casting of unwanted offal into the river. The streets were black with inky mud that served as excellent manure. In Elizabeth's rein Borough householders were required to hang out lamps on winter nights to light up a district of small shops and saddlers, grocers, linen-drapers, barber-surgeons, hatters, shoe-makers, pastry cooks, poulterers and taverns. Piecemeal industrial development also occurred on Bankside, including large soap works and glassworks. From 1750 the tanning industry proliferated in nearby Bermondsey, with its accompanying vats of dog excrement for steeping skins and wool fulling for felted material to make heavy coats and hats. The Skin Market behind Cardinal Cap Alley on Bankside supplied rabbit skin, plucked and brushed with mercury to keep the rain out, for hats. Rennie's engineering works grew up in Holland Street

Corruption, theft and smuggling were constant irritants throughout, and in Elizabethan times, twenty 'legal quays' were established. These were named after the person who operated them, and it was forbidden to land goods anywhere else, or – with the exception of fish – anywhere at all in the dark. London's population doubled

Previous page: Trade card of Philip Fruchard, coal merchant, etching, c1750 (British Museum)

to 200,000 in the forty years to 1600, and went on rising. After 1663 'sufferance wharfs' were developed to cater for the explosion in trade and its accompanying delays, pilfering and over-charging. Pilots, watermen, lightermen and porters all gained from the increased activity, and the men who worked the boats underpinned intense rivalry with camaraderie. Already there were signs of organised labour: a brotherhood of corn and salt porters was set up at Queenhithe in the thirteenth century. Demarcation disputes arose between street porters and those who tended British and foreign ships. The streets close to the river wharfs grew into a warren of workshops for coopers, sailmakers, blacksmiths and tailors. Taverns, brothels, doss houses and cheap lodgings for sailors extended from the Tower to 'sailortown' at Limehouse.

In April 1651 Alexander Hay took over the site of the Abbots of Battle Inn on the south bank, a monastic property near London Bridge that was to become the largest wharfingering and warehousing business in the Port of London. Hay began as a brewer, but soon let the brewery and concentrated on his wharfs and warehouses along what is now Tooley Street. Every week one bylander (coaster) and three hoys (sailing barges) brought tallow and fats from East Anglia for soap making, and hides and skins from Ireland and the West Country for the tanners of Bermondsey.

In 1656 part of the wharf was let to the New River Company, the nucleus of the Metropolitan Water Board. The wharf became known as Pipe Borer's because Hertfordshire elms were hollowed out there by giant gimlets for London's first water mains. Another enterprise involving Hay was the first fire office, set up with his neighbouring wharfingers Chamberlain and Beale, after numerous fires damaged their premises. Unsurprisingly watermen, with their experience of tackling conflagrations from the river, were much in demand by fire offices.

From times Roman, the most important commodity was fuel. Fuel agents known as woodmongers were well-established in the middle ages - there is reference to a 'misterie' of woodmongers in 1376 – and they transformed to coal merchants from the seventeenth century when coal replaced timber for heat and power in the cities. Markets developed in Newcastle to exploit the outcrop coal seams found near navigable water, and in London, a huge receptacle at the other end of the voyage between Tyne and Thames. Bulk transport was a major factor in the fuel trade.

Coal found on Tyneside was used by the Romans for smelting and domestic heating, but the main fuel sources for 800 years since their departure were wood and charcoal. The latter gave its name to coal, hence prefixes in common use such as pit-coal and sea-coal. Timber was plentiful and cheap before the seventeenth century, and charcoal was used by charcoal-burning 'colliers' for finer work. London's chief source of charcoal came from the colliers of Croydon. By Elizabeth's reign, demand for wood and charcoal outstripped supply – hardly surprising when four thousand great oaks were required to build a man-of-war. In 1578 three breweries consumed 2,000 wagon loads of firewood.

Thus alternative fuels were required in the sixteenth and seventeenth centuries to supply a growing population. Estimates for coal coming to London amounted to 24,000 tons in 1586, rising to 74,000 tons by 1606. By then woodmongers dealt more in coal than in wood. By 1700 demand for coal in the Thames Valley reached 455,000 tons. Coal had its downside, of course. In John Annals under the date 1616 is a marginal note says that 'nice dams of London would not come into any house or room when sea coales were burned, nor willingly eat of the meat that was either sod or rosted with sea cole fire'.

In 1605 the woodmongers achieved their pinnacle of power when they gained jurisdiction over the carriers in the City known as carmen, whose fraternity dated from 1517. The rot set in for the carmen when, in 1528, woodmongers were allowed a cart for use at their own wharfs, an allowance extended to an additional general goods cart in 1546. In 1605 the Woodmongers Company was formed, one William Cory being a member of its first court. The struggle for control over distribution between woodmongers, carmen, wharfingers and others resulted in the dramatic and sudden downfall of the first when merchants transferred their interest in land transport to water. As the seventeenth century progressed, it was lightermen who gained the upper hand in the unloading of bulk carriers and the sale and distribution of fuel.

An Act of Parliament in 1529 removed control of Tyne coal shipping from the Church and vested it in the Company of Hostmen who were householders charged with the duty of entertaining strangers. The hostmen thus acquired a monopoly of the coal and grindstone trades, the latter another speciality of Newcastle. Because thirty-five of the original forty-two hostmen were associated with the Newcastle Merchant Adventurers, a snug relationship was ensured. The venturers' 'foreign bought and sold' rule stated that all goods shipped or unloaded on Tyne must be brought in to Newcastle, and only freemen could buy or sell goods of foreigners, who were defined as people who were not freemen.

The coal trade was a good source of revenue for the Crown, which in Elizabeth's day applied a duty of one shilling per chaldron. A chaldron - a corruption of 'cauldron' - was a vague measurement by volume. In 1694 a Newcastle chaldron used for all coal shipped from the north-east was fixed at 53cwt, while a London chauldron, the standard for south and east England, was '36 bushels heaped up', or approximately 28cwt. Value depended on size of lumps and water content. Chaldron became the legal limit for horse-drawn wagons, and railways used standard chaldron wagons measuring 10ft by 6ft 3in high.

The coal duty and the coal monopoly were, naturally, unpopular and subject to disruption. Ship owners and masters imposed a two-month boycott of the hostmen in 1605. In 1622 ship owners combined with the woodmongers of London to complain about good and bad coals being mixed together. Next year ship owners of London, Ipswich, Harwich and other ports petitioned the Privy Council against the prevention of free trade for coals. In 1637 the Tyne producers were boycotted by London merchants and East Anglian shippers after Charles I imposed another shilling per ton duty in a contract with the hostmen. The new duty was abandoned in the following year. Between 1665 and 1667 – the years of the Dutch wars, the Great Plague and the Fire of London - the price of coal rose from 30 shillings to £6 a chaldron. The market was depressed during the Civil War and by the 1700s the hostmen's role had changed from one of producers to one of agents, termed 'fitters', who arranged cargos for ship owners and moved the black stuff from staithes to ships.

Over the seventeenth century the average size of a cargo of coal rose from 50 to 250 tons. Coal was the bulkiest commodity to transport in proportion to its value, and bad weather often spelt danger for the hundreds of ships engaged in the 350-mile two-week voyage from Tyne to Thames estuary. The first attempt to chart the North Sea did not take place until 1693, there were no lights until the 1700s. There were even threats from Dunkirk pirates.

The burgeoning coal fleet overloaded the quays and promoted barge trade at both ends – lighters on the Thames and keel-boats on the Tyne - as more and more colliers moored in the river. The vast pool of experienced seamen tempted the press gangs and caused similar strains as those between watermen and the navy. The king had a stark choice between going without seamen or colliers. This rose to a head in 1667 during the second Anglo-Dutch war when a fleet of eighty ships commanded by Admiral de Ruyter arrived off Harwich and sailed into the Thames and the Medway. Besides intensifying impressment, the Medway raid was both costly and embarrassing for the English. (A large dish, presented to the Company after peace was signed at Breda, was stated to be the property of Admiral de Ruyter, the commander of the Dutch fleet.)

It appears that the Company sensed which way things were going. In the year of the raid on the Medway the woodmongers were in trouble with parliament for fraudulent dealings and were prohibited from 'keeping carts of their own for carrying abroad their fuel'. Their charter was declared illegal. At this time, the official history points out, the Company consisted of watermen and wherrymen only. 'The lightermen appear to have been members of a livery company of the City of London (No 63 in the list) but little is to be ascertained on the subject beyond this statement'. Difficulties had arisen between watermen and lightermen who were 'free of the city' and 'most likely did not confine themselves to carrying goods on that part of the river within the city'. The king referred the subject to the Lord Mayor to reconcile differences. The mayor was silent on the matter until 1673, a year when the king demanded 200 watermen for navy service in the next Dutch war.

The mayor's court decreed that henceforth masters and owners of lighters, being freemen of the City of London, shall have equal privileges with the Company, and that lightermen and their apprentices should be bound by the same rules as watermen. Spasmodic argument continued until the watermen promoted a bill incorporating lightermen into the Company in 1695 that was enacted in 1700. The preamble set out the purpose as 'for the explanation and better execution of former acts, made touching watermen and wherrymen rowing on the river Thames, and for the better ordering and governing the said watermen, wherrymen and lightermen upon the said river between Gravesend and Windsor'.

Henceforth, watermen and lightermen were joined. Under William III, the Company of Watermen and Lightermen of the River Thames came to pass. And it was the lightermen who carried the coal.

1 8

Prote

Cust

Cu

13
THREE SQUARE MEALS
A DAY

The Utrecht treaty of 1713 did not bring an end to war or impressments. The eighteenth century was full of conflict. Press gangs were at work in half of the sixty years between the Utrecht treaty and the start of the American War of Independence in 1776. An amnesty for buccaneers in 1716 brought some respite in the Caribbean, although whereas six hundred turned themselves in, fifteen hundred did not. It took until 1730 for the navy to rid the Atlantic of pirates. The British saw action in the War of the Austrian Succession (1740-48), the Seven Years War in Europe and North America (ending in 1763), the American War of Independence (1775-83) and the prolonged Napoleonic Wars that followed the French Revolution of 1789. That struggle kept the press gangs at work until 1808. All of these conflicts were global in the sense that they involved the Americas, India and the Pacific as well as the great powers of Europe, and they kept the British navy busy in several theatres simultaneously. The Caribbean continued as a hot spot fuelled by privateers and the War of Jenkins' Ear against Spain (1739-48).

George Anson, 1st Baron Anson, after Sir Joshua Reynolds oil on canvas, 1755 (National Portrait Gallery, London)

Consequently, the century was one of great change and expansion in the navy. By the 1720s there were two dry docks and two wet docks at Portsmouth, and bases at Plymouth and Devonport were developing fast. The main theatres of naval action were the Channel and the Atlantic approaches, and these dockyards were better placed for maintenance than the bases of the Thames and Medway, which increasingly became storage depots. In 1672 a method was found to bolt sheets of copper to wooden hulls, giving them protection from weed and shipworm and a durable smooth surface. Time spent in dockyards for hull maintenance was thus reduced greatly. By 1761 Earl Sandwich, First Lord of the Admiralty, had coppered 82 battleships and 115 frigates. The copper sheath gave them more speed and lighter handling. Sandwich also adopted an advanced type of gun, the squat but powerful 32-pounder called a carronade, developed by the Carron Iron Works in Scotland.

Battle techniques changed, an example being Admiral Rodney's first use of an attack from the leeward side against the Spanish at Cape St. Vincent in 1779. This was a century when the nation went to sea, whether voluntarily or by compulsion. The number of sailors in the navy rose from 10,000 in 1755 to 85,000 by 1760, the latter figure almost matched by those in the merchant fleet. Their welfare and management

Previous page: 1803 document requesting Samuel Grey be spared from impressment

changed for the better, and there were willing recruits because of competitive pay of 22s.6d a month guaranteed, often with an added bounty, and the opportunity to hit the jackpot if prize money was paid out. Furthermore, a typical man of war had a crew of 400 against 120 for an equivalent size of East Indiaman, so life was generally easier with the navy.

Nevertheless, the attractions of going to sea in the service of the Crown did not produce sufficient recruits, and so reliance on press gangs continued. This was less because the navy was a cruel taskmaster, more that British society gave it no other option for manning its ships. The Impress Service's powers were both legal and circumscribed. Categories of seamen such as sailors who manned colliers, fishermen, whalers, apprentices and certain watermen were exempt, although as we have seen, the quest for skilled men led to many abuses. Resistance compelled the navy to use force, and force bred further resistance. Magistrates often impeded the service's work. Local authorities attempted to assign drunks, criminals and the mentally retarded to the navy. Riots occurred in ports, sometimes sparked by deserters. For these reasons, captains often preferred to do their own pressing. They required hands with specialist skills, men who could 'hand, reef and steer', i.e. handle sails and rigging and tie thirty kinds of knot; men who knew hundreds of parts of the ship by name; men who could furl a sail in the rain or dark while balancing on a foot rope a hundred feet in the air; men who could take a turn at the wheel. Men with experience were rated as an ordinary seamen, while those with skill were able seamen. Men who couldn't do these things were 'landsmen' and worked on deck as 'waisters', hauling sheets and halyards, or 'idlers' who assisted carpenters, cooks and sailmakers. Hence the temptation to grab merchant seamen and watermen to man your ship.

John Montagu, 4th Earl of Sandwich after Johann Joseph Zoffany oil on canvas, feigned oval, c1764 (National Portrait Gallery, London)

Modernisation of the navy was carried out by the Earl of Sandwich, three times First Lord of the Admiralty, and George Anson, an experienced captain who was given a seat on the Admiralty board in 1744 and became First Lord in 1751. Crucially, the Admiralty called the shots over the Navy Board. The fleet was reorganised so that each class of ship reflected uniform tonnage and firepower. First, second and third class vessels carrying sixty guns or more were termed battleships of the line; four, five and six raters, the frigates and sloops, were renamed cruisers and assigned to patrol work and convoy protection — a system that would last for two hundred years. Thirty ships of the line formed a western squadron later to be known as the Channel Fleet to patrol La Manche and its approaches round the clock and round the year, thus bottling up the French in their Atlantic ports. This was made possible by the introduction of fresh vegetable supply ships that plied from the Channel ports to the Mediterranean to keep the dreaded scurvy at bay and enable warships to stay at sea for months at a time. By the end of the century lime juice was being added to navy rum as an antidote to scurvy. There appears to have been another welfare development hinted at by the Gentlemen's Magazine. In 1746 it reported that 'numbers of women have entered the fleet bound for Cape Breton,' being allowed £10 each and provisions, 'and are to receive further encouragement.' Whether their duties were on board ship or at Cape Breton is not specified.

The 60-gun *Eagle*, the ship that able seaman James Cook signed on to in 1755, enjoyed a surgeon and a chaplain as members of the crew. Each lieutenant had personal charge of a division of the ship's company, with a midshipmen supervising each sub-division. They had to make sure that every sailor had proper clothes and a twice-weekly change of linen, and that his hammock was washed and stowed. Hygiene and discipline had become tenets of the navy. Sailors received a daily allowance of half a pint of rum mixed with a quart of water when at sea and a gallon of beer when in port. This practice was introduced by Admiral 'Old Grog' Vernon in the 1730s to reduce drunkenness. The crew of the *Eagle* enjoyed three meals a day, served on the gun deck on square wooden plates – hence the phrase 'three square meals a day'. The future Captain Cook, whose first seagoing experience was learned on East Coast colliers, rose to master's mate in less than a month.

Edward Vernon by Thomas Gainsborough oil on canvas, c1753 (National Portrait Gallery, London)

So as the century progressed, life on the ocean wave improved for the impressed as for the volunteer. But the process of impressment was laced with deviancy and dispute. If, for example, you had happened to the Monument on the fifth of August 1738, curiosity may have drawn you to a large crowd of idle persons loitering round its base. The attraction was a live turkey tethered to the top of the great tower built to commemorate the Great Fire. The hapless bird had been trapped there by a press gang who were then able to pick off any men who fitted their profile. They had the idea from an incident a few days beforehand when two large birds settled on St. Paul's church and caused a large crowd to assemble. Those wishing to avoid being impressed would have beenwell advised to stay at home at this time. In anticipation of war with Spain, the Admiralty ordered the rulers of the Watermen's Company to raise a thousand sailors and the Company issued impressment orders on the first of August. At the same time the London Magazine reported that 'the press on the river was so hot to man several ships, that between Wednesday and the following day, fifteen hundred men were impressed'.

In 1739 there were further hot impressments, and the Company report says that many freemen appear to have obtained small freehold properties in order to obtain protections from forced service. The Government introduced a Bill for compulsory registering addresses of all watermen, lightermen, fishermen, keelmen and bargemen, with the threat that they would be deemed deserters if they refused to comply and answer the call. The Bill was strongly opposed by the Company, and failed its second reading. The Company was summoned to the Lords Commissioners of the Admiralty to discuss the difficulties of finding enough men and produced a litany of obstructions to raising the numbers demanded:

'…that men under twenty and over thirty, however lusty and strong, and those who had not been before at sea, were refused by the officers of the navy; that great numbers of serviceable men were protected by ambassadors, the nobility, and members of Parliament, that many of them not having badges, bought their own liveries and badges; and the numbers of men protected by the navy and victualling officers, shewed that many more were protected than required for service.'

It also said that several freemen had small estates conveyed to them by friends, which though they appeared to the Company collusive, were deemed valid by the regulating captain.

Watermen and apprentices were seized for all manner of expeditions, examples being Admiral Byng's fleet which destroyed what remained of the Spanish fleet and forced Spain to accept the terms of the Quadruple Alliance, and Admiral Vernon's adventure to Porto Bello in Panama in 1739, during which the keys of the city were acquired for Watermen's Hall. In 1740 bounties of 2 guineas were offered for signing on for the navy (i.e. £2:2s for sailors aged 18-54, £1:10s for ordinary men, plus six months' pay). Constables received £2:2s for every man they impressed. The London Magazine records an early morning press below the bridge on 2 June 1741, the hottest since the war with Spain began, when 2,370 men were taken in 36 hours. At the close of 1743 there were impressments to fit out ships at Chatham to meet the anticipated descent of the Pretender and his adherents on the coast of Kent. The year of 1754 saw 2,000 impressed to an East Indies squadron. Bounties were doubled next year and the Company supplied upwards of five hundred young men for increasing the fleet owing to troubles in North America.

On 2 August 1756 a great fight broke out when a press gang attempted to press about forty sailors bound for the Custom House to renew their protections. Several were wounded, including one of the lieutenants in charge. Opposition to impressment was so great that some homeward bound ships in the Thames turned their guns on the gangs, resulting in serious fights. 'One or two laden ships were sunk in the river,' says the Company report. On 19 September 1770, impressed men forcibly opened the hatches of a tender sailing downriver and overpowered the officers and crew.

They sailed the boat to Grays and escaped, a hundred and ten of them. In another incident that same year at Gravesend, a boat's crew from the navy sloop Lynx boarded the *Duke of Richmond*, bound for the East Indies, to impress crew members. The officers and men of the trader resisted; the press gang disembarked, but later the Lynx was brought alongside. Battle ensued, with one death and several wounded. The men of the East Indiamen all escaped ashore. In 1777 the Commons voted 60,000 seamen towards carrying on the American war, a struggle for independence in part brought about by taxes imposed on the New World colonies to fund the navy.

In short, there were many disputes and wrangles over manning the navy. Some concerned exemption for Sunday ferrymen with families to support; some with under-age boys on the river; some over increasing apprentice numbers to compensate for loss of manpower to the navy. Ingenious methods of pressing, albeit not as inventive as stranding a turkey on top of the Monument, were employed before the Napoleonic Wars. In 1770 a press gang picked fifty men off streets with a long boat on wheels drawn by horses. In 1778 galleys were filled from Tower Hill. In 1779 a prize fighters' stage was erected in St. George's Fields to draw a crowd who soon discovered the true nature of the fighters — press men and recruiting constables.

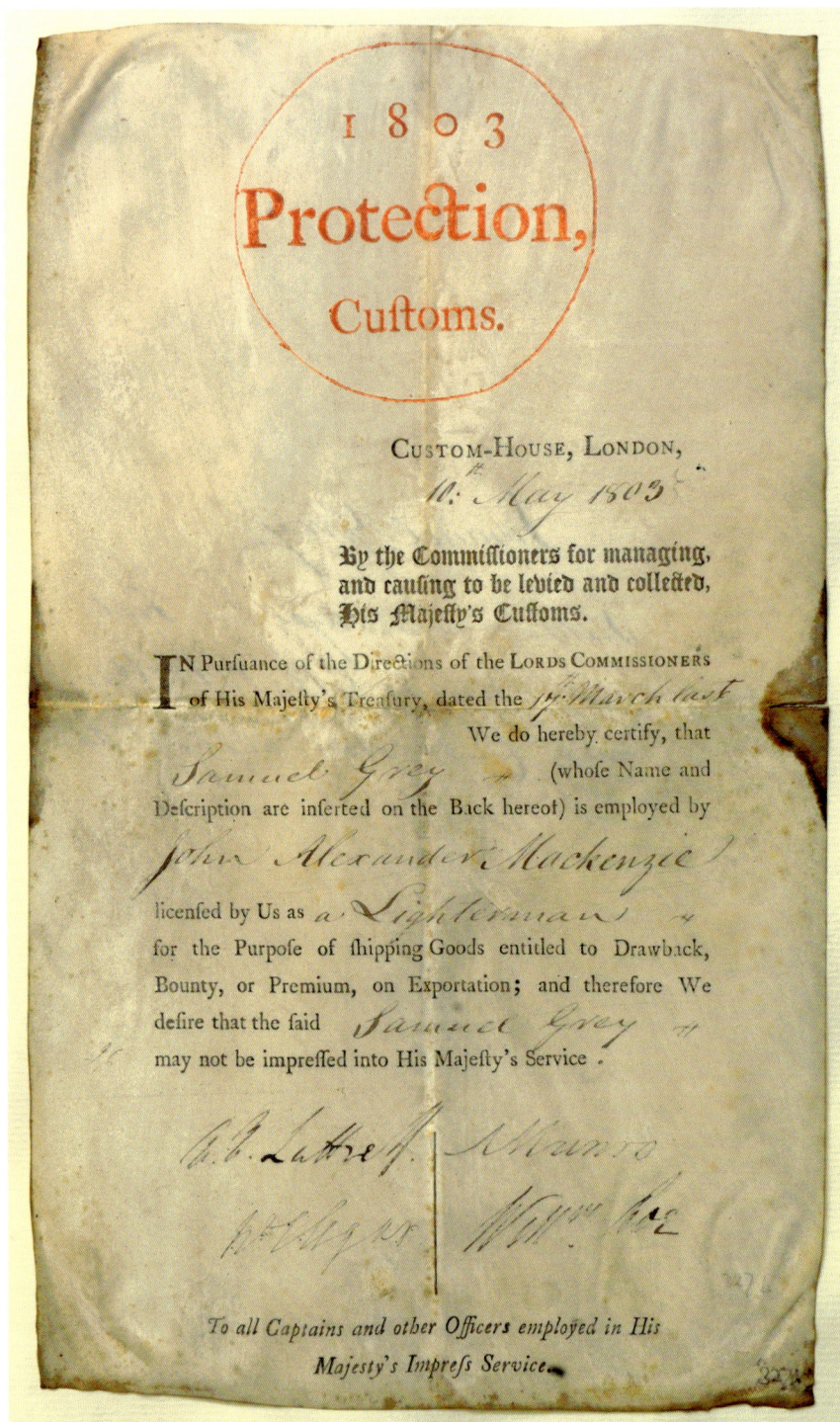

1803 document requesting Samuel Grey be spared from impressment

14
BRIDGE OF SIGHS

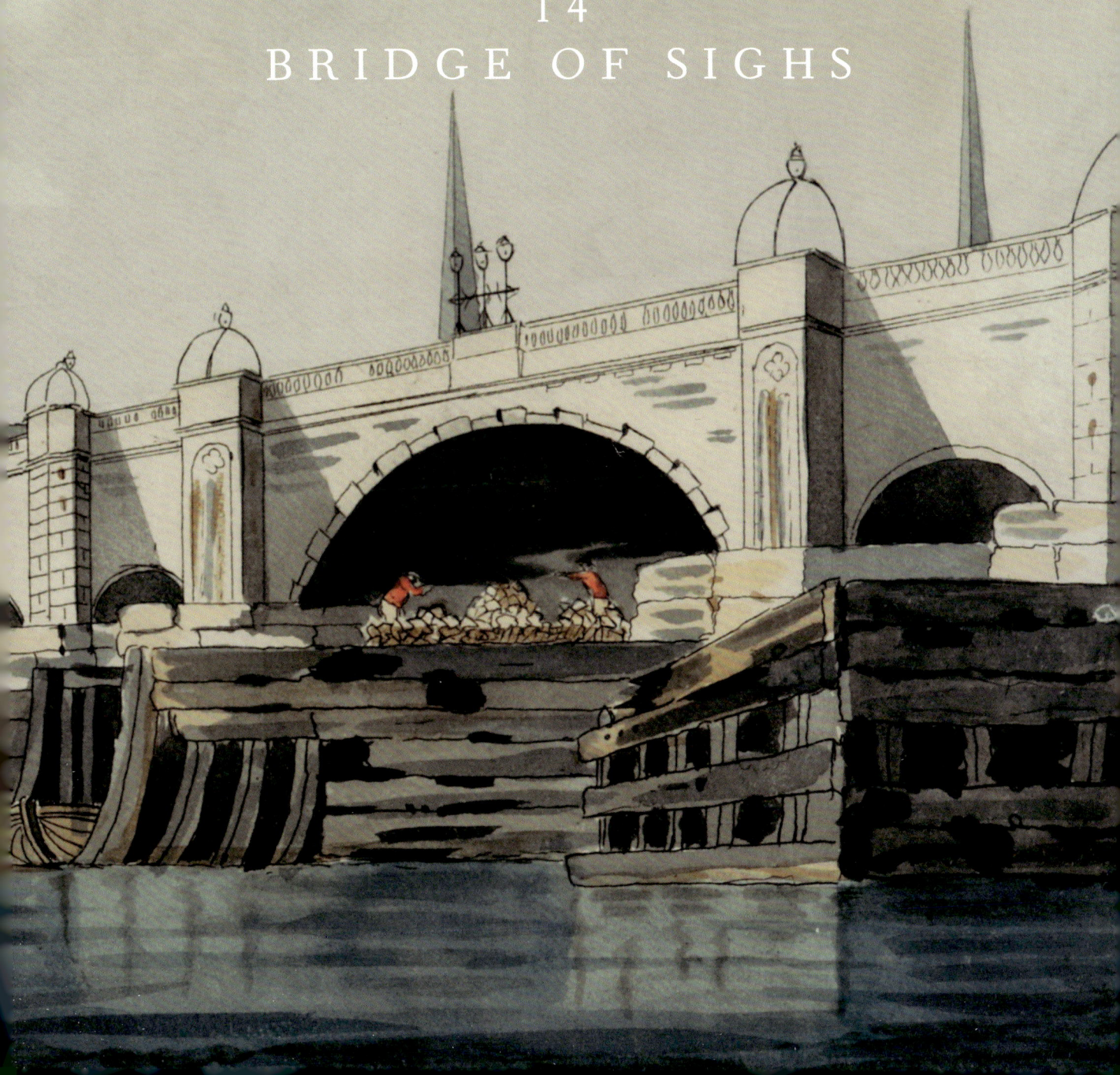

London Bridge is falling down,

Falling down, falling down.

London Bridge is falling down,

My fair lady.

Build it up with iron bars,

Iron bars, iron bars,

Build it up with iron bars,

My fair lady.

Iron bars will bend and break,

Bend and break, bend and break,

Iron bars will bend and break,

My fair lady.

Build it up with gold and silver,

Gold and silver, gold and silver,

Build it up with gold and silver,

My fair lady.

There was seldom a dull day at London Bridge. During a rebellion in 1264, for example, Henry III's queen, Eleanor of Provence, was stuck in the royal apartments at the Tower after Henry had retreated to Kent and sent a fleet from the Cinque Ports to blockade the Thames and stem the supply of provisions to London. Eleanor, terrified of the neighbourhood, resolved to go to Windsor Castle by water, but 'as she approached London bridge in her gilded barge, accompanied by her ladies, the populace assembled against her, there was a general cry of "drown the witch", and besides abusing her with the most opprobrious language, and pelting her with rotten eggs and dirt, they had prepared large stones to sink the barge when the royal party should attempt to shoot the bridge.' Fortunately for the

Previous page: London Bridge 1829 (Reginald Francis Print Collection)

Queen, the mayor interposed for her protection, and conveyed her in safety to St. Paul's.'

London Bridge was prone to damage by frost, fire, siege, falling masonry and shipping disasters.

By way of example, five arches were carried away by ice in 1281 (the bridge at Rochester on the Medway was destroyed in the same freeze). In 1437 the stone gate and tower at the Southwark end collapsed into water, and in 1481 a portion of the bridge fell into the river.

In 1382 it was decreed that all horses, oxen and cows unfortunate enough to fall into the river from the bridge became the property of the Constable of the Tower , together with animals passing under the bridge, though it doesn't specify if the latter refers to stock conveyed in boats or creatures in the water, having fallen out of boats. The Constable enjoyed many dues in kind. Cargo carriers, for example, were required to pay him 'one maud' from every boatload of oysters, cockles and mussels, 'as much as a man could hold between his arms' from a cargo of rushes, and two gallons of wine from Bordeaux ships.

Temporary London Bridge on fire on 11 April 1758 (Reginald Francis Print Collection)

There is a record of a jousting match on the bridge in 1390 between Sir David Lyndesey, Earl of Craufurd, and Lord Wells, watched from the river by courtiers. Craufurd was victorious. Royal processions turned out to be fatal for some, an example being in 1396 when nine persons were pressed to death on the bridge while trying to get a glimpse of Richard II's new bride, Isabella of Valois during the royal couple's progress from Kennington to the Tower. No such disaster is recorded in 1415 when the Lord Mayor met Henry V on the bridge on his way home from the Battle of Agincourt.

The bridge naturally played a strategic role during rebellion and conflict, as we have seen in the case of Queen Eleanor. In 1425 the mayor and aldermen had to mediate a violent argument between the Bishop of Winchester and the Duke of Gloucester. Twenty-five years later Jack Cade's rebels occupied the southern side of the bridge and set fire to it. Their action was pardoned but Cade himself was hunted down and killed. In 1471 there was another rebellion led by Thomas Neville, the illegitimate son of Lord Falconbridge. Three thousand of Neville's men crossed to the northern

London Bridge 1745 (Reginald Francis Print Collection)

bank from Southwark by boat but failed to capture the bridge. Neville was executed and the Lord Mayor and nine aldermen were knighted on the spot for their spirited defence.

The hazards of shooting the bridge are illustrated by the experience of the Duke of Norfolk in 1428. He set sail in his barge from 'Seynt Marye Ouerye' in Southwark. Through 'misgovernance of steering' the barge fell upon the piles and was overwhelmed. The duke and several of his men leapt onto the piles and were saved by ropes cast down to them. It is this kind of misadventure that caused many, including Cardinal Wolsey, to avoid being rowed under the bridge. During Henry VIII's reign the increase in the number of barges kept by the nobility contributed to the chaos on the water and led to his Act to regulate watermen in 1514.

A seventeenth century French writer, Balthasar de Monconys, remarked that: 'The watermen's boats plied to carry persons to the City of Westminster, by way of avoiding the rude English coaches and the ruder paved streets of London... [Watermen] never go below the bridge, although there is not any place to which they cannot be had, but it is considered dangerous for these small boats to go under the bridge when the tide is running up, for the water then has an extreme rapidity, even greater than when it is returning, and the two currents are united.'

Normal tides were one thing, but the river is prone to freak weather conditions. In 1539 it is recorded that sea water flowed freely above the bridge when extreme drought caused by extreme summer heat drained the river of fresh water. In 1591 there was another drought and a curious situation arose in September when a very boisterous south-westerly blew for three days, forcing out the fresh and keeping back the salt, so that a collier on a mare was able to ride from north to south and back on both sides of the bridge — 'not without danger of drowning', said the

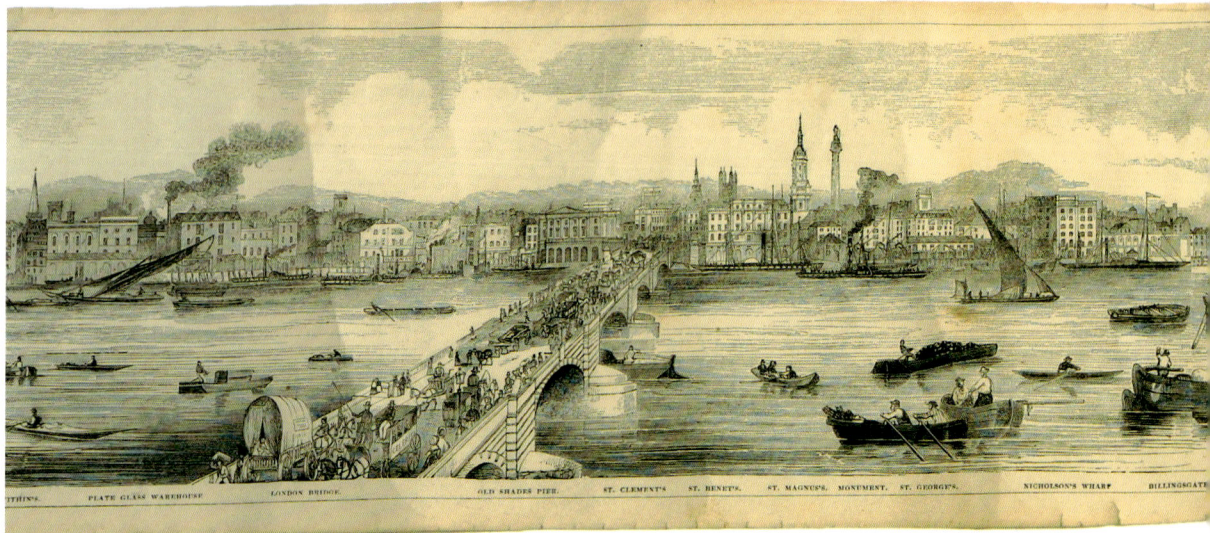

Early panorama of London scroll c1851 (Watermen's Hall Collection)

witness. In 1608 there was a freak tide recorded by Edmund Howes in Stow's Annals: 'When it should have been dead low water at London Bridge, contrary to course, it was then high water; and presently it ebbed almost half an hour the quantity of a foot, and then suddenly it flowed again almost two foot higher than it did before, and then ebbed again until it came near the right course, so the next flood began in a manner as it should.' All this happened before twelve o'clock in the afternoon in calm weather.

In 1582 works were erected to pump a water supply from the Thames to Leadenhall, and by 1701 such machinery occupied four arches of the bridge. From 1588 four of the southern arches were occupied by water wheel-powered corn mills, a development permitted after consultation with the navy, Trinity House and the Watermen's Company concluded that navigation would not be impeded.

In 1635 the bridge was partially destroyed by fire, and it did not escape damage during the Great Fire of 1666, a year which began with a severe January storm that drove ships against it and through it, causing severe damage and havoc on the river. These were bad times generally for the citizens of London. An estimated 100,000 people died of plague in 1665, but dwellers on the bridge escaped infection — saved, according to Daniel Defoe in his historical novel Journal of the Plague Year (1722), by the ceaseless rushing of the river beneath it.

In 1687 came a hurricane which kept the flood tide out of the Thames and enabled people to cross on foot at several points above the bridge. Two years later Mr Temple, the secretary for war, jumped out of a wherry near it and drowned, leaving his hat, sword, a shilling for the waterman and a letter of explanation on the seat. 'My folly in undertaking what I could not perform, whereby some misfortunes have befallen the King's service, is the cause of my putting myself to this sudden end,' he wrote.

The first half of the 1700s was plagued by navigational difficulties. In 1703 the bridge was blocked by storm-blown vessels. The Company's history records severe problems in 1708, 1716 and 1722 when the draw bridge was taken up for repair. Fire destroyed houses and two arches on the south side in 1725. In 1756 a Bill was passed to 'improve , widen and enlarge the passage over and through London Bridge' by widening some arches, demolishing houses on and contiguous to the bridge, and introducing tolls for loaded vessels passing through. The Company did not succeed in squashing the sliding scale of cargo tolls to be paid by every loaded hoy, barge, vessel, lighter or other craft. The only exceptions were barges laden with straw, manure, dung, compost or lime for tillage. At the same time the court of the Company appointed a committee to oppose the bill for erecting a bridge at Blackfriars. The opening of Putney Bridge in 1729 had reduced the distance to the next Thames crossing to approximately eleven miles. The writing in the ripples spelt danger for wherrymen in 1750 when Charles Labelye's Westminster Bridge opened. Like Putney, but in the heart of Westminster, it changed the routes and habits of people movement. A bridge at Blackfriars would be right on the edge of the City, and a massive threat to watermen's livelihood.

In 1757 a temporary wooden bridge was erected while works to London Bridge were carried out, and on 11 April next year a portion of the old bridge and the wooden bridge were destroyed by fire. Vast timbers fell across the arches, trade above the bridge was distressed, and all communication between the City and Southwark was suspended except by boat. The Company provided forty extra watermen to work the ferries on Sundays.

The fire was discovered at both ends at the same time, leading to suspicion of deliberate incendiary devices and pointing the finger at both reactionary watermen and supporters of developments at Blackfriars. A reward was offered for discovery of the incendiary, and an inquiry interviewed many witnesses without result. But two days after the fire, the court of common council appointed a committee to erect a new bridge at Blackfriars.

On 23 August another attempt was made to fire the bridge, and as a consequence the Lord Mayor created a night watch of five watermen armed with blunderbusses and cutlasses positioned in a boat under the great arch. Watermen thus stood both as the accused and as the custodians of the city's only bridge.

In June 1758 the mayor petitioned Parliament for a grant towards bridge works on the grounds that the cargo tolls were not meeting their projected income. Surprisingly, it was proving difficult to collect the revenue when the tide was strong or darkness fell. Barge owners petitioned against the continuance of the tax, and when £15,000 was granted for the bridge works, the tax was dropped. Special provision was also made that any person setting fire to, burning or blowing up the bridge should be punished by death without benefit of clergy.

The new arch, formed by removing the old middle pier and laying the two adjoining locks into one, opened for free passage of boats on 28 January 1760. Eleven months later a large old French ship stuck in the arch, her beam being 18 inches wider than the lock. It took several weeks to break her up and free the navigation. Meanwhile, on 17 June the first pile of Blackfriars Bridge was driven into the middle of the Thames, only to be broken down by a west country barge that ran out of control. The man in charge was fined for attempting to navigate two barges at the same time, a practice as forbidden as it was money-saving. At the end of October the first stone was laid, with the Lord Mayor and aldermen dancing attendance.

Robert Mylne's Blackfriars Bridge, designed in Italianate style, became the third bridge in the built-up area of London when it opened in 1769. Judging by the number of proposals flying about at Westminster in the mid-eighteenth century, there was plenty to keep the court of the Watermen's Company busy compiling objections to projected spans and compensation claims once objections foundered in the mud. In the watermen's world, London Bridge was tumbling down.

THE OPENING OF NEW LONDON BRIDGE.

FROM THE PICTURE IN THE ROYAL COLLECTION

The opening of new London Bridge 1860 (Reginald Francis Print Collection)

15
THE KEYS TO
DARIEN'S ISTHMUS

Portobelo is a sleepy town with a deep natural harbour enjoying world heritage status on the north side of the isthmus of Darien, in Panama. Once upon a time it was a key staging post on the Spanish Main, serving as the assembly point for the bullion fleets that brought untold wealth to Cadiz. Porto Bello (as it was then spelt) was thus of more than passing interest to British privateers and buccaneers for two centuries, and strikes a special resonance with the Company of Watermen and Lightermen because the keys of the city ended up at Watermen's Hall after Admiral Vernon destroyed its defences in 1739.

The Spanish explorer Francisco Velarde y Mercado founded Porto Bello in 1597, a year after the adventurer Francis Drake died of dysentery while at sea close by. Its proximity to silver mines and its excellent anchorage made it a natural base for treasure galleons, and defences were built accordingly to protect it from marauders. In 1668 the port was plundered by Captain Henry Morgan, a privateer who captured it with a flotilla of twelve ships and 450 pirates. He used women, friars and nuns as a human shield to take the fort, put many of the garrison to the sword, exacted 350,000 pesos from the governor on pain of burning the city, and returned to Port Royal, Jamaica, a wealthy hero as a result of a fortnight's looting and raping.

Keys to the city of Porto Bello

There was an unsuccessful attempt to blockade Porto Bello by Admiral Hosier in 1726, but in 1739, during the War of Jenkins' Ear, Vice-admiral Edward 'Old Grog' Vernon captured the town in an action that received popular acclaim in England. Vernon, who had taken part in the unsuccessful assault in 1726, claimed that he could take Porto Bello with only six ships, believing that small fast-moving and hard-hitting squadrons held better prospects than large disease-prone slow movers. By 1739 he was the commander of the British base in Jamaica, and on 20 November his six ships caught the Spanish garrison of the Todo Fierro harbour fort unprepared.

Landing parties of sailors and marines scaled the walls and replaced the Spanish colours with a British ensign. All but 40 of the 300-strong garrison fled the fort. Vernon's ships then attacked the Santiago fortress and sank a Spanish sloop. The Spaniards requested terms on the next morning and the governor, Francisco Javier Martínez de la Vega, surrendered in the afternoon. The cost of the action to the British was three dead and seven injured. Three prizes were taken and, over the next three weeks, the fortress and other buildings were demolished. Porto Bello's main function as a major maritime base was at an end.

Vernon distributed $10,000 amongst his men, several of whom were watermen and one, 'Pug' Mason, was allegedly first to enter the fort. He secured the keys and sold them to the Company, and it is said that the cottage he built on the proceeds gave London's Portobello its name. The keys are displayed at Watermen's Hall with the inscription:

Previous page: The Capture of Porto Bello 1739 by Peter Monamy (Watermen's Hall Collection)

From their lofty ships descending

Thro' the flood, in firm array,

To the distant city bending,

My lov'd sailors work'd their way.

Strait the foe, with horror trembling,

Quits in haste his battwe'd walls;

And in accents undissembling,

As he flies for mercy calls.

Vernon's Porto Bello adventure caught the popular imagination at home and raised him to an exalted position among sailors, opponents of the government and the populace. Streets and districts were named after the battle in Britain and America, the action being particularly welcome in the latter because it had suffered much from Spanish coastal raiders. Compared with Porto Bello, the Battle of Cartagena de Indias, fought along the coast in present-day Colombia two years later, was soon forgotten. Cartagena was one of the largest naval and amphibious campaigns in Britain's military history and the most important engagement in the 'Jenkins' Ear' theatre of the War of Austrian Succession. The British fleet under Vernon lost 50 of 186 ships and 18,000 sailors and infantry dead, mainly felled by yellow fever. Porto Bello returned to Spanish hands, but its economy did not recover until the building of the Panama canal.

Medal commemorating the capture of Porto Bello by Admiral Vernon on 22 November 1739 (Watermen's Hall Collection)

British efforts to disrupt the Spanish galleons and their trade on the Spanish Main failed. Part of the cause may have been that during the period leading up to the war of Jenkins' Ear — so-called because Robert Jenkins claimed that the Spanish coast guard had boarded his ship Rebecca and severed his ear, which organ he pickled and sent to the House of Commons — British merchants were engaged in valuable trade with the Spanish, both by treaty and black market, including the trafficking of slaves. The Spanish thwarted British belligerence by switching from large fleets calling at a few ports to small fleets making numerous stops. The Spanish also took to voyaging round Cape Horn to trade directly with the South American west coast instead of carrying cargo overland to Caribbean ports. By such measures, their ships became less vulnerable to attack.

16
STOP THE PRESS!

The Royal Navy took on the French five times during the hundred years before the revolution that started with the storming of the Bastille in 1789. While Louis XIV, the Sun King, presided over France, parliamentary politics was developing in Britain. During Louis XV's reign, Britain created an empire, enhanced her place in the world economy and became a major player in global affairs. Louis XVI ran foul of popular demands for a new dawn and rights of man, but the revolution soon deteriorated into despotism and a police state, and soon brought on foreign adventures. Prussia and Austria declared war on France in 1792 and Louis XVI was guillotined in 1793. France's invasion of the Netherlands — at that time part of the Austrian empire — closed the Scheldt estuary to maritime traffic and thus breached a treaty with Britain, causing Prime Minister William Pitt to prepare for war.

War was declared on 1 February 1793, and after fours year of struggle all but two of the protagonists were virtually eliminated. French ports were blockaded, and their defence was hampered by the suspicion that much of the French navy's sympathies were royalist. The French fleet in Toulon surrendered to Admiral Sir Samuel Hood, and sailors at the Brest naval base mutinied on hearing the news. Hood sent one of his captains, Horatio Nelson, to Naples to recruit troops to occupy Toulon, and while there Nelson met the British ambassador, Sir William Hamilton, and his striking young wife, Emma, who was an artist's model. Back in Toulon, Lt. Sidney Smith set fire to several French ships while evacuating 15,000 people in the face of a brutal assault on the town and its royalists led by a young French artillery officer, Lt. Napoleon Bonaparte. The French navy was kept out of the war for six months while France set about recruiting a mass conscript army.

Napoleon was forced to give up his planned invasion of Britain by the Royal Navy's command of the seas. His notion of a world network of trade and commerce governed by centralised bureaucracy and military power was but a dream. By the same token Britain's coast was safe before the decisive naval engagement at Trafalgar in 1805. The evolving British system of limited government with parliamentary sanction emerged as a triumphant alternative to French centralism once the Duke of Wellington had finished off Napoleon's army at Waterloo ten years later.

Through all of the above there was, needless to say, no let-up in impressment. The Watermen's Company ordered a new six-oar for the use of rulers engaged in it. In 1805 daily summoning and impressing of watermen was carried out at the hall for three months, starting in July. Further, the Company received an order to supply five hundred men to the Admiralty's new force of river fencibles to defend the river. In 1807 the Lord Mayor required apprentices to be pressed into the navy, while the Company objected that during the war the river Thames had 'more than once or twice been cleared of all persons capable of serving in the navy, to the amount of about three thousand persons entitled to the privileges of the company'. It was no longer possible to find the number required nor justifiable to impress apprentices. The Lord Mayor and the courts demurred. On 27 October the Admiralty issued a proclamation for seamen, and apprentices were apparently taken. In the same year 375 volunteer watermen went to Copenhagen to bring 33 ships of the surrendered Danish navy to the Thames. This averages at skeleton crews of eleven men per ship.

Previous page: Naval Review at Spithead, 1767 by Francis Swaine (© National Maritime Museum, Greenwich, London)

In 1808 the rulers resolved to prepare a list of watermen and lightermen at sea and the ships on which they served, and lists of those known to have met death, been taken prisoner or invalided on his majesty's service. The beadles were to obtain lists of watermen employed by fire offices, the city, the treasury, the crown, the West India and London Docks companies, and those protected by the victualling board, excise, customs, navy, transport board, Board of the Green Cloth (the royal household's auditors), ordnance, magistrates of the Thames police, river fencibles, harbour marines and Greenwich fencibles.

Manning the Navy by George Barnard O'Neill (© National Maritime Museum, Greenwich, London)

The war with the American colonies, as the Company history still called them, broke out in 1812 and rumbled on for three years. The demands of the navy in blockading the American seaboard exacerbated the general problem caused by the press gangs, namely a chronic shortage of labour on the river. The admiralty's somewhat unsatisfactory answer was for more and more apprentices to be indentured to work the river and in turn be impressed when they could serve in the navy. Upwards of four thousand watermen and lightermen were thought to be serving as seamen at this time, with another thousand in the river fencibles, plus wives of serving or deceased freemen.

On 7 February 1812 an Admiralty warrant to impress five hundred men arrived at the Company, and for the next six months argument about how best to man the navy flew back and forth between interested parties. The Admiralty wanted a reduction in the protections against impress, while the Company, 'desirous of rendering every assistance to procure men in crisis', put forward cogent proposals for raising men by ballot, thus protecting activity in the port. The main points were that parliament would enable the Company to raise men annually from watermen aged 18 to 45 by ballot with the privilege of finding substitutes; apprentices having served four years be obliged to submit thereto; invalids and widows to be placed on the pension list; persons owning 100 tons of craft be allowed three apprentices and an additional one for every additional 100 tons, plus one for every apprentice entering the navy; that all craft and tonnage be registered with the navy. On 8 May the Admiralty approved of the plan and consequently several corps of fencibles disbanded and gave up their arms. But protests and public meetings were held and petitions advanced by various interests, including those engaged in the iron, coal and deal trades and lightermen and merchants concerned with manpower for handling cargos. On 14 May the Company wrote to the Admiralty giving the numbers of lightermen requiring protections for dock work, viz.: 250 for export and import trade, 150 for corn, 200 for coal, 100 for deal &c. Among other categories deserving of exemption were those involved in recovering the Danish fleet as above. On 9 July the sum of £3:15s. was set as the watermen's subscription for finding a substitute. On 11 July Captain Richbell, regulating captain of the Port of London, received names of those who had subscribed, and between July and October 531 protections were issued.

The Company history records No 312 issued to Mr. C. Lucey:

LIGHTERMEN AND WATERMENS' HALL

We do hereby Certify, that Charles Lucey, eighteen years of age, five feet nine inches high, fair complexion, grey eyes and dark hair, is one of those persons who have furnished a substitute, to serve in His Majesty's fleet, in compliance with the instructions of the Lords Commissioners of the Admiralty.

This certificate is issued to protect the said Charles Lucey from being impressed.

Signed by two rulers of the Company and Captain Richbell.

Thus a considerable advance seems to have been made in procedure for forced manning of the fleet, although there remained a sticking point caused by the Admiralty's nervous refusal to set a time period on the exemptions. Freemen and apprentices journeying to Watermen's Hall to make protection payments were wise to avoid approaching the premises via Cross Lane or Thames Street because press gangs had set ambushes there.

Napoleon, crushed at Waterloo, abdicated in 1815 and consequently great numbers were discharged from the navy. But in 1816 Lord Exmouth mounted an expedition to punish Algerine pirates, and many watermen volunteered. After a successful outcome, during which 1,200 Christian slaves were freed in Algiers, Exmouth declared 'there were never any, on whom he could place greater dependence, or upon whose courage and presence of mind he could more firmly rely, than upon those who had joined him from the river Thames'.

In 1818 the freemen, overseers and rulers of the Company drew up a petition to the House of Commons praying for powers to raise watermen by ballot for service in the navy, replacing the 'objectionable' press gangs. The petition also addressed consolidation and amendment of various acts of parliament involving the company. This was laid on the table. Six years later another petition to the Commons from watermen, lightermen and seafaring men appealed for a system 'more consonant with justice and humanity' for recruiting to the navy. Again, nothing happened, and in 1826 a petition was again presented advocating 'the abolition of that odious system of impressments for the navy, which since the abolition of the slave trade is the foulest stigma which attaches to the national character'. Britain had banned slave trading in 1807 (four years after Denmark, the first country to do so). Henceforth slavers were treated as pirates, punishable by death, and the navy set about abolishing the trade on the high seas.

In 1827 the proposed bill for regulating the Company was under discussion with representatives of the City and Sir George Cockburn, a Lord of the Admiralty, who was concerned that those balloted for naval service, and their named substitutes, should be members of the Company. The Company approved of the bill, but it foundered at its second reading, whereupon the Commons committee reluctantly withdrew the impressment clauses. After much coming and going between Lords and Commons, the statute book recorded 'an Act for the better regulation of watermen and lightermen on the river Thames, between Yantlet Creek and Windsor.' It dealt with all manner of things, but did not mention the press gangs.

Petitions against impressments continued, and in 1833 Mr. Buckingham moved that forcible impressment of seamen for the navy is unjust, cruel, ineffectual and useless. He urged the House to promote some means of manning ships for war without violence to the liberty of the subject. The Government opposed his argument and, after a long debate, the motion was lost by 54 votes to 50. The subject was pressed again in 1834, and this time a government amendment was carried for registration of merchant seamen and selection of a certain number by ballot for the navy. Impressment was to continue, but would only be enforced in times of necessity. An act next year provided that 'the general register office of merchant seamen' be established. But the question of impressments remained a vexed one. A bill entitled 'the seamen's enlistment bill' was considered objectionable by the court of the Company when it was published that same year. Representations to the Lords of the Admiralty elicited their opposition to exempting members of court, the clerk, beadles, Sunday ferrymen and masters of vessels above forty tons, all of whom hitherto had been free from impressment. The act for the encouragement of the voluntary enlistment of seamen and for more effectual manning of Her Majesty's navy was duly passed, without referring to impressments. Abolitionists appeared to be getting nowhere.

Then came the war against Russia in the Crimea in 1854. Despite the popular conception of a land war centred on the siege of Sevastopol and the disastrous charge of the Light Brigade, the Crimea was principally a navy action. The Royal Navy sent fleets to the Baltic and the Black Sea to contain the Russian navy, and manned its ships without resort to the press gang. It was a close run issue, but impressment was terminally ill.

In February 1855 the Admiralty sent a polite request to the Watermen's Company to calculate the number of persons between the ages of 19 and 45 eligible for call up 'without material detriment to the navigation of the river Thames'. The previous lists dated from the close of the Napoleonic wars in 1815. Law stationers were engaged day and night in copying out the list of freemen made since 1831. On 6 March the clerk, Henry Humpherus, wrote to the Admiralty disclosing 3,345 freemen and 960 apprentices aged 19 or more on the books, including about 486 registered master lightermen, owners of craft, Thames and Channel pilots and others who claimed exemption from naval service.

His letter also pointed out that of this number many were dead, a great number had left the Thames for Australia and others were currently serving in the navy, merchant shipping, coastal trade or had found pursuits on land. Consequently, inconvenience to trade on the Thames and in the port would ensue from the withdrawal of numbers of freemen. To assist Her Majesty's service, Humpherus said, public notices would be affixed to plying places informing freemen of the advantages of volunteering for the navy.

The Lords of the Admiralty were keen to recruit watermen to man gunboats for the Baltic and Black Sea expeditions. They hoped that the Company could achieve this through volunteers – they were reluctant, they said, to resort to impressment, but neither were they offering bounties. They placed the onus on the Company to find the manpower. Watermen and lightermen were reminded that they had to register their places of work and abode on pain of a considerable £10 fine.

The Company's navy recruitment notice read:

> Desirable opportunity now offers to Watermen & Lightermen between the ages of 19 & 45 years of entering the Royal Navy. Applicants must be active and able bodied, 5 feet 6 1/2 inches high & in all respects healthy and fit for service. Further particulars may be known by Application at Watermans Hall.

> Watermans Hall 6th March 1855;

> Henry Humpherus. Clerk.

The result was a large number of recruits for the Baltic and Black Sea fleets without the navy resorting to press gangs. The admiralty also issued notice for men for service in a boat expedition up Russian rivers. In the event, the corps was disbanded in June 1856 following the end of the Crimean war. The outcome was more a stalemate than an Allied victory, but the British navy had succeeded in closing the Mediterranean to the Russian fleet and taken control of the Black Sea and the Baltic. The navy was now committed to the age of iron ships, steam power, screw propulsion and officers with an engineering and scientific bent. It had cleared another important hurdle in becoming a professional service.

In 1858 the Admiralty was on the recruiting warpath again, and the Company prepared a similar placard to that of 1855 soliciting watermen, lightermen and their apprentices between the ages of 20 and 45 to join up. This time there was the added incentive of a bounty ranging from £2 to £10.

In 1860 the world's first iron-clad battleship was launched. The *Warrior* was revolutionary in design and formidable in firepower. She was Britain's answer to France's *Gloire*, outclassing her in every respect. The *Warrior* was also the first ship to be manned by professional seamen, extending to all ranks the security of employment hitherto only available to officers. The process began in 1853 during recruitment for Crimea, when new entrants were invited to sign on for ten years for a higher pay level and offered a pension after twenty years service.

Her Majesty's navy was now a professional, all round the years', service with a career structure for all ranks. There is no further mention of impressment in the history of the Company or the navy. Watermen were, of course, still in demand for their specialist skills, as shown in 1873 when they were recruited to man the 26-oar yellow-coloured surf boats built by Mr. Forrest of Limehouse for landing troops and materials on West Africa's Gold Coast. In 1874 General Garnet Wolseley commanded a large force against the Ashanti who claimed the territory that Britain had purchased from the Dutch three years previously. He achieved a quick victory, despite the British government's refusal to take measures against British arms manufacturers who were busy supplying both sides. But Wolseley's rapid departure left a vacuum on the Gold Coast which soon erupted into conflict in the absence of any administration or governance.

The action, incidentally, was well publicised by war correspondents, including Henry Morton Stanley the explorer and George Alfred Henty, the latter a profuse writer of adventure stories and a keen member of London Rowing Club.

Press gangs had been the bane of life to men who worked on the Thames for five hundred years. The death of forced labour in the Royal Navy was more of a blessing for watermen than some of the other threats to their livelihood because, unlike wheels and bridges, it opened an alternative career to them, and an increasingly attractive one. The close relationship between seamen and the river men would continue without the antagonism threaded through it hitherto.

Manning the Navy from Attic Miscellany 1790 (© National Maritime Museum, Greenwich, London)

17
WHERRIES AT THE CROSS ROADS

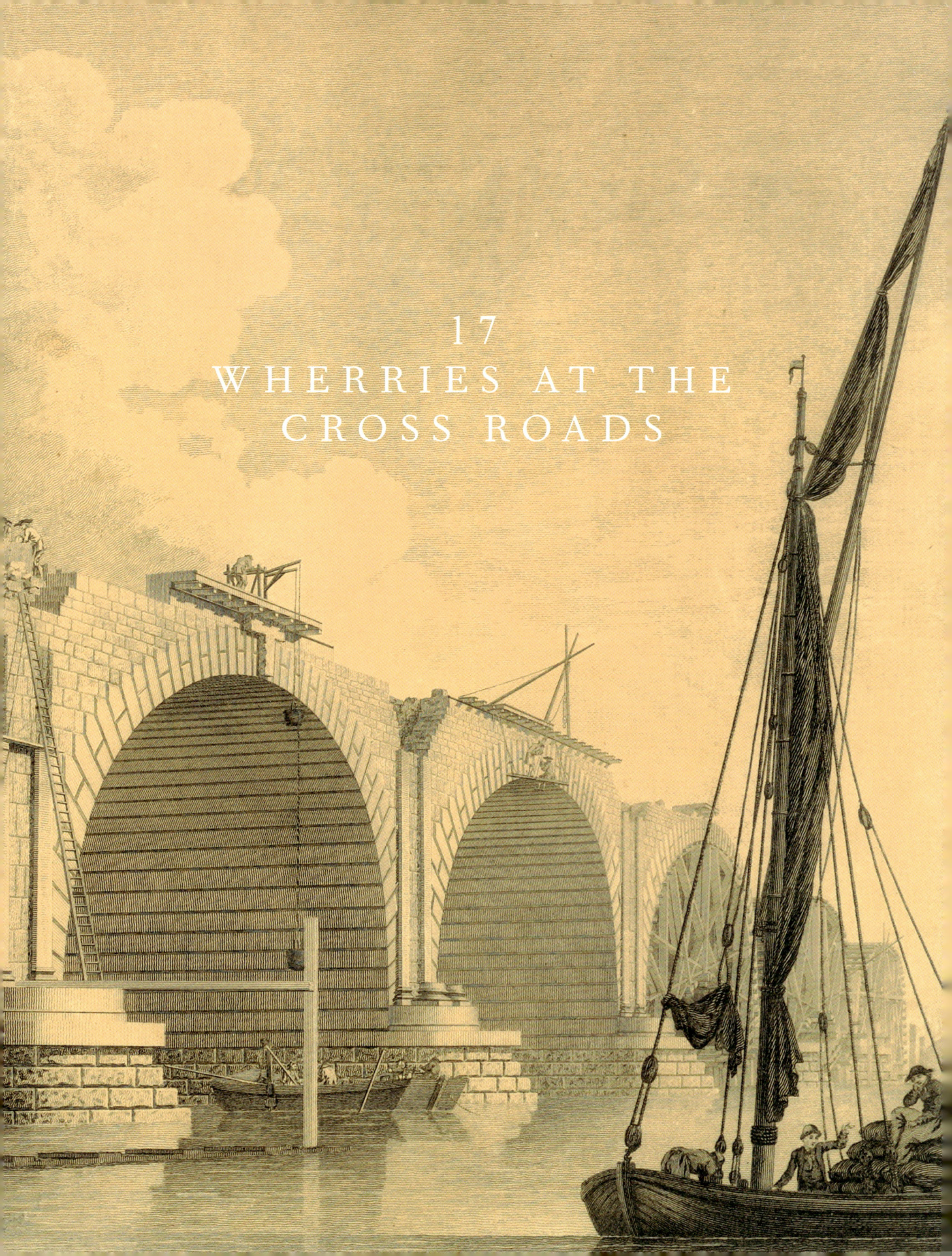

Confusion and bad luck, I say,

To all these precious schemers-

May every bridge be swept away,

And Satan seize the steamers!

— Anon

The rot set in for the wherry trade during the eighteenth century, and continued in the next one. First came horse drawn carriages, followed by the encroachment of bridges and improved roads that ate into their near-monopoly of human river traffic. If the proliferation of crossing places wasn't enough, the invention of the steam engine and its application to trains and boats was the killer.

1722 was a red-letter year for the watermen. A bill was under consideration in parliament for the building of a bridge from a place called The Prince's Waste to the opposite shore near Peterboro' House, and the Company was quick to gather opposition to it. On 24 January a petition of bargemen and watermen from Kingston, Richmond, Mortlake, Barnes and other places was presented to the House of Commons, declaring that such a bridge would be pernicious to navigation, detrimental to trade in London and Westminster and the ruin of thousands of families. The Lord Mayor's court also petitioned against the bridge, and petitions followed from watermen in places such as Queenhithe, Deptford and Bermondsey. Pamphlets circulated expounding the consequences of bridge building on watermen's livelihood. Progress on the bridge was bogged down for some years, but 1722 was also a year when London Bridge was closed for repairs, an occurrence that no doubt served supporters and detractors of bridges. Its closure restricted watermen's upstream-downstream traffic but increased crossings between the banks, while the lack of a foot and cart passage between London and Southwark illustrated the usefulness of bridges.

By 1726 there were proposals for bridges at Lambeth and Fulham. The Fulham project was opposed by the corporation of London, the trustees of St. Bartholomew's Hospital who were large landowners in Southwark, the watermen of Putney and the tenant of the Chelsea to Battersea ferry. The bill was amended and passed, with compensation for watermen written into it. Recompense of £9,655 was paid to the existing horse ferry. Revenue from tolls was to be put towards watermen, their widows and children as compensation for loss of earnings. The Duchess of Marlborough as the Lady of the Manor of Wimbledon received £64:10s for her interest in the ferry. The Bishop of London, whose palace was close to the bridge in Fulham, received £23 plus free passage for himself and his servants for his interest in the same.

Previous page: Blackfriars Bridge under construction in 1766 (Reginald Francis Print Collection)

View of Fulham Bridge looking towards Putney 1760 (Reginald Francis Print Collection)

COMPLETED IN 1729
REMOVED IN 1880
OLD·PUTNEY·BRIDGE
FROM · A · SKETCH · TAKEN ·
JUST · BEFORE · ITS · REMOVAL
H · H · STATHAM

Old Putney Bridge from a sketch by H H Statham before its removal in 1886 (Reginald Francis Print Collection)

A wooden structure of twenty-six arches by Sir Joseph Acworth was preferred to John Price's design in stone, and Thomas Phillips built the new bridge. It opened in 1729, curving through the churchyard of St Mary's, famous for the Putney Debates of the Levellers in 1647, and ending at a tollgate downstream of the present bridge on the Fulham side, near what is now Fulham's bus and Underground station, known as Putney Bridge. The bridge's twenty-five piers were close together and its roadway low over the water, offering a considerable challenge to navigation. The Company history says it 'much interfered with the watermen's labour at the ferries above and below'. Numerous accidents occurred with vessels hitting the bridge, and the loss of life to passengers was noted in the Commons when Westminster Bridge was being debated in 1736. Putney's arches later became known as 'the Scylla and Charybdis of amateur boatmen'. In 1870 a barge damaged three central sections, and in 1871 two piers were removed and replaced by an iron girder to make a wider passage. The Metropolitan Board of Works purchased the bridge in 1879, and the present graceful bridge in Cornish granite by Sir Joseph Bazalgette, with its magnificent trident lanterns on the balustrades, opened in 1886 and was widened in 1933.

Fulham Bridge from Putney 1760 (Reginald Francis Print Collection)

The Company of Watermen and Lightermen was not alone in opposing bridges in their early days. Vested interests from landowners to ferry licensees, from shipping interests to barge owners, from wharfingers to fishermen were all against. So were the City's mayor and corporation, the aldermen of Southwark and the Church, the latter because it owned a horse ferry. Arguments mustered against bridges included interference with currents, disruption of upriver trade, threat to naval manpower as a result of reduction of skills and the river's workforce, inhibition of sewage dispersal, affect on fish stock and catching same — you name it, bridges were bad for it.

But in 1736 parliament passed an act for the Earl of Pembroke's scheme to build a bridge from New Palace Yard in Westminster to the Surrey shore. Ironically, there was a great flood in February that year as the proposal was under debate. It exceeded previous records by 18 inches, filling the cellars of great houses in Westminster and Southwark and putting large areas of Essex, Kent and Middlesex under water. There was two feet of water in Westminster Hall, and watermen were rowing their boats across Palace Yard to ferry judges to their coaches. The watermen blamed the flood on the effect of Putney Bridge on the current of the river.

The new bridge was seen in Westminster as a victory over London and the Church, while those interests dubbed it the 'bridge of fools' because it was proposed to finance it by lottery. The rulers of the Company saw a threat to ferries between Vauxhall and Temple. Lightermen in the coal trade petitioned against on the grounds of navigation problems likely to ensue. Inhabitants of Southwark feared injury to trade and a run on parish funds to support ruined watermen.

There were delays caused by the failure of the lottery funding scheme, but the Company succeeded in negotiating recompense for loss of Sunday ferries from Millbank to Vauxhall, Westminster to Stangate and the Horseferry to Lambeth. The

Westminster bridge and Abbey 1799 (Reginald Francis Print Collection)

bridge commissioners applied for permission to exact tolls on Putney Bridge (halfpenny per passenger on weekdays and 1d on Sundays). The first pile was driven in on 9 June 1738 'with great concourse of persons in boats and barges,' with watermen reaping a rich harvest. The first stone was laid on 29 January next year. Construction was disrupted by frost and thawing flood water that washed away the piles. The Spanish navy sank some of the ships bringing stone from Purbeck and Portland, and the navy contributed by impressing some of the workforce conveying stone up the river. The stone barges sometimes collided with the structure, and at least one pier was sunk in this way. A dozen almshouses, mostly occupied by watermen, were demolished to make way for the bridge approach and rebuilt in St Anne's Lane, off Little Smith Street.

Westminster Bridge was built by the Swiss engineer Charles Labelye who constructed caissons, or huge boxes, on shore that were floated into position, driven into the riverbed, pumped out and filled with stone. The weight of the masonry piers fixed them in place, and the new bridge withstood an earthquake in 1850. Opinions of the bridge differed, of course, but its fifteen semi-circular arches which diminished in size from the centre and its fine stone balustrade with turrets at intervals was hailed as elegance personified. Canaletto created twenty images of it between 1746 and 1756, and the poet Wordsworth declared that 'earth has not anything to show more fair,' a sight touching in majesty. Watermen may have thought differently. The Westminster to Lambeth crossing of many arches, like the Fulham to Putney bridge, was sometimes a hazard to navigation, but it gave direct passage from Westminster to the Surrey shore. Navigation was made easier when the bridge was rebuilt in 1862 to a wrought iron seven-arch design by Thomas Page with Gothic detailing by Charles Barry, architect of the Palace of Westminster.

The construction of Westminster Bridge provoked the City to demolish buildings and widen London Bridge, and to go ahead with a scheme for a new bridge near its western boundary at Blackfriars, where the saline Thames gave way to the freshwater river. In 1754 the Company petitioned against this idea. Apart from providing a crossing, the William Pitt Bridge, as it was christened, was to serve as a social engineer in opening up the burgeoning urban area south of the river round the Elephant and Castle junction and shortening the journey time to the south coast ports.

On the north side, traffic in the Strand and New Oxford Street bound for London Bridge would be eased by the new crossing, and the notorious black spot along the valley of the tidal inlet known as the Fleet through Holborn and Farringdon would come in for regeneration. The open sewer of the Fleet — clogged with dead livestock, excrement and industrial waste — sludged through appalling slums and passed near the Bridewell and Newgate prisons, the latter described by Henry Fielding as 'a prototype for hell'. It was a no-go area for the forces of law and order.

The Scots engineer Robert Mylne secured the contract to build the Pitt bridge after he lost the competition to design it. Although they had crowned another as winner, the judges eventually decided that Mylne's elegant structure was what they were after. Work began on his nine Portland stone elliptical arches in 1760. A huge hoard of skulls was found in the riverbed during construction of the sixth arch. The bridge was 303 metres long, 13 metres wide, resting on slender, pointed cutwaters and supported by double ionic columns. The carriageway was 8.5 metres wide with footpaths either side and sheltered spots above each pier.

By 19 November 1769 when the bridge opened, Pitt's star had waned and the name was changed to Blackfriars after a Dominican monastery that once stood on north bank. Blackfriars began life as a toll bridge, though in 1780 Gordon's rioters against the Papists Act – which repealed some penalties and restrictions on Catholics including membership of the armed forces when Britain was up against France, Spain, the Dutch Republic and the revolting American colonies – robbed and then destroyed the toll gates. Charges on weekdays were abandoned in 1785 and on Sundays in 1811. The bridge was replaced by a five-arch wrought iron structure by Joseph Cubitt in 1869, and widened in 1907-10.

The easing of congestion on London Bridge by removal of shops and houses in 1763 and the opening of crossings at Westminster and Blackfriars fatally holed watermen's trade right where it had been most prolific and profitable.

View of Black-Friars Bridge 1798 (Reginald Francis Print Collection)

Doggett's Coat and Badge cements the Company of Watermen and Lightermen's link – and history's link – with the working river in the age of the oar. It was not the first competitive event on the tidal Thames by any means, but its annual endurance since the first race in 1715, for which we have Thomas Doggett and the Fishmongers' Company to thank, makes it the iconic reminder of flashing blades in the great scheme of things. Its first winner was unknown until recently, when Robert Cottrell's diligent digging disclosed John Opey or Opie of Saviours Mills to be accorded the first Coat and Badge.

Doggett's is the oldest continuous sporting event in the British sporting calendar. But other, long forgotten, competitions for coats and badges, and sometimes for wherries themselves, were part of the life of the river. During the eighteenth and nineteenth centuries challenges, matches and regattas thrived alongside Doggett's all along the tidal river from Gravesend. During the nineteenth century there are references to regattas at the Adelphi, Bankside, Hungerford Market, Westminster Bridge, Whitehall, Poplar Blackwall, the Tower, St. Katharine's, Custom House, St. John's and St. Margaret's as well as many at Gravesend and Greenwich.

For the populace, such occasions were entertainment on a summer night with cabaret provided by rowers, but for participants, prizes and prowess were at stake and reputations to be made or wrecked. Betting and its attendant opportunities for corruption and cheating often fuelled both kinds of event. One reason for Doggett's quick rise to prominence in the rowing calendar may have been attention to rules, judging by several occasions when the race was re-started or re-rowed. A voyage through some of the prominent dates in the rowing calendar, often on troubled water prone to accident and interference, gives a flavour of the times.

In 1721 and again in 1726 there was trouble in Doggett's when contestants jumped the start. In the latter case, three are said to have put off before the signal was given, and the race was run again, the result being the same as for the disallowed contest.

In 1723 on 'King William of Immortal Memory's birthday', a boat and oars were offered to be rowed for by eight bachelor watermen of the Tower liberties. The course was from Wapping New Stairs through London Bridge to Whitehall and back to Tower Watergate. Each pair was distinguished by caps of red, blue, black and yellow. Samuel Lecounts and Richard Wright, the red caps, won and were shouldered at the Tower to collect their prizes.

An apprentice named Jack Broughton won Doggett's in 1730. Broughton was unusual in that he was the grand old age of 20 when he was bound in 1723. He was 5 ft. 11 ins. and weighed 14 stone, and he took up boxing in the year that he won Doggett's, punching his way to champion of England four years later. Broughton became known as the father of English boxing after he opened an amphitheatre near Oxford Street in 1743 where his teaching brought some science and humanity to a barbarous activity. In the code that he promulgated, Broughton introduced defensive guards and banned hitting a man when he was down. He himself retired from the ring in 1750 to become a connoisseur and dealer in furniture and curiosities. His London Prize Ring Rules

Previous page: The Grand Metropolitan Regatta 1849 by James Baker Pyne RA (River & Rowing Museum)

were revised in 1853 before being superseded by the Marquis of Queensberry Rules in 1867 - rules actually written by John Graham Chambers, a Cambridge University oarsman.

Prince George's twelfth birthday was celebrated in 1749 by a race for seven pair-oars from Whitehall to Putney for a cup valued at 25 guineas. A great many nobility and gentry accompanied the race in barges rowed by watermen. *Frederick*, a barge containing a band led the procession, followed by the Prince and Princess of Wales's barge, followed by the racing wager men, followed by the future George III and young princesses in a new Venetian-style barge with watermen 'dressed in Chinese habits which made a very splendid appearance'. Ten days earlier, the Duke of Richmond burned money on a grand scale on an entertainment for the Duke of Modena that consisted of a pyrotechnic display off the Privy Gardens and a Thames crowded with watermen's and other boats. The bill of fare included 200 water mines, 200 air balloons, 200 fire trees, 5,000 war rockets, 5,000 sky rockets, 100 fire showers, 20 suns and 100 stars, 'concluding with a grand illumination'.

In 1751 there was a scheme afoot to raise a subscription for a boat to present to the winner of Doggett's, but nothing seems to have come of it. Four years later six watermen rowed from Westminster Bridge to the Hoop, Battersea, for a new boat, coat and badge in honour of the Prince of Wales's birthday. Charles Bernard of Whitehall won the prize that was presented by the Society of Anti-Gallicans, whose members were opposed to French cultural influence and imports. Prince George's birthday was also marked by the launch of his new ten-seat leisure barge at Kew Gardens. The *Princess Augusta* was named for his mother, and was built by J. Rich Esq. to an unusual design:

> 'It is finished in a taste entirely new, and made to imitate a swan swimming; the imitation is so very natural, as hardly to be distinguished from a real bird, except from its size; the neck and head rise to the height of eighteen feet, the body forms a commodious cabin…'

It is not clear from the description if the boat accommodated ten oarsmen or ten persons in total.

John Sugden, a Southwark ironmonger, had the misfortune to have his skull fractured by a bottle thrown at him while watching the Coat and Badge race in 1766. King George III gave prizes – five guineas for first place — for a race between six young watermen at Kew in 1768. In 1772 there was a grand regatta on June 23 for watermen of private barges, organised by west end clubs, including Boodle's, White's, Stapleton's, Almack's, Savoir-Vivre and Goosetree's. Three hundred watermen attended Mr Roberts's in Lambeth to draw lots to determine who should row, for competitors were limited to a dozen two-man boats. Tickets were limited to 1300 to see the race from Westminster Bridge to Watermen's Hall and round a moored vessel to race back to Westminster. The winners received ten guineas and coats and badges, while second and third received seven and five guineas respectively and inferior coats and badges. Afterwards, ticket holders were entertained to supper and an orchestra at Ranelagh Gardens.

There was a grand regatta at Ranelagh in May 1775. Supper tables were laid out in the rotunda to form an amphitheatre for the 1,300 subscribers who included the royal family, the prime minister, Lord North, and the French, Spanish, Prussian, Russian and Neapolitan ambassadors. A 240-strong orchestra 'of the most capital vocal and instrumental performers in Great Britain' occupying the centre. A pavilion was erected for dancing and elaborate decorations graced the gardens.

SCULLING-MATCH ON THE THAMES FOR THE CHAMPIONSHIP OF THE WORLD: THE RACE AT BARNES RAILWAY-BRIDGE.

Ed Trickett of New South Wales leading James Sadler at Barnes Railway Bridge for the professional sculling Championship of the World, 27 June 1876 (Watermen's Hall Collection)

Only watermen were permitted as competitors. Lots were drawn on May 13 to select 24 from the entry list of 200. This allowed only ten days for training. A seat in a barge to watch the exertions cost half a guinea. By six o'clock the Thames was overspread with boats. At seven o'clock the director's barge, displaying a large blue ensign with 'regatta' in gold letters embroidered on it, rowed to its station on the west of the centre arch of Westminster Bridge. A ballast barge contained 'the finest ballast in the world – about a hundred elegant ladies'. At 7.30 the Lord Mayor's barge described a circle by the bridge, and 21 cannons were fired.

Henry Humpherus quotes the *Morning Chronicle's* description of the proceedings while pointing out that the reporter considered the actual business of the evening, the races, as the least important feature of the regatta. There was, of course, no such thing as a sporting press at this time, and certain facts were wanting, such as whether the boats were pair-oars or double sculls or whether the contest began with trial heats or went straight off as a grand final. 'The several candidates for the regatta honours,' said the

Chronicle, 'started at Westminster Bridge, twelve boats, two men in each, in three divisions, habited in the colours of the royal navy, white, red and blue, rowed down to Watermen's Hall and went round a vessel placed there for the purpose, and then made up again for the goal, which was first gained by one of the red squadron, who had each for their reward a new boat, with furniture compleat, coats and badges, and an ensign, with the word "regatta" in gold letters inscribed thereon.'

The crew of the second boat earned eight guineas apiece (£8:8s), and those of the third, five. There is not a line of description of the racing, nor of names. There followed a great procession through the 'floating town' to supper at Ranelagh, laid on for two thousand souls by Mrs Cornelly who received 700 guineas for her services. Four people were drowned in the melée on the river. The spirit of the occasion was captured by a ballad:

> *We've friends in the Court, and we've friends in the City,*
>
> *No doubt then, our place is both useful and pretty,*
>
> *Since the Six Clubs have joined to defray all the charges,*
>
> *And the Lord Mayor and Aldermen leant us their barges.*
>
> *Did ye mind how each candidate tugg'd at the oar?*
>
> *How the managers storm'd, how the constables swore?*
>
> *Shall ye ever forget how the mob were delighted,*
>
> *When the boat all ran foul, and the ladies were frighted?*

Later that year there was a sailing race from Westminster Bridge to Putney and back for a 20-guinea silver cup presented by Prince Henry, Duke of Cumberland. There was also a regatta at Walton in August, attended by the Prince of Wales and Princess Amelia.

1776

Next year a sailing regatta took place for a 20-guinea silver cup presented again by the Duke of Cumberland. On 22 July a regatta was held between Richmond and Kew for George, Prince of Wales's birthday. Although members of the royal family and crowds of people were present to witness 'some very curious fireworks on an aite on the river', there was very little diversion according to the account in the Company's history.

There was a neat illustration of the dangers of dipping for both victim and perpetrator in 1777. A gent watching Doggett's from the Steel Yard had his pocket picked by a genteel young fellow who was caught in the act. The mob were for ducking him, but the gent delivered him into the hands of the officer in charge of an impress galley that was near at hand.

On 25 June 1781 eleven sailing boats slipped their cables at the Temple and set off to race to Blackfriars via Putney for a cup worth £50 donated by the Duke of Cumberland. Unfortunately the royal duke's barge was tardy by an hour or so in reaching the start, so that when the *Eagle* that led the squadron reached Battersea, she could not get under the bridge. Watermen in attendance declared a record number of boats containing an estimated 30,000 onlookers, with another 100,000 on the banks. The fleet anchored off Chelsea church and the duke arranged a new meeting in July to settle the matter, but there is no record of this taking place. That year Doggett's was re-run on 2 August after foul play at the first attempt.

A race for a new wherry was held in 1786. Seven pairs were chosen by ballot from 180 hopefuls to compete from Blackfriars to Chelsea and back to Vauxhall stairs. William Dawsley of Vauxhall and William Surall won the race. Competitors wore white waistcoats, blue silk sashes and white caps. Eight, six and four-oared cutters plus a multitude of small boats followed the race. A seven-gun salute was fired as competitors passed freeman Roberts's garden, where his guests included the Archbishop of Canterbury.

On 8 September 1788 two eight-oared cutters raced from Westminster Bridge to Richmond against wind and tide for a wager of 60 guineas. Invincible cleared Kew Bridge three hundred metres ahead of Chatham but was caught at Sion House and driven ashore by *Chatham*. Two of *Invincible's* men landed at Kew the worst for wear, and another 'died on his oar'.

One Saturday evening in 1795 a man watching a rowing match on Mill Bank put a lighted tobacco pipe into a hollow willow that was not discovered until the tree was completely enflamed. With great difficulty it was cut down in time enough to prevent the fire communicating to adjoining trees.

In 1797 Thomas Watford, a waterman, was killed when the wadding of the gun he was firing at a match for a silver cup at the New Swan, Chelsea injured his side. A subscription for his widow and five children was opened on the spot.

In 1799 the Cumberland Society gave an annual silver cup for sailboats from Blackfriars Bridge to Putney and back to Vauxhall Gardens. The proprietors of the gardens and 'Astley the rider' offered a new wherry each year to be rowed for by 'jolly young watermen' in two-man boats.

A rowing match in 1803 between the six-oars *Eclipse* and *Hector* from Westminster Bridge to Kew against the tide for a wager of 23 guineas got out of hand after the boats reached Putney. The engagement was built up to the best match ever known, with the London watermen of Hector supposedly superior in strength and the Gravesend crew of *Eclipse* in skill. *Eclipse* led to Putney, where *Hector* 'got foul of her', and one of *Eclipse's* company 'by dexterous manoeuvre knocked one of *Hector's* oars out of the boat'. The man who had lost the oar rose to recover it and thereby lost the wager as, according to the agreement, 'no man was to quit his seat'. The case was referred to the

Society for the Suppression of Vice — dedicated to opposing indisciplined radicals — who requested the Company's rulers to use their authority to prevent any thing so indecent and unlawful from being committed in future.

Whatever the outcome of the vice squad's deliberations, *Hector* and *Eclipse* were scheduled to meet again at the end of January in 1804 when Captain Durand MP sponsored a race of unusual length from Gravesend round the Nore light and back to Rotherhithe. The London watermen took up quarters in Gravesend on the night before, 'where they fared sumptuously and rose in the morning like giants refreshed.' High expectations were doomed, however, when the crew of *Hector* was overpowered by sickness before they reached the Nore, and were taken on board Captain Durand's pleasure steamer *Rambler. Eclipse* completed the 67 miles in 8 hours 17 minutes and was adjudged the prize.

We can already see that prizes in kind or cash were often substantial. Challenges were sometimes against the clock and sometimes offered to other than waterman. On 14 May 1824 there was a wager for 600 guineas between Sir John Burgoyne and Captain Short that six Guards officers belonging to aquatic clubs should row a six-oared wherry from Oxford to Westminster Bridge in sixteen consecutive hours. The 118 miles was accomplished in 15¾ hours.

In 1825 Mr. Kean, the performer, gave a prize wherry to be rowed for by seven pairs; first heat from Westminster Bridge round a boat moored near Lawn Cottage to the Red House in Battersea which, notes the Company report, is said to be 50 yards from the spot where Caesar crossed the Thames. In the same year a crew of Westminster schoolboys rowed an eight-oar from the Horseferry at Westminster to Windsor Bridge and back, a distance of about 60 miles, in about 20 hours, including a stop for lunch at Eton.

A parade of city barges commemorated the Battle of Waterloo on 18 June 1828, followed by 'a magnificent déjeuner' in the state barge's cabin.

There were sometimes diversions of a different nature. In June 1840 a man wagered to jump from the centre arch of London Bridge and swim to Greenwich in one and a half hours. He leapt in at 4 a.m. when the tide was on half ebb and completed his swim in an hour and 20 minutes. 'He did not appear the least exhausted', said a report.

On 26 July 1842 the Westminster scholars raced the Eton scholars from Barkers Rails to Putney Bridge. The exact location of Barkers Rails is open to question, but they were – or perhaps are – close to the finish of the Championship Course, the great S-bend used by professional scullers from Putney to Mortlake that was to become the University Boat Race course when Oxford and Cambridge migrated from Westminster in 1845. The Westminster scholars won.

On 23 April 1844 there was a great 12-mile rowing match for £100 on the canal from Ostend to Bruges between Robert Newell of Battle Bridge and five Belgian watermen. Newell reached Bruges three quarters of a mile ahead of his opponents. Steamer No 10 made the 140-mile passage from London to Ostend, in 9 hours 26 minutes to witness the event. Another match took place on 27 May over the same ground with the points reversed. Four Flemish watermen in a London-built boat defeated Newell

The final heat of the Champion Prize at the Thames Grand Regatta, Putney 1848 by J F Martin (River & Rowing Museum)

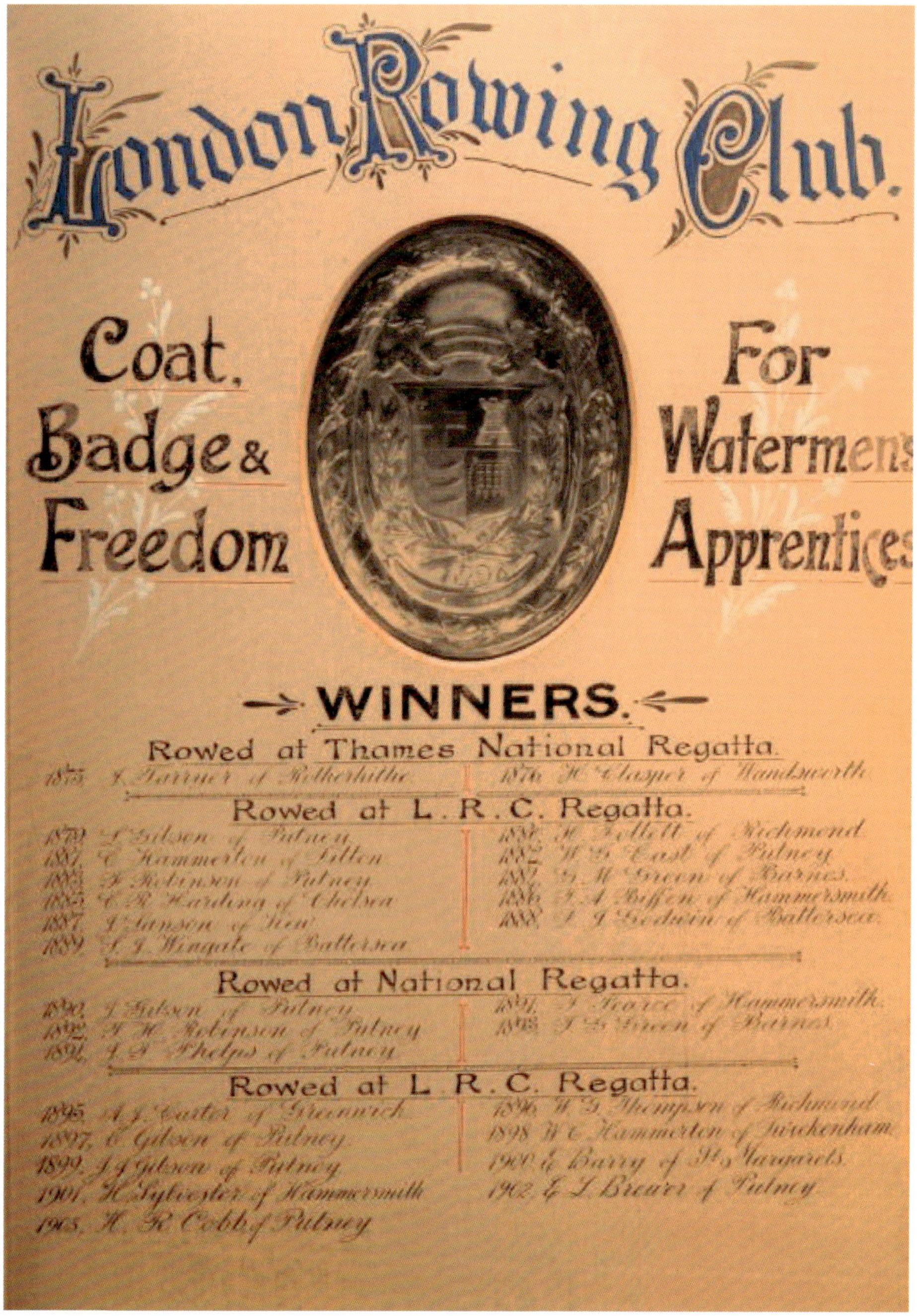

London Rowing Club's winners' board (London Rowing Club)

by two minutes. Their time was 1 hour 53 minutes. Newell 'lost in consequence of wind'.

There was quite a furore on 20 June when a Newcastle boat builder named Harry Clasper turned up in Putney with a four-oared outrigger, the *Lord Ravensworth*, built in mahogany by himself and his wife. The boat weighed 145 lbs. and was 37 ft. 6 inches in length and 12 and a half inches deep. The wonder was the breadth of only 2 ft., counteracted by rowlocks mounted on iron rods that protruded about 8 ins. outside the boat. The iron thole pins were covered with leather. She moved through the water beautifully, and the Tyne men (R. Clasper, E. Hawks, W. Clasper and H. Clasper) won a fifty sovereign prize by beating three other crews from Putney to Chiswick. Next day, however, they were beaten for the £100 prize for four-oars by the London crew consisting of T. Coombes, J. Phelps, R. Newell and R. Coombes. But the visit of the Claspers advertised the growing prowess of professional scullers and oarsmen from the Tyne and their accompanying skills at racing boat building and design. They returned the following year and beat the Thames men.

At Bankside Regatta in 1844 the dummy and the bridge leading to the pier at Blackfriars Bridge gave way just as a shot was fired for the commencement of a wager race. Watermen's boats rescued numbers of the great crowd, but five drowned. On 23 September, Barry, the resident clown at Astley's, sailed from Vauxhall to Westminster wearing his clown's attire while seated in a washing tub drawn by two geese.

In 1856 the Company history records that a coat and silver badge, paid for by a penny subscription from no less than 3,864 watermen, were presented to William Edward Blackwell for the manner in which he had run Horselydown Regatta for many years. The presentation was made at Victoria Theatre, Lambeth. Here is a rare piece of evidence that the races for Doggett's and fêtes afloat were only the tip of the iceberg as far as rowing and racing on the river are concerned. Horselydown was a parish in Southwark in the vicinity of Tooley Street with a population of 11,360 in the 1851 census. It was a riverside community taking its name from the grazing meadows opposite the Tower, a community dependent on riverside activity, and enjoying a regatta in the summer when its drab streets would be decorated, and watermen would compete for catch prizes and new wherries.

Prince Regent's Coat and Badge 1851 won by George Robbins of Battle Bridge

The year of Blackwell's recognition was notable for another development in rowing at the opposite end of the social scale. In August 1856 London Rowing Club began life in Putney. It was formed by amateurs with the aim of giving men who worked in the City the opportunity of forming crews to win pots at the most prestigious amateur regatta, Henley Royal. The adoption of Putney as its headquarters was made possible by the efficient train service from Waterloo and had the effect of reviving amateur rowing in London when it was threatened by water pollution in the city and the unfavourable rowing conditions caused by steamers, sailing barges and lighters.

The founders of London aimed to create a big club which was affordable, and its immediate success led to a further decline in small clubs that were essentially groups of friends who rented or held shares in a boat in favour of a place that could afford to maintain a fleet without calling upon charges beyond members' annual subscriptions. Leander Club moved to Putney soon after London came into existence, and Thames Rowing Club was born five years after London, to be followed by many more. The Tideway above Putney Bridge became the preferred water for competitive rowing among the city's oarsmen, amateur and professional alike.

Josias Nottidge, a founder of London, revived the old Royal National Thames Regatta in 1854, a regatta that had events for amateurs and professionals. London's annual report for 1856 stated: 'Such being the leading objects which the committee are earnestly resolved in carrying out, they cannot but indulge in a well-grounded hope that this club will infer most valuable benefits on the deserving watermen, as well as the gentleman amateur, and that from its establishment may hereafter be dated the revival of rowing on the Thames.'

The schism over the definition of amateurs and professionals was another thirty years in the making — in 1862 the Rowing Almanack was classifying clubs under the headings 'gentlemen', 'tradesmen' and 'watermen'. Through most of its history, London Rowing Club has resisted a hard-line approach to the class war in rowing that lasted until the 1970s. The associated Thames Subscription Club was offering coats and badges for watermen apprentices, while in the twenty-first century there are Doggett's winners who have rowed at and for London. In 1866 Herbert Playford, captain of London, started the Metropolitan Regatta which became London's own, soon ranking second to Henley in the domestic calendar and mutating to the multi-lane course at Dorney Lake, site of the 2012 Olympic regatta, in the twenty-first century.

The schism caused by wrangling over the definition of amateurs and professionals raged for a hundred years and did much to befog the transformation of rowing from a way of life to a pastime of sport and leisure. When attitudes changed and the fog lifted – just as the London smog itself wafted away – after the Second World War, it became clear once more that rowing in the twenty-first century owes its roots and its skills to men who worked waterways as much as to its Johnny-come-lately amateur pioneers.

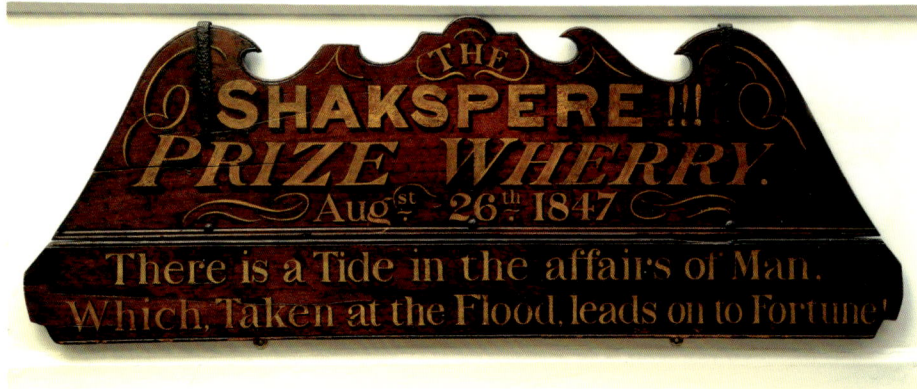

The Shakspere Prize Wherry backboard, 26 Augst 1847

103rd Annual Greenwich Regatta 1880 won by John J Williams

Backboard commissioned by the Company to commemorate the Queen and Duke of Edinburgh's visit to Watermen's Hall on 27 March 2014

19
THE THAMES FINDS
A CHAMPION

'Great race between Coombes and Campbell, 1846' (River & Rowing Museum, gift of British American Arts Association from the Collection of Thomas E. Weil)

A really significant event in rowing history occurred on 9 September 1831 when Charles Campbell, a waterman of Lambeth, became the first champion of the Thames. Campbell was a powerful sculler and a 'thorough waterman in the strictest sense of the word', according to Henry Humpherus in the Company history. After two years as an apprentice he joined a man'o'war for three years, and on the day of his return 'unwittingly laid the foundation of his future greatness as the original champion of the Thames'. Landing at the Old Swan near London Bridge with his sea chest, Campbell hailed a wherry to take him to Lambeth. Once afloat, he told the waterman to 'sit down, Mr. Holmes, I'll scull her up'.

Holmes was reluctant until he found out who Campbell was. It so happened that Paddy Noulton, who had a reputation as a sculler, had just rowed a fare from Westminster to London Bridge and started back ahead of them *sans* sitter or sea chest. Noulton, in a new fast boat, was hard pressed to hold Campbell off, and on reaching Lambeth and finding out who it was that had so warmed him, remarked that he must

Previous page: Robert John Jenkins Coombes, World Champion 1846-1852. Coombes was probably unsuccessful in the lottery for Doggett's entries in 1834. (Watermen's Hall Collection)

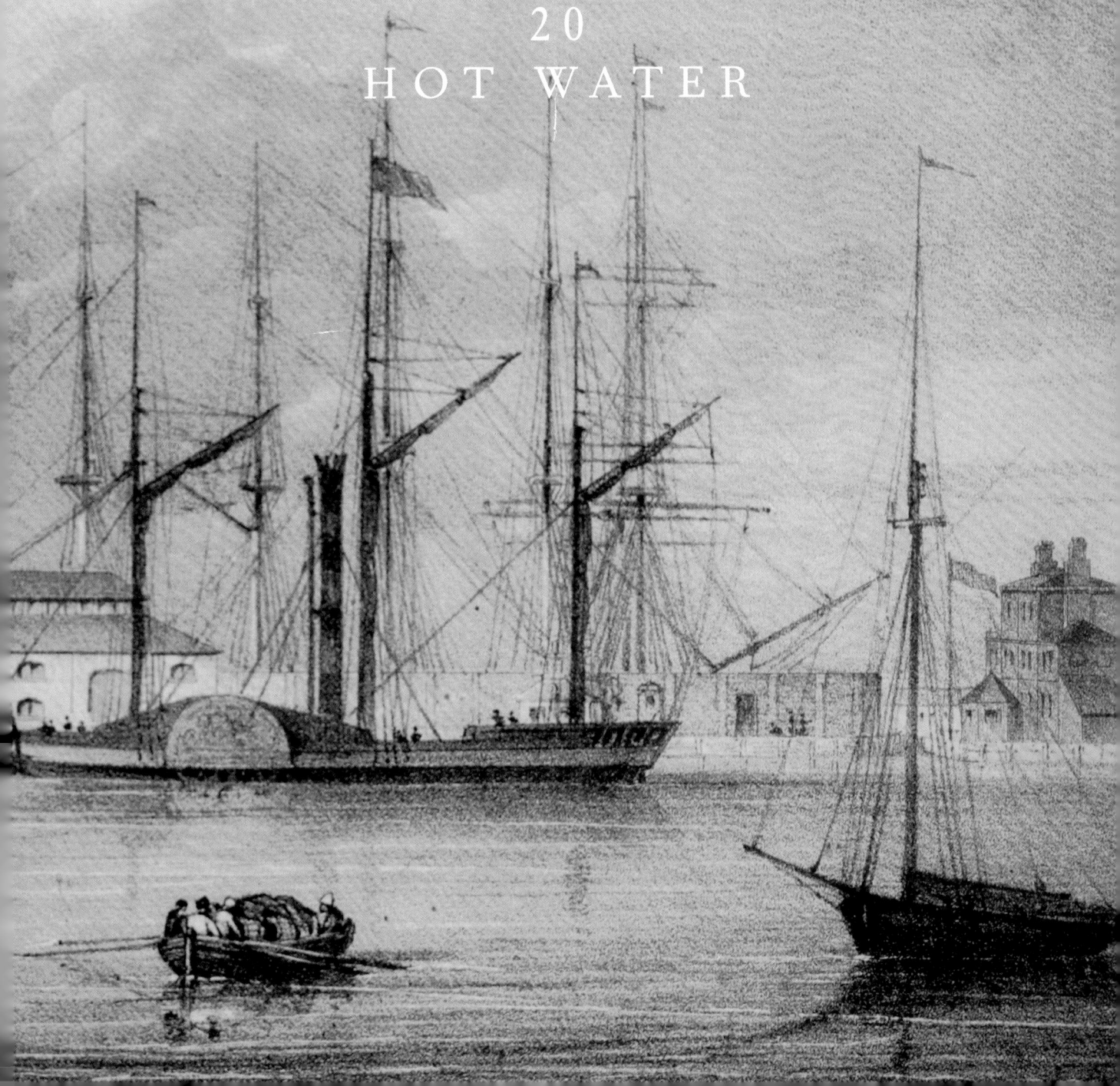

20
HOT WATER

Until the late eighteenth century, mist and fog were the only threats to visibility and movement by water craft. But in 1783 the London Chronicle made reference to an experiment with steam-powered oars. Five years later, James Taylor tried out a steam engine on his lake at Dalswinter, near Dumfries. In 1786 there was a steam boat on the Forth and Clyde canal – far enough away from the Thames to sound a warning as yet, but this was the start of something big. Lord Dundas's *Charlotte Dundas*, designed as a towing boat for the canal, drew 70 tons at 3¼ m.p.h. into a headwind, but her wash damaged the banks and curtailed her activities. In the same year another experiment in Edinburgh tried a human-powered paddle wheel which failed because the quantity of labour required was unsustainable.

Brunswick Steam Wharf, East India Docks 1845 (Reginald Francis Print Collection)

In the same year, a steam powered barge proved manoeuvrable on the Thames, making 2½ m.p.h., and in 1803 Robert Fulton, an American, tried his 70-foot steam boat on the Seine. By now the threat of steam power was beginning to penetrate the oar-powered psyche. Here was a new evil to rail against — a well-chosen word, that, for steam engines mounted on rails would soon become as big a threat as fired up ships. All kinds of activity and legislation kept the Company's rulers busy. In 1812, for example, there was a proposal to bridge the river at Vauxhall, and one to create a horse and carriage ferry between the Isle of Dogs and Greenwich, not to mention a proposed tunnel under the river at the same point, and a bill in Parliament for a canal from Paddington to Limehouse. The Company history notes that unsuccessful attempts to navigate boats by steam power 'seems to have led to further improvements, and to the adaption of paddle wheels for the purpose.' Mr. Bell of Glasgow built a steamer called Comet of three horse power which conveyed passengers between Glasgow and Greenock, and Mr. Lawrence of

Previous page: Brunswick Steam Wharf, East India Docks 1845 detail (Reginald Francis Print Collection)

Bristol brought his large prototype to the Thames, only to encounter the wrath of the watermen. 'The Company… made so strenuous an opposition to what was considered an innovation of their vested rights, that the proprietor was obliged to return with his steamer to Bristol.' It quotes a ditty attributed to Darwin, though which Darwin is not clear. If contemporary, it was perceptive to say the least:

Soon shall they arm, unconquered steam! Afar
Drag the slow barge, or drive the rapid car;
Or, on wide waving wings expanded bear
The flying chariot through fields of air.

Battling against steam power was a hopeless cause. By 1814 there was a steam packet service between London and Richmond, and the Steam Packet Company was formed by the engineer Ralph Dodd to run boats upstream to Kingston and downstream to Gravesend. In January 1815 a notice startled adventurers and watermen and lightermen alike:

'The public are respectively informed that the new London steam packet *Margery*, Captain Cortis, will start precisely at ten o'clock, on Monday morning, 23 inst. from Wapping Old Stairs, near the London Docks, to Milton, below Gravesend, and will return from thence, at the same hour on the succeeding morning to the same stairs, the said packet having superb accommodation.' The fare was four shillings in the main cabin or two in the fore cabin.

Captain Cortis was proceeded against for his trouble under the Watermen's Act, and replaced by John Pashley, who was a freeman of the Company, as skipper. Next year the unreliable *Margery* was re-fitted and sent to the Seine, to be replaced by the 74-ton *Thames* that made the round trip to Gravesend in a day.

Steam was unreliable and dangerous, but also challenging, exciting and above all, popular. To oppose it was to stick one's finger in a dyke. But steam also possessed positive attributes for watermen. It threatened old occupations but created jobs requiring new skills. If the man-made clouds that propelled vehicles could not be halted, then best to ensure that the hands on the tillers of tugs, barges, ferries and excursion boats belonged to watermen steeped in the ways of the river and its navigation. Small boats remained essential for ship to shore business, especially as it would be some years before piers became common.

In 1817 parliamentary and public debates on safety were sparked by such catastrophes as the bursting of the Richmond packet's boiler upstream of Westminster Bridge and the burning of the *Regent* off Whitstable— all passengers and crew mercifully rescued by boats from the shore. After debating boiler safety, the parliamentary committee's conclusion was that legislative interference with private concerns and property was inexpedient, 'and the mechanical skill and ingenuity for which the artists of the country were so pre-eminent, and of which the introduction of steam was a most powerful agent, as shewn with what advantage that power had lately been applied to propel vessels both of burthen and passage [made them] averse to propose any measure, by which the science and ingenuity of our artists might even appear to be fettered or discouraged.'

The parliamentarians did, however, propose a bill requiring registration of steam packets and two safety valves for wrought iron or copper boilers.

On May day 1818 the rulers of the Company gave a licence to Joseph Jones as master of the packet *Sons of Commerce*, the first waterman formally qualified to navigate a steam boat. *Sons of Commerce* was one of several packets on regular runs to Gravesend and round the Kent coast of the estuary to Margate. The London and Margate Steamboat Company's passenger figures were 27,291 for 1821 and rose to 71,469 four years later. Only a shortage of combustible material would check the rise of steam.

In 1822 the Commons received a petition from coach proprietors and innkeepers on the London to Dover road complaining of loss of business and asking for a compensatory tax on steamboats. Experimentation continued unabated: a 106-feet iron steamboat was demonstrated between London and Battersea bridges on 9 May. She had a 30 horsepower engine with 'Oldham's revolving oars' and was intended to go into service between London and Paris. In September a patent was taken out by Van Heythuysen for paddle-propelled barges for rivers and canals. An axle fitted with paddles passed through a tread wheel at one end of the boat and projected twenty inches over the side, and was put in motion by watermen propelling the wheel.

Another glimpse of the future occurred in 1824 when the 300-foot 3,900-ton *Columbus* loaded with 6,300 tons of timber — the largest ship ever seen in the Thames — was towed from Gravesend to Blackwall by three steam tugs.

Excessive speed and safety continued to be a problem. In 1823 the Lord Mayor cautioned steamers to ease off when passing barges and passenger boats, and to avoid reckless overtaking.

Parliament enacted a new law in 1827 that repealed a bunch of old acts regulating watermen and their activities and laid down 107 clauses concerning the governance of the river and the Company, including regulations for construction and use of vessels from Richmond to Yantlet Creek. The act vested powers to set fares in the Lord Mayor and powers over employment, apprentices and licensing of vessels and their masters in the Company. Inevitably, the mayor's attempt to regulate steamboats by byelaw led to frustrating disputes. In 1828 the parties were at loggerheads over speed restrictions and the ratios of passengers to tonnage of steamboat. The ferry companies argued for more speed and a five passengers per ton, the Company for less speed and two passengers per ton. Once compromises had been reached and byelaws of the City and the Company completed on 15 April, they were submitted to the Privy Council for approval, and the court of the Company began the process of examining steamboats and issuing licences for their operation. Watermen who supplied verified dimensions of their boats were licensed to carry the appropriate number of passengers. By 13 August, 1,857 licenses had been issued. Six steamboats were licensed in that month, the largest being the Favorite for 320 passengers.

All was not well, however. On 25 September upwards of a hundred and twenty watermen were arraigned before the master and wardens at Watermen's Hall for variously abuse of passengers, landing passengers from steamboats out of turn, working boats without names and numbers, carrying more than the permitted number of passengers, and being unlicensed. Fines were up to 20 shillings, and only six men were acquitted. Over the course of the half year 320 were summoned. The master, Mr. Drinkald, congratulated his colleagues that the act that was causing so much bother — boards showing fares were vandalised by tar — in all probability would 'soon be in perfect operation, and the watermen brought into a habit of conforming to it, which would be no less beneficial to themselves than to the public'.

A snapshot of the river in 1828 shows a plethora of management issues other than speed and safety caused by steam power. There was dispute and discourse and sometimes legislation over pilots, piers, navigation aids, the town quay at Gravesend, stairs and platform opposite Blackwall, docks and dock access, bridge proposals and even one for a canal from Rotherhithe to Spithead!

One by-product of steam power was pollution, both in the air and in the water. In 1828 the clerk of Billingsgate market said that fishing in the river had been almost destroyed by steam navigation, sewers, gas works and other manufactures discharging obnoxious matter. Gone were the days when 50,000 smelts and up to three thousand salmon arrived at Billingsgate in season.

By the 1830s steamers had transformed river transport between London Bridge and the estuary. The jetty that opened at Northfleet, near Gravesend, on 10 July 1831 was used by 40,000 passengers before the year was out. Watermen indicted the pier as a nuisance, and formed the United Gravesend and Milton Watermen's Club that attracted three hundred members. Ranks closed against the proposed Gravesend pier that would undermine the packet-to-shore passenger trade. Steamboats were also laying wakes on the upper river and laying waste the watermen's trade in those parts. Construction of piers like that at St. Katharine's Dock, with waiting rooms and modern comforts, gave passengers direct access to ferries and at the same time created additional navigation hazards near bridge works. A frequent steam service between London Bridge and Hungerford began in 1831, described as the 'last and most severe blow dealt on the poor watermen', numbers of whom were forced into the workhouse. A new type of steam boat arrived in the Thames from the Tyne – designed for towing. Not for much longer would small flotillas of watermen's boats be berthing and manoevring shipping.

The increase in numbers and speed of steamers increased the scale and frequency of accidents. In 1831 the new government steamer *Firefly* ran into the Venus with 280 passengers on board, wrecking both ships. The *Pluto* ran down a sand barge, drowning three, and the *Comet* caused five to drown when she swamped a boat off Woolwich. Further obstructions arose on the river when barges were moored below stairs to aid passenger embarkation.

Unsurprisingly, a bill to regulate steamboats was soon laid before Parliament. The Company appended a petition listing accidents that had resulted in damage or loss of life. The inventory of steamboats on the Margate and Ramsgate run and points between had grown from three in 1820 to twenty by 1830, divided between five companies. The bill did not progress, but a select committee was appointed by the Commons in 1831 to examine calamities and how to avoid them. It reported on 14 October. It found that persons navigating small boats and barges were exposed to serious inconvenience and personal risk from the manner of navigating steam vessels without reference to time or speed. It recommended that speed be regulated between London Bridge and Deptford, that all vessels should be surveyed and licensed and not allowed to carry more than three passengers per ton on the river or two on the sea, and that provision should be made for lights, lifeboats &tc. The committee drew attention to the shallow build of some wherries as being unsafe in waters churned by steamboats.

William George Bowyer struck a blow for watermen in 1832 when he took proceedings against Richard Grant as pilot of the *Royal Sovereign* before the Lord Mayor's court at the Mansion House. Bowyer was a freeman of the Company, Grant was not. Bowyer and the Company used the argument that watermen had been in the habit 'from time immemorial' of piloting vessels up and down the river and, since the introduction of steamboats, piloting those also. This was a demarcation dispute that Bowyer won after the court's lengthy deliberations and an extraordinary degree of interest in the case.

Watermen thus secured the right to pilot steamboats and the liability of misbehaving on the water. Two steamers were convicted for racing at speeds above 10 m.p.h. in 1832, and in the next year there was another petition against reckless driving. By now the Gravesend trade was running at 290,000 passenger journeys per annum and rising, and making the voyage under sail was no longer an option. The last sail boat to operate was the *Duke of York*, withdrawn in 1833.

In 1835 a public meeting of the inhabitants of Rotherhithe debated alarming losses of life and property caused by steamers, and in December merchants called a meeting at the London Tavern to discuss regulation and speed restriction of steam vessels. The Company's solicitor was among the throng, and resolutions directed at the government were passed recommending, among other things, that boats and wherries should be increased in size to cope better on the river. The Company also petitioned the Chancellor of the Exchequer to relieve stamp duty on bindings, assignments and freedoms of watermen in the light of distress caused by loss of employment caused by steam.

These developments came at the end of a year that contained a catalogue of accidents. A man was drowned when the *Greenwich* and the *Red Rover* were racing each other. A coal porter drowned when a steamboat wash knocked him off his plank. Four were drowned off West India Dock when their boat was upset by wash from three steamers. A Company beadle named Cutler was run over by the steamboat he was monitoring. The *Red Rover* was involved in another accident that resulted in loss of life; the *Royal Adelaide* drowned two men; a waterman's apprentice was drowned by the *Monarch*, and in November the *Princess Victoria* ran over a boat with eleven people on board and drowned three of them. Several of these incidents resulted in prosecutions of captains, but none in conviction. It can be assumed that some if not all of these skippers were freemen of the Company, causing friction in fraternal relations and conflicts of interests. In 1836 several freemen were engaged by the Company to check the speed of steamers, and some proceedings were taken and convictions obtained. Public notices were given against watermen working unlicensed boats. In October that year, the infamous *Red Rover* met her end in a collision with another Margate boat, *Magnet*. She went down in eleven minutes, while the Magnet rescued all passengers and crew.

A select committee looked into the state of pilotage on the Thames in 1836. Eleven new byelaws came into force governing the size and dimensions of wherries, skiffs and square-sterned wherries for carrying eight, six or four passengers; the licensing of existing boats not of the required dimensions; and defining future construction requirements.

Royal Adelaide steam packet (Watermen's Hall Collection)

They also set regulations governing plying for and taking fares at other than marked plying places on weekdays and Sundays.

In the same year the master, clerk, several court members, pilots and lightermen of the Company gave evidence to a parliamentary select committee appointed to investigate the state of the port of London. Evidence from coroners' inquests during 1834 and 1835 showed that 197 persons drowned, eighteen of them in incidents caused by steamboats. There were 2,085 licensed watermen's boats for passengers below the bridge and 643 above (1,582 for eight passengers, 997 for six, 149 for four, plus 103 boats licensed by Trinity House). There were 8,000 freemen and apprentices of whom 3,000 worked wherries and 5,000 were lightermen.

A hasty assessment by the Company in 1854 gives a more informative breakdown of the skills and occupations. Freemen totalled 7,786, apprentices 1,680, owners of cargo vessels 800 with 5,000 barges and lighters registered to them, and a further 1,200 barges registered to coal merchants and woodmongers. The occupations of the 7,786 freemen are listed as 2,500 lightermen, including 800 who own craft; 1,500 watermen, scullers and those employed in the Customs, Admiralty, Thames Police and Harbour Service; 500 on tugs and steamboats; 800 pilots and attendants; 700 hundred employed on fishing boats and yachts; 300 in the navy and merchant marine, 500 pensioners and inmates of Greenwich Hospital, and 1,000 abroad or not presently engaged on the river.

In 1839 the Company again provided statistics to another parliamentary committee inquiring into accidents. From May 1834 to December 1838 there were 120 personal accidents and 71 involving vessels.

Before the 1830s were spent, numbers of steamboat passengers passed two million per annum. There were regular ferries of the London and Westminster Steamboat Company between Hungerford Market and London Bridge, and the Blackwall and Woolwich Steam Navigation Company was also in business. Freemen of the Company enjoyed a monopoly of employment in and about such vessels. By 1844 there were two hundred steamers on the river, and landings at Gravesend totalled 330,000 passengers for the year. There were 28 boats on the Gravesend run, 28 to Greenwich and Woolwich, ten between London and Herne Bay, and tug boats for towing were growing in number.

Public and official dissatisfaction with speed, safety and service was rife, from both sides of the argument. Delays in regulation measures were criticised, and when the regulations did come along, their restrictive nature was taken to task. The Company's officers who were given watches to check times between half mile and mileposts came in for mobbing and insults from passengers and crews alike. Prosecutions and accidents, run downs and exploding boilers were regular occurrences. An example occurred in 1843 when Captain Read incurred proceedings for carrying passengers on his steam tug without license. The mayor's office saw fit to issue a notice in May 1844 that read:

'Whereas numerous accidents, attended in many instances with loss of lives, have occurred upon the River Thames, from the practice of carrying in the boats plying upon the river more than a proper number of passengers, the Lord Mayor deems it necessary to caution all captains of steamboats, watermen and others, that any future infringement of the bye-laws of the court of Aldermen, or any other misbehaviour on the part of those navigating the river Thames, will be punished with the utmost severity, the police having received orders to prevent any infraction of the law.'

The act that required all sea going vessels to carry boats and passenger vessels to be inspected and issued with a certificate by the Board of Trade was extended to Thames steamboats in 1846. Thirty-eight masters of steamboats were summoned by the Company, although a deal was struck with the steamer companies that charges would be dropped if they took out licenses for their vessels. Thus cases were dropped against the London and Westminster, Citizen, Westminster, Eagle, Falcon, and Watermen's companies (the latter entirely unconnected with the Watermen and Lightermen's Company). It was not only passenger packets that were increasing in number and size. In 1838 the *British Queen*, launched at Curling and Young's Dock in Limehouse, was the largest vessel seen so far, 275 feet in length. In 1845 Isambard Kingdom Brunel's Great Britain, built in Bristol and 320 feet long, arrived at Blackwall. Sightseers were charged half a crown to go on board.

What with proliferation of ocean-going steam ships, packet boats, steam tugs and docks and piers to serve them, the landscape of the Thames and the riverside was becoming more complex, not to mention polluted. The Big Stink would cause the final act of

enclosure of the Thames in mid-century when Parliament sanctioned Sir Joseph Bazalgette's construction of underground sewers and overground embankments to clean up the river. London had long since closed its front door to the river. Pleasure seekers and sportsmen in racing boats moved to rural Putney, fifteen minutes from Nine Elms by train. Traditional watermen's work declined rapidly in the second half of the century, but growing numbers were engaged on and about steamboats and tugs, while work for lightermen grew with burgeoning trade and industry.

The Boat Race c1867 - crews approach the finish at Mortlake with paddle steamers in pursuit, oil on canvas, James Baylis Allen (Private collection, England)

And it should also be remembered that through the stench and the loitering mist, fog and smokestacks along the Thames, spars and masts were still plentiful halfway through the nineteenth century. One of the fastest clippers of all time, the *Cutty Sark*, was launched in 1869 – the year that the Suez Canal sliced off a continent on the passage between Thames and Cathay. The ship that bore the name of a Scottish chemise — nickname of a fictional witch — may have been behind her time, but sail would hold its own in the scheme of things into the next century.

PART 2
LIGHTERMEN'S WORLD

21
UNDER LOCK AND QUAY

As the 1700s drew to a close, crowded shipping and the ever-increasing demands of trade were clogging up the Port of London. Eleven miles of almost continuous wharfs extended downstream from London Bridge servicing the to-ing and fro-ing of thousands of coastal packets, Tyne colliers, Baltic timber vessels and ships bearing riches from the east and the Americas. The Industrial Revolution made London a huge manufacturing centre, and a large part of the port's business was in exporting technology and all manner of finished goods to the world – governed, to no small extent, by the relentless tide as captured by Rudyard Kipling:

I walk my beat before London Town,

Five hours up and seven down.

Up I go and end my run

At Tide-end-Town, which is Teddington.

Down I come with mud in my hands

And plaster it over the Maplin Sands.

The eighteenth century trade balance showed a healthy superiority of exports over imports. In 1700, imports were worth £4,785,538 and exports £5,387,787. By 1792 these figures had almost tripled to £12,071,674 and £14,742,516 respectively. In the second half of the century coastal trade doubled, reaching nearly 12,000 vessels in 1795, while overseas trade increased by a third, growing from 1,700 ships and 235,000 tons to more than 3,600 ships and 620,000 tons.

This burgeoning business of ships and wharfs and their attendant wherries and barges was gradually squeezing the oxygen from the river. The Thames was polluted by the detritus of the city and choked with its traffic. In 1793 the Company history comments: 'From want of accommodation for landing and storing goods at the quays and wharfs, lighters were frequently detained a month or six weeks before they could be discharged, and so becoming floating warehouses of valuable property.' In addition, thievery was rife. In 1795 the West India merchants requested cooperation to curb enormous plundering of merchant ships. The Company's court resolved that it was the indispensable duty of wherrymen, watermen and lightermen to assist in detecting and bringing to justice persons engaged in embezzling, carrying away or receiving 'from any ship, lighter or boat on the river Thames any sugar or other West India produce'. Aiding or assisting anyone convicted of such offences resulted in the removal of Company privileges and benefits. There can be no doubt that innocence was not abroad among the watermen and lightermen.

Previous page: West India Dock 1810 (Reginald Francis Print Collection)

Shipping and trading interests, faced with paralysis, embezzlement and the threat of competition from other ports, cast around for solutions. Willey Reveley proposed cutting a channel from Wapping to Woolwich Reach, slicing off three of the Thames's horseshoe bends and the peninsulas of Rotherhithe, Isle of Dogs and Greenwich. Nothing came of this except a canal that cut across the Isle of Dogs. The solution that eventually took root was 'wet' docks — docks on a much greater scale than the centuries-old muddy holes where the water rose and fell with the tide.

In short, the 1800s brought enclosures to the Thames – docks that were to keep the port in business as the world's busiest for another century, while locking London outside its walls. The process turned the riverbanks into a series of vast high-walled fortresses to trade and commerce, designed to keep cargos accountable and plunderers out. The quays and warehouses were impenetrable save to those employed in and around them. It began in Deptford, where there were naval dockyards in the 1700s. The Duke of Bedford had a great wet dock there that was rented by the South Sea Company for its ships engaged in the Greenland whaling industry, hence known as the Greenland Dock. In 1807 the Howland Great Wet Dock (1696) and Greenland Dock were incorporated into Surrey Commercial Docks. As whaling declined, the main business became timber and grain from Canada, and granaries were soon a feature. The site grew into a network of nine connected docks plus timber ponds covering 460 acres that the writer Joseph Conrad described as imposing by the vast scale of ugliness that forms their surroundings.

On the north bank, Mr Perry began construction of Brunswick Dock at Blackwall for the East India Company in 1781. It opened in 1790, and its mast house, with a tower

Floating dock at Rotherhithe 1815 (Reginald Francis Print Collection)

and crane on top and a long body for stowing spars and sails, became a symbol of home for returning East Indiamen. A whole suit of masts and bowsprits could be raised and fixed in 3 hours 40 minutes.

The London Dock opened in 1805, a place that quickly gained an aroma of spices. The first ship to enter it was a packet bringing wine from Oporto. In 1820 a dock was added to the Regent's Canal junction with the Thames at Limehouse. In 1827 work began on St. Katharine Docks in the parishes of St. Botolph Without Aldgate and St. Katharine's, near the Tower. The earth removed by creating what Conrad described as a quiet pool among rocky crags was used to fill in old reservoirs on Millbank. Ten acres of water were hemmed in by sheer Georgian warehouses on massive cast iron Doric columns. But the entrance to the docks only measured 180 feet by 45, so most cargoes of tea, shells and essential oils entered by barge. St. Katharine's opened in 1828.

View of the proposed St. Katharine's Docks 1825 (Reginald Francis Print Collection)

More docks, further downstream and designed to cater for larger and larger ships, came in the second half of the century. Millwall Dock opened in 1868 and the South West India Dock in 1870, preceded by the first of the Royal Docks, the Victoria in 1855. Royal Albert Dock joined the Victoria in 1880. Tilbury, far downstream on the Essex shore facing Gravesend, opened in 1886. The last major dock to be built on the river was the immense King George V, the third element of the Royal Docks that started construction in 1908. This ocean terminal was the only dock built by the Port of London Authority, which had been formed in the same year to take control of the port and possession of all the docks from Tower and Tilbury.

Among practices changed by the advent of wet docks was that of victualling outgoing ships at Gravesend, together with the market in personal effects for sailors. In future ships and their crews would embark ready serviced. The 'bumboat' trade of small vessels plying the river to sell supplies to ships in the roads died out. Bumboats derived their name from the Dutch words for canoe (*boomschuit*), tree and boat.

In 1869 Deptford dockyard closed after building its last warship, the corvette Druid. The Corporation of London opened a cattle market on the site in 1871, capable of landing stock at any state of the tide.

Needless to say the Company, in common with other interests, resisted the movement towards docks. A pamphlet entitled 'The Story of Tom Cole, Waterman, with Old Father Thames' Malediction of the Wapping Docks' appeared:

'Tom', says Old Thames, 'what news, my lad, what cheer?"

'Please you, my Lord, bad news I fear.'

'Speak out then lad, and tell us what is doing;

What schemes afloat? Is any treason brewing?

Do the French threaten they will burn my shipping?'

'Oh, d--- the French,' says Tom, 'we'd send them skipping.

Worse than the French; some folks a plot have laid

to starve poor Watermen, and take their bread.'

The bill placed before Parliament on 18 February 1796 'for making wet docks, basins, cuts &c for the greater accommodation and security of shipping' was opposed by a committee formed for the purpose, and another committee was charged with inquiring into the best mode of providing sufficient accommodation for trade and shipping in the port. It reported that there were 2,196 coal barges, 400 deal barges totalling 85,103 tons capacity; 402 West India trade lighters, 441 punts, boats, sloops, cutters and hoys employed in the export trade, plus 3,000 wherries for passengers and parcels and 155 bum boats licensed to hawk goods among shipping. There were 8,283 freemen of the Company and approximately 2,000 each of persons not free and apprentices. The committee estimated that the commerce of the river employed at least 120,000 people, employers and employees all.

The breakdown of the estimated 10,250 employers includes 4,100 merchants and ship owners, 2,200 manufacturers of exports, plus brokers, warehousemen, rope and sail makers, master lightermen, wharfingers, carmen operating 420 carts, master coopers, trunk box makers and lumpers, coal merchants and officers of the City, Trinity House and Revenue Boards. The persons employed total 122,320, including 33,000 seamen,

St. Katharine's Docks from the Basin 1828 (Reginald Francis Print Collection)

52,000 clerks, journeymen and labourers, 3,000 lightermen and 5,000 watermen. There is a long list of journeymen's trades, including shipwrights, rope-spinners, block and oar makers; carmen, coopers, trunk and box makers; coal heavers, porters and carters; corn, salt and fruit meters, plus 200 pilots, a thousand watchmen and 1,250 fishermen.

Before steamships, the docks were enclaves of masts and spars, of clippers and windjammers. They gave seafarers like Conrad an uneasy feeling. In 1857 he wrote:

'The view of ships lying moored in some of the older docks of London has always suggested to my mind the image of a flock of swans kept in the flooded backyard of grim tenement houses. The flatness of the walls surrounding the dark pool on which they float brings out wonderfully the flowing grace of the lines on which a ship's hull is built. The lightness of these forms, devised to meet the winds and the seas, makes, by contrast with the great piles of bricks, the chains and the cables of their moorings appear very necessary, as if nothing less could prevent them from soaring upwards and over the roofs… the least puff of wind stealing round the corners of dock buildings stirs these captives fettered to rigid shores.'

Conrad found an inspiring spectacle in a fleet of clippers moored along the north side of the New South Dock – a quarter mile of them in a long, forest-like perspective of masts, moored two-and-two to many stout wooden jetties. 'Their spars dwarfed with their loftiness the corrugated iron sheds, their jib booms extended far over the shore, their white and gold figureheads, almost dazzling in their purity, overhung the straight, long quay above the mud and dirt of the wharfside.' Men moved to and fro twixt clippers and wharf, dwarfed under their soaring immobility. A sailing ship in dock, he says, is a prisoner meditating upon freedom while surrounded by quays and walls. Chain cables and stout ropes keep her bound to stone posts at the edge of a paved shore, and a berthing master with brass buttons on his coat walks about like a weather-beaten and ruddy gaoler, casting an eye on the fetters.

Conrad likens the stretch of Thames from London Bridge to the Albert Docks as a virgin forest, not as a garden as in other ports he knows. River ports like Antwerp, Nantes, Bordeaux or Rouen lie open to their stream, with quays like broad clearings and avenue-like streets cut through thick timber for the convenience of trade. 'Night-watchmen of ships, elbows on rail, gaze at shop windows and brilliant cafes, and see the audience go in and come out of the opera house,' he says, 'but London, the oldest and greatest of river ports, does not possess as much as a hundred yards of open quays upon its river front.'

City Basin, Regent's Canal 1828 (Reginald Francis Print Collection)

Conrad's river comes alive when the tide nears the top, when big ships move off, pilots go aboard, lines are thrown to tugs that tow them to dock entrances. On the river barges, launches, skiffs, lighters abound, while the tide does most of the work. Coasters and short-sea traders coming up searching for quays. Cranes lift boxes, crates and barrels on to quays or through loopholes or doorways, while lighters load on the other side of the ship. Nothing arrests the sleepless industry but a heavy fog, which clothes the teeming stream in a mantle of impenetrable stillness. 'After the gradual cessation of all sound and movement… only the ringing of the ships' bells is heard, mysterious and muffled in the white vapour from London Bridge right down to the Nore.'

Dock and Thames landscape lay in the eye of the beholder. Wordsworth romanticised it in 1802 from his vantage point on Westminster Bridge, a safe distance from the business end:

Earth has not anything to show more fair:

Dull would he be of soul who could pass by

A sight so touching in its majesty:

This city now doth like a garment wear

The beauty of the morning; silent, bare,

Ships, towers, domes, theatres, and temples lie

Open unto the fields, and to the sky.

In 1928 H. V. Morton saw nothing more wonderful than the silvery dawn light followed by a chilly greyness coming up over the tangled shipping of the docks: 'then a flush in the east, and, with startling suddenness, every mast, every funnel, every leaning crane is silhouetted jet black against the pearl-coloured sky…' Mast lights grow pale on tall ships, bacon fries, men awake… 'As light grows, one's sense of smell improves. This is strange. The air is now full of a pungent smell of hemp and tow and tar… as the dawn wind blows.'

The journalist H. J. Massingham took a boat trip from the Tower to Greenwich at the zenith of the port. He claimed to be the only Englishman on board the pleasure steamer, and was quickened by two sights on the voyage among the gloom of the warehouses, cranes and ships from all over the world. The first was the sight of the Royal Naval College 'set like a jewel of unexampled lustre in that drab scenario between the Surrey Commercial Docks and the opening curve of the Blackwall Reach. Its quadrants dominate and transform all of the riverfront on its own bank and the Millwall Docks on the other. Its calm majesty lofted the mind above all the confusions of our immediate age into the falcon's kingdom where all things could be seen in just measure and appraisement.' Massingham's second quickening was in Gallions Reach near the entrance to the Royal Docks where 'a beflagged fishing fleet with furled brown sails lay snugly at anchor. The water flowed bluer here, the air flew sparkling and the herring, black-headed and lesser black-backed gulls swung in full sail above the rigging of the fleet.'

During the heyday of the docks there were few vantage points giving insight to this secret world. In 1929 the journalist A. G. Linney suggested Richmond Pier for the river of pleasure, Westminster Bridge for liquid history, Shadwell Memorial Park for commerce, the gardens at the tip of the Isle of Dogs for history and trade, and the Tilbury Hotel for the Thames gateway (in 1991 Chris Ellmers and Alex Werner added London Bridge, Tower Bridge, Greenwich and Blackwall piers and Gravesend's waterfront to his list). A voyage downriver from London Bridge began with Billingsgate fish market and the Customs House on the north side, opposite Hay's Wharf, past the Tower and through Tower Bridge to the jumble of begrimed walls of St. Katharine Docks, the Wapping entrance to London Docks, and the waterfronts of pubs, sail lofts, barge yards and warehouses along the opposing Limehouse and Rotherhithe shores. On the south side came the entrances to Greenland and South Dock, where Cunard White Star and Canadian Pacific liners waited to be locked in. Then came Georgian rum warehouses and the Admiralty's victualling yard, the cattle market on the slipway of the former Deptford Naval Dockyard, On the north bank were Millwall docks and the colour works at Burrell's Wharf, once the shipyard where John Scott Russell built Brunel's *Great Eastern* in 1858. Opposite was the repair and maintenance base for the General Steam Navigation Co. at Deptford Creek, followed by Greenwich pier, the naval college and Royal Observatory.

Lighterman outside Braithwaite and Deans, showing the Angel public house, Rotherhithe, in the foreground (Watermen's Hall Collection)

In Blackwall Reach, east Greenwich peninsula was a hive of industry, including barge building, cable manufacture and the South Metropolitan Gas Works. On the north side were the entrances to the West and East India Docks near the mouth of Bow Creek and Trinity House's wharf, landmarked by the lamps and mirrors of an experimental lighthouse. Here was the House's maintenance depot for buoys – important aids in the management and safety of the river. Here could be seen a wide variety of shape, size, decoration and trimmings; anchored floats to indicate a fairway, shoal or reef;

mooring, wreck and spar buoys; conical, spherical, cylindrical; black, white, red, piebald; distinguished by staff, ball, cone, diamond, triangle or combinations thereof; green for wrecks, red and white for navigation; bell buoys, whistling buoys, foghorns, fog bells and fog sirens, submarine bells, air diaphones; buoys lit by acetylene or oil gas.

Bugsby's Reach leads to the entrance to Royal Victoria Dock, while north and south banks of Silvertown and Charlton have industrialised waterfronts. Paddleboats serve the Woolwich free ferry, and sailing barges awaiting orders are moored to 'Starvation Buoys'. The Royal Arsenal at Woolwich is opposite the entrances to Royal Albert and King George V docks.

Here in Gallions Reach, where blow the ugly breezes of Beckton Gas Works and the tanker jetty for London County Council's northern sewage outfall (the southern outfall is across the river at Crossness), the river is crowded. The waterfront of Halfway Reach is Ford's motor works. Erith on the south side has coal and timber yards, cement works and board and paper mills. There are petroleum depots between Dartford, Purfleet, Greenhithe and Grays. And so to Gravesend, the gateway to the port and the boundary between the fiefdom of the Thames and the open sea. Gravesend has the Port Sanitary Authority, Trinity House pilots and cutters and moorings for tugs awaiting orders. Customs officers boarded ships to lock holds pending payment of duty. Once duty was paid, officers were present as cargo was craned into bonded warehouses.

The Pool of London seen from Tower Bridge 1908 by Alfred Egerton Cooper (1883-1974). (Guildhall Art Gallery City of London)

Tilbury, on the north shore, is the last of the docks handling the greatest of the ships - the Clan Line, Ellerman Line, Orient Line and Peninsular and Oriental Steam Navigation Company. Lower Hope Reach, beyond Gravesend, has Thameshaven Oil Refinery on the north bank, and is otherwise bordered by flat and desolate marshland, described by the journalist Charles Dickens:

'Ours was the marsh country, down by the river, within, as the river wound, twenty miles from the sea… The dark flat wilderness beyond the churchyard intersected with dykes and mounds and gates, with scattered cattle feeding upon it, was the marshes; and that low leaden line beyond was the river.' At the end of the winding river came Southend-on-Sea and the Nore Light vessel, the very outer limit of the port.

When the docks came, they severed the river from London and Londoners at the same time as creating close-knit communities for thousands whose livelihood depended on them in a great diversity of trades. 'Few European cities have a finer river than the Thames,' said the writer Henry James, 'but none certainly has expended more ingenuity in producing a sordid riverfront. For miles and miles you see nothing but the sooty backs of warehouses, or perhaps they are faces: in buildings so utterly expressionless it is impossible to distinguish.'

The docks changed the working lives of the men who worked the port. Another awesome threat to the water taxi business arrived when passengers and crew could simply walk ashore. Docks were less of a threat to lightermen because the latter secured and safeguarded the task of moving goods between ship, dock, quay and warehouse. But it was not long before the docks acquired direct rail connections for national distribution. The Royal Docks, Millwall and Tilbury were built with integrated rail facilities, and the older wet docks were eventually given connections so that by the 1930s the Port of London Authority operated 140 miles of track with 40 locomotives. Horse-drawn transport held its own in the docks until the 1930s, when improved roads and motor lorries made their presence felt.

When the Thames and the Pool ebb and flow into the nineteenth century, the river that is a God-given highway is under lock and quay. It is no longer a Grand Canal. The palaces and grand hotels turn their backs to it; streets no longer lead to it, citizens no longer flock to it for sport or entertainment. When the century is out, the shores upstream of London bridge will be embankments instead of strands, and the waters be-smogged and inky. Commuters have gone underground, and London's great Tideway is a mysterious place, unloved save by those steeped in the life of dock and wharf.

22
CHALDRONS, CRIMPS
AND CARGOES

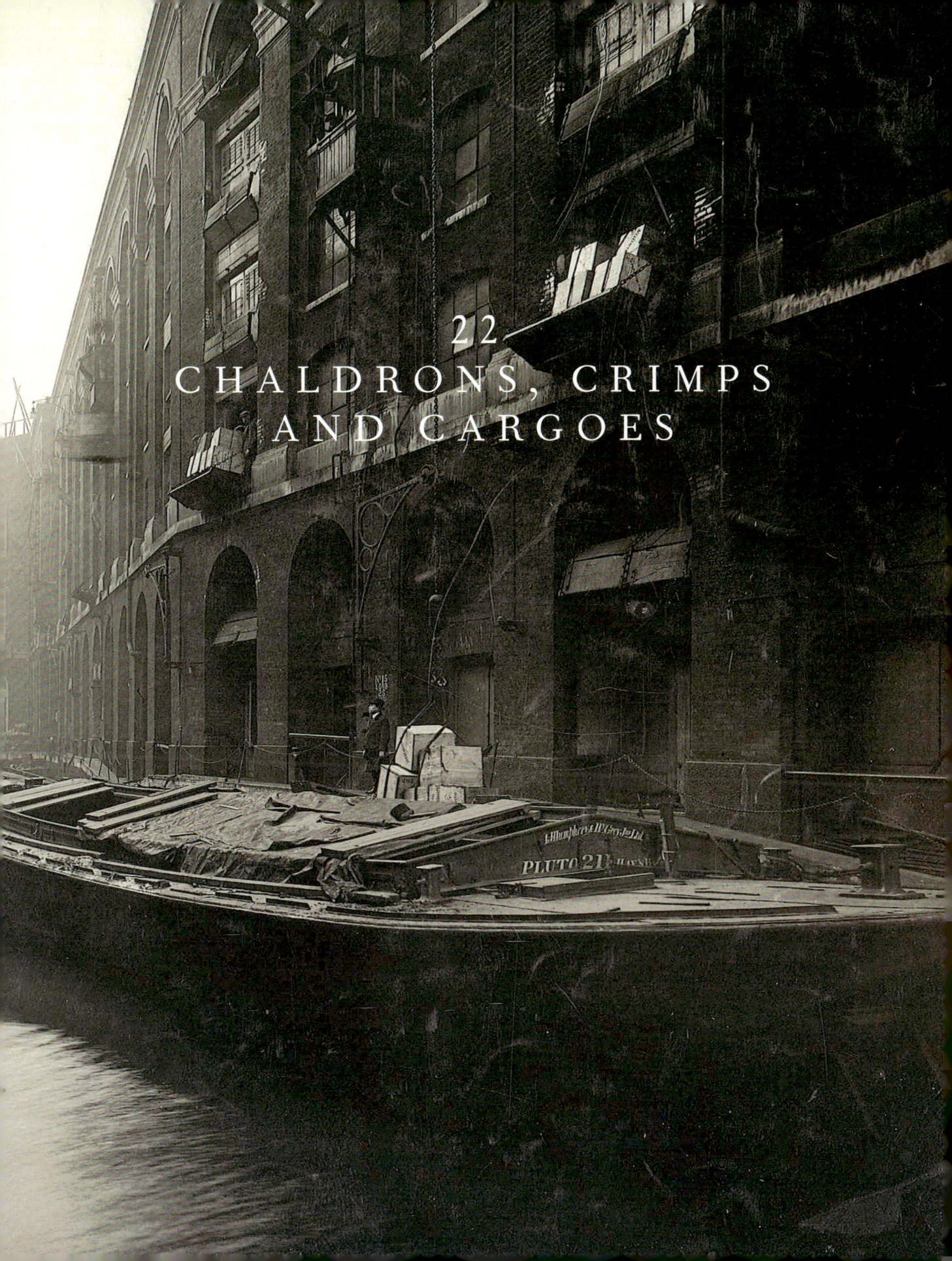

In 1675, James Howell noted that 'while Venice is steeping and pickling in salt water, London sports herself upon the banks of a fresh stately river, which brings on to her bosom all the spices of the East, the treasures of the West, the gems of the South, and the rich furs of the North'. True enough, but as we saw in Chapter 12, the strength and riches of London's trade lay in more basic commodities – wood and coal.

An anonymous pamphlet written in 1743-44 is quoted by the coal trade historian Raymond Smith:

'In process of time great ships being employed in the coal trade, whose ladings were too large for any one or two woodmongers either to purchase or dispose of, the lightermen took hint to do what the woodmongers could not: by which means from carriers they, at once, became traders of a superior class, and found themselves in a capacity to treat those who had been their masters, as their customer; I had like to have said their dependents and understrappers. Nor did they stop here: for having taken possession of the hive, they resolved to keep all the sweets for themselves, which they soon accomplished after this manner: When a fleet of ships was expected in, fifteen of the most considerable of these upstart-engrossers used to hold a cabal, in which having first settled the market price to their own minds…'

Speculation and concentration into a relatively few wholesalers who commanded necessary capital was no surprise, given the risks involved in the London coal trade. Supply was limited by encumbrances in the long line of communication with the north. Production, transport, storage and marketing on the Tyne were all prone to problems. The sea passage was beset by storm, press-gang, navigation hazards and sometimes by the King's enemies. Unloading, measuring, river transport and marketing in London also involved challenges, and labour troubles, actual or potential, were present throughout the process. The coal trade also required money for wholesale dealing, the purchase or hire and maintenance of carts and lighters, the purchase, handling and storage of hundreds of tons of stock, to say nothing of spreading turnover across seasonal trade and elapsing months between purchase from ship-master and sale to retailer.

Thus in the eighteenth century the coal trade became a struggle between ship owners and barge owners. As Smith observes, 'Whether the ship owners were shore merchants, colliery-owners, fitters, financiers, coal dealers, ship masters or others, and whatever parts they held, they collectively formed a separate branch of the trade as a body of dealers, and cohered sufficiently from time to time to present a formidable bargaining front, reinforced by the interests of ship masters as agents, to the northern owners or the southern buyers.'

In 1605, 1622, and 1637 those interests united against the Newcastle hostmen, and in 1710 and 1728 took on the northern 'regulation' and the London lightermen. A Commons inquiry into the excessive price of coals in 1702 had blamed high wages of seamen in the collier fleet and onerous deals between Newcastle merchants and London lightermen. Lightermen were acting as 'crimps' or brokers who set high

Previous page: Barges unloading tea at Hays Wharf Dock c1920 (Southwark Local History Library)

prices. The Commons inquiry also identified the practice of laying up private stores of coals by investors and large users, as a list of hoarders in two parishes of Southwark published in 1703 reveals: Ashurst, a sugar-baker, had 300 chaldrons; Richard Oldner and William Smith, lightermen, 150 each; Rowl. Gideon, a Jew merchant, 300; Ryall, a lighterman, 100; Dawkins of Rotherhithe had 100 chaldrons stored in Ipswich; Newell, a goldsmith, had 400 and Sheppard, a brewer, 200. Other brewers and coal merchants were also listed.

The dispute in 1710 involved between six and seven hundred colliers laying up at Harwich and refusing to abide by the terms laid down by the hostmen and lightermen. Next year, legislation forbad contracts in restraint of trade between coal owners, lightermen, fitters, ship masters, ship owners, crimps, coal factors or others. It required certificates to be registered with the Lord Mayor and issued to ship masters showing dates, quantities, sorts and prices.

Billingsgate, London 1801 (Watermen's Hall Collection)

By 1729 the buyers and lightermen were opulent and few in number. It was estimated that half the coal trade was in the hands of a dozen watermen, one of them being George Oldner who was selling in the order of 25,000 chaldrons a year. The other fifty per cent of trade was shared between another forty watermen. Further inquiry heard ship owners, crimps and dealers giving evidence against lightermen and their restrictive practices, and in 1730 Parliament decreed that dealers in coals could use their own lighters anywhere on the river, but that lightermen manning them must be duly qualified, and lightermen were forbidden from acting as a crimp, agent or factor. In 1734 a register was established to record the unloading of ships by turn, with required certificate of unloading for captains.

The ship owners' stand against the lightermen was a prime cause of eventual statutory recognition of coal factors, who thereby became the chartered agents of the shippers. The Society of Coal Factors was born in 1750. Thus the eternal dialectic of trade, practice and dispute continued, one factor being that the Company and the lightermen played a significant role in the working of the port through the century that saw lightermen link arms with watermen and witness the coming of enclosures – the locked-in world of the docks. Just as lightermen grasped a lion's share of the coal trade in the role of merchants as well as movers of the black stuff, so they obtained the keys to freedom of the docks when it came to moving cargo about quay and wharf. The coming of the docks was another giant step in the long process of turning the capital city's back on its grand canal of colourful, sparkling pageantry. The public face of pomp, parade and wealth now eschewed the river and took to the streets, while real wealth and real poverty grappled with each other in the ebb and flow of what became an awesome backwater, lined with satanic stores and larders. During the nineteenth century, coal fired its engines, lit its streets and warmed its population. Enterprise and empire brought a myriad of growth and variety to the workings of the port, but it was accompanied by a steep decline in the fortunes of the Company's watermen.

Although London differed from other growing ports such as Liverpool, Cardiff, Newcastle or Glasgow in that its river flowed past great affairs of state as well as acres of industry or, in some cases, landscapes of natural resources, the eclectic trades and

Black diamonds at Bugsbys Hole, W L Wyllie (Watermen's Hall Collection)

occupations brought together along the tidal Thames formed its industrial population. Writing in Temple magazine in 1897, Millicent Morrison referred to 'the endless offspring of the animal, vegetable and mineral kingdom brought hither by both sea and land to render willing service to civilized man. [The docks] tell of a world-wide industry centred here in epitome – the Emporium of the World.'

No wonder that John Masefield could write:

You showed me nutmegs and nutmeg husks,

Ostrich feathers and elephant tusks...

Cinnamon, myrrh, and mace you showed,

Golden paradise birds that glowed,

More cigars than a man could count

And a billion cloves in an odorous mount

And choice port wine from a bright glass fount.

You showed, for a most delightful hour,

The wealth of the world and London's power.

In short, the port dealt in and developed a deep knowledge of a great range of commodities that began to be locked into docks from the opening of West India in 1802. Spices, drugs, tea, coffee, cocoa, sugar, dairy produce, meat, fruit, grain, flour, wines, spirits, tobacco, ivory, shells, silk, wool, leather, hides, skins, furs, feathers, bristles, carpets, oils, waxes, gums, curios, paper, timber, hemp, jute and rubber were all staples.

Dan Wills, a sailing bargeman, said that he could feel his way on the Thames by nose. 'You could smell where you were from the different smells from the factory. If you were in the 'Mudhole' you could smell all your pepper and things like that... we'd smell a gasworks, the sewerage places... enough to knock you back at times... that's how you used to feel your way.'

The sound of the docks was a blend of humming ropes, rattling chains and hooves on cobbles. At the London Docks there was a heady scent tinged with the odour of dry rot of wine vaults. There was a rich pungency of tobacco at Victoria Dock, mustiness of oriental carpets in Cutler Street; a blended whiff of straw and eggs, butter, cheese and bacon at the Greenland Dock.

The two miles of quaysides and the imposing stone warehouses of London Docks dealt in Guinness, dried fruit, canned goods and three-quarters of the country's imports of wine, sherry and port. A warmish dusky silence permeated the labyrinth of vaults housing hogsheads and casks from Europe, North Africa, Madeira, Australia and South Africa. Wool, spices, drugs and ivory arrived from lower docks by lighter. The wool samples floor was larger than Wimbledon tennis courts, and on buying days, 300-400lb bales were stacked three high and manhandled by men with hooks for inspection by white-coated buyers dressed like cricket umpires. The grease from the wool was used in face cream. The spice warehouses smelt like an apothecary's as garblers dealt in 20,000 tons per annum of pepper, nutmeg, capsicum, cloves, chillies, cardomoms, cassia, cinnamon, ginger, mace and pimento. A hundred and fifty tons of elephant tusks passed through the ivory warehouse in a year, and narwhal tusks, rhino horns, hippo and walrus teeth were traded for fashioning into billiard balls, piano keys, umbrella stands and curios.

The Millwall and West India docks, developed from 1802 and 1870 on 160 acres of the Isle of Dogs, where William Cubitt built a model housing estate for his workers. There could be found rum warehouses, hard woods from Central America, India and Africa, sugar bags drying in the sun, granaries and grain elevators, McDougall's flour mills and dried and fresh fruit. Surrey Docks (150 acres) served Baltic steam tramps, storm-battered sailing ships and trans-Atlantic liners among stacks of softwood, rafts of logs and granaries. The East India Docks handled chilled meat and Jamaican bananas and was the terminus for ships of the Union-Castle, Ellerman, Blue Star and Ben lines.

The largest complex, however, was the Royal Docks, 244 acres of continuous water set in bend of river between Bugsby's Reach and Gallions Reach. Spread over three miles, it was the largest dock in the world once the King George V dock, with its 800 x 200ft entrance lock, joined the Victoria (1855) and Albert (1880) in 1921. Vessels from the Blue Star, British India Steam Navigation, Cunard, Peninsular and Orient Steam Navigation and Shaw Savill & Albion lines shipped in tobacco, frozen meat, grain and general cargoes as well as passengers.

The nearest dock to the open sea is Tilbury, a long way downriver on the north bank facing Gravesend and opened in 1886. Improvements and extensions gave it a thousand-foot cargo jetty and a passenger landing stage with a customs and baggage hall designed by Sir Edwin Cooper that impressed Prime Minister Ramsey MacDonald with its 'dignity, great calm, beauty and idealism in the simple walls and proportions' when he came to open it. Tilbury impressed Linney also when he noted the P&O's 'towering white hulls and buff funnels of the *Strathnaver* and the *Strathnairn*.' Tilbury was home to lines such as Anchor Brocklebank, Bibby, Clan, Ellerman, Harrison, Orient and Rotterdam Lloyd.

Tilbury contributed four miles of quays and 105 acres of water to the Port of London's total of 35 miles of quay and 720 acres of water over its seven dock systems at their zenith. This, plus 1,500 working wharfs on 26 miles of river from London Bridge to Gravesend, constituted the world's largest port. From 1908 it has been governed by the Port of London Authority, and it has handled virtually every cargo known to man. Between the two world wars there were 1,000 arrivals and departures each week served by 250 tugs, 8,000 lighters and 1,000 sailing barges. It remained the largest port into the 1930s, and sustained its place among the largest until containers and bulk carriers broke the locks and quays in the 1960s. Tilbury is the only system surviving, able to handle container ships and harbour cruise liners.

One commodity became a casualty of dock development, and that was the fish of the river. In 1800 salmon still swam up to town, but by 1856 when the Metropolitan Water Board was born, they could no longer be found. In the 1830s men fished from the starlings of London and Blackfriars bridges, and in the 1850s the docks contained large numbers of fresh water fish - perch, bream, roach, pike, rudd, even carp – fished by rod. Above Chiswick, roach, gudgeon, dace, bleak, perch and bream were to be found, and eels and lampreys were trapped in grig wheels, a grig being a species of small eel. Two dozen professional fishermen operated in the upper reaches. But in the 1920s the journalist A. G. Linney reported Inspector Rough as saying that no sprats had come up to Kew for 30 years, and he noted that the London County Council's chief chemist himself doubted that fish existed at all in the Thames. Apprentice fishermen were a thing of the past, and Billingsgate only dealt in sea catches or fish from other parts of the British Isles, brought in by road or rail.

Both sides of a medal issued In commemmoration of the opening of the new Coal Exchange 1849 (Watermen's Hall Collection)

23
CAMPBELL, CRIMEA
AND CIVILITY

Waterman William Henry Campbell signed on for the navy in 1851 and joined Admiral Sir James Dundas's *Britannia* that was fitting out in Portsmouth. Campbell was the nephew of Charles Campbell who became the first champion sculler in 1831, and like his uncle, he was skilled and successful at the oars, winning the Royal Thames Regatta in 1849 and Doggett's Coat and Badge in the first year of his freedom in 1850. He also liked the sea, spending 1846-48 on a voyage to the Mediterranean.

Britannia was the flagship of the Black Sea fleet during the Crimea war. British naval strategy required Dundas to attack the Russian fleet at Odessa and Sevastopol and prevent access to the Mediterranean while Admiral Charles Napier was to contain the Russian Baltic fleet at Fort Revel to prevent it passing through the straits of Denmark. This was accomplished with relative ease when the Russian fleets were reluctant to do battle, but the Russian land mass was not too hampered by naval blockade. The navy was engaged in supporting the British and French armies in their troubled attack on Sevastopol, and Campbell was propelled into the thick of it. He was selected for a flotilla of rocket boats that bombarded the Odessa forts with Sir William Congreve's missiles. He then assisted in the landing of British troops at Old Fort, near Eupatoria, and on the same day was engaged in bringing wounded soldiers to hospital ships after the Battle of the Alma.

Campbell was then appointed to the naval brigade, a force of 1,200 sailors sent to man shore batteries. He took part in an attack on Sevastopol on 17 October 1854, and on 5 November was making fireworks at the battle of Inkerman. When removing casualties from the Inkerman battlefield, he was wounded in the arm by a sniper. He was slightly wounded again in the trenches four days later, and spent the evening of Christmas Day removing bodies under intense Russian fire. After enduring the hard winter of 1854-55, Campbell sailed for Plymouth aboard the *Vengeance*, arriving home on 1 May.

Two weeks later he reported to the Victory at Portsmouth, sailed to Sheerness on board *Retribution* and was drafted to *Glatton*, a floating battery under Captain Cummings that was one of the first iron clad men-of-war in the navy. *Glatton* took Campbell to the Black Sea for the second time, and he served there until being paid off in Portsmouth on 18 June 1856. He had helped the navy help the army, and for his pains he received the Crimea Medal with clasps for Sevastopol and Inkerman, and a medal from the Sultan of Turkey.

Although the Crimea was an expensive campaign in every way for the allies, it succeeded in stemming Russia's ambitions in eastern Europe for almost a hundred years, and prepared a new map of Europe in which Italy and Germany would unify and Austro-Hungary would decline. It also closed the Mediterranean to the Russian fleet and led to the 1856 Declaration of Paris that renounced privateering and reinforced freedom of the seas. It proved the worth of steam and screw-propelled ships to the Royal Navy.

Previous page: The First Shot of the War, 6 April 1854 by Richard Henry Nibbs (© National Maritime Museum, Greenwich, London)

In February 1859 Campbell was appointed an admiralty waterman. Two years later he became a Queen's waterman, undertaking attendance on the likes of the Sultan of Turkey, the Shah of Iran and the Khedive of Egypt during their stays at Buckingham Palace. He also undertook guard of honour duties as a Doggett's winner at Fishmongers' Hall on numerous occasions when princes, dukes, lords and even sultans were presented with the freedom of that worshipful company. Campbell was also appointed almoner at Westminster Abbey.

During his lifetime Campbell saved about twenty lives on the Thames, including that of Miss Mary Ann Elsley who attempted suicide at Waterloo Bridge, an incident that laid our hero at death's door for two months with bronchitis. He was a great promoter of benefits got up on behalf of widows and orphans of watermen, and was rewarded for his public service by testimonials that included £25 raised at a complimentary benefit, a gold watch, a gold Albert and locket and a handsome timepiece and gold medallion from his brother watermen.

Henry Humpherus remarked in the Company history that Campbell was a shining example of how 'even a waterman may get on by civility and good conduct to his superiors'.

William Henry Campbell of Westminster (Watermen's Hall Collection)

"CIVIL WAR" ON THE THAMES, BETWEEN

24
TROUBLE AND STRIFE

We have noted that the construction of wet docks created an industrialised society along the Thames, marked in the docks by demarcation of skills and outside by manufacturing and servicing trades. The clerks, coopers, lock keepers, dock police, engineers, carters, warehousemen, stable boys, smiths, porters, stevedores and dockers employed by the dock companies and their clients were served by laundresses and needlewomen, shirt makers and street sellers, beer house keepers and shopkeepers. The docks also led to the growth of organised labour to protect jobs and increase wages, with attendant inter-labour and worker-employer disputes.

The business of the port was not always plain sailing to prosperity. Many cargoes were seasonal, and therefore work fluctuated with the shipping patterns. A lot of competition came from ports close to manufacturing areas such as Manchester, Hull, Newcastle and Glasgow, or places located closer to the Atlantic, thus reducing voyage time, such as Liverpool, Cardiff, Bristol and Southampton. The channel from Gravesend to London was not deep enough for larger ships. The Suez Canal, expected to enhance trade when it opened in 1869, instead enabled shippers to unload cargoes in Mediterranean ports and distribute by rail, an unforeseen development that snuffed the boom at birth.

The watermen and lightermen and their apprentices voyaged through this new landscape of complex working practices and labour relations until the docks closed in the 1960s. On 14 August 1894, for example, Harry Harris was apprenticed to his father Charles, and in 1903 became the sixth generation of his family to earn his freedom. His son Bob would become the seventh. Harry was brought up at 77 Park Street, Southwark, and educated at St. Peter's National School. One of the perks of singing in the school choir was that the choirboys visited Sadlers seed-crushing mill in Great Guildford Street to bathe in the hot tank at the top of the building, which Harry says was hotter than a hot bath. His swimming exploits and mucking about on Bankside were forbidden; highlights of his boyhood were being rowed to Richmond and back by his father to celebrate Queen Victoria's jubilee in 1887, seeing Canadians demonstrating log rolling on the Thames, and the visit of the Shah of Persia when the torpedo boats that accompanied his yacht got into a pickle with their navigation.

There was also the annual Bankside regatta. The races were followed by a brass band seated on the top deck of a disused tramcar mounted in a barge's hold and towed by a tug. The tow couldn't keep up with the races, so it turned halfway to meet the scullers returning while the band played 'See the Conquering Hero Comes'. Spectators sat on the top decks of other trams in their riverside graveyard. Harry saw people throwing barrels at the leading sculler to slow him up. At the end of important races Bobby Bush, the lighterman who organised the regatta, came ashore and accompanied the band in a march along Bankside and down Emerson Street. Dressed in breeches, silk stockings and buckle shoes, Bush looked straight ahead, keeping time with the band, dignity and importance personified.

Harry's father was foreman at W. Pells & Son and gave him some experience there before he was apprenticed. He witnessed the opening of Tower Bridge from a Pells

Previous page: Civil war on the Thames between watermen and City authorities 1846 (Watermen's Hall Collection)

barge in the roads below London Bridge. His employment began at Pells where he received a spartan training, and moved to quay lighterage with H. Grey Jr.

Unlicensed apprentices were usually employed as second hands to freemen in craft registered to carry more than 50 tons. Dumb barges had a fixed rudder or budget, oars up to 30ft. long, and carried between 15 and 120 tons of cargo. A punt was up to 29¾ tons, built of wood with flared sides, carried up to 50 tons, and was driven by one man. Apprentices had to learn to 'drive under oars', the art of navigation. The essence of 'taking your oar aft' is to grasp the handle in one hand while the other hand cants or slants the blade with a turn of the wrist causing the blade to plane away from the barge's side. If this canting was not achieved, the oar would come parallel to the gunwale and the handle would go beyond reach, giving the oarsman the split-second choice of letting go or being pitched into the 'ditch'.

The Opening of Tower Bridge by W L Wyllie 1895 (Guildhall Art Gallery City of London)

One of the earliest lessons Harry learned was that abstainers were neater, cleaner and kinder to the boys. Another was the practice of drawing off of cargo. The majority of men carried gimlets [screws] to tap a cask, gently tapping the hoops towards the tapering end and boring two small holes. After the 'waxer' or illicit taster had been drawn, the holes were neatly spiled or plugged and the hoops hammered back over the holes and secured. No evidence was thus visible from the outside. 'I never drank, but I didn't refuse a tin of 'pines' or similar goods,' Harry wrote in his memoirs.

In August 1896 Harry obtained his two-year licence, and was put in charge of punts loading cotchels or small quantities of cargo for a variety of wharfs, ships and docks. Then he moved to Farmiloes Wharf at Nine Elms to learn lightering as an above bridge man. Farmiloes handled lead and glass and operated above Battersea as well as downriver to the Pool. Now he was working double-handed barges with a junior to steer and help headway by laying the oar well round the stern. Every bridge from Waterloo to Kew is on a bend, and the tide sets away from the point. By steering at a slight angle to shape for the hole (the lighterman's term for a bridge arch), the hand aft rows against the man forward to edge the barge up against the tidal set and increase the headway. Before entering the hole, the barge is straightened up and the bridge shot. After shooting Vauxhall on a strong spring tide a barge would gather enough headway to shoot her into the wharf a mile above the bridge with little effort even though a strong set of tide came off Nine Elms Pier. If wind was hard out of the wharf and the cargo was a stack of plate glass, hard rowing and careful watching were the only the means of 'fetching' the wharf.

Accompanying Harry and his raw recruit on a voyage from Nine Elms to the Tower on the barge *Jubilee* is instructive of skills and unforeseen circumstances. As they left the wharf in a south wind, the apprentice was told the importance of establishing a rhythm of swinging out and pulling steadily. They were blown across to Pimlico to get favourable position to shoot Vauxhall. A waterman who acts as bridge pilot to sailing barges, known as a hoveller (pronounced huffler), is in his boat nearby. Harry spots a mate on the pier and signifies by two waves from elbow and one from shoulder that he is bound for the lower reaches, and a scissor wave to indicate that he will not be at their regular Friday night date at Gatti's music hall.

To clear the bridge, it is necessary to hold up to the north buttress of the chosen arch. Harry takes the aft oar and tells the boy to pull steadily and to watch him when he gives the order 'other way', when the oar is reversed at the stern post. They shoot Number 3 arch.

As they pass the statue of Britannia outside the Tate Gallery, Harry points out that she holds her trident in her right hand, whereas on the penny coin she holds it in her left.

A boat comes alongside with a mop hanging over the stern signifying that the occupier purchases old rope. On the Lambeth shore the river police are rowing up against the tide. A sculler is paddling up abreast of Doulton's Pottery, and Harry recognises him as George Odell of Lambeth who is training for Doggett's. Harry thinks his finish was all wrong, but he won anyway, whatever his finish.

Approaching Lambeth Bridge he tells his boy not to look at his hands so often, then he'll forget their blistery condition. The tide is at full ebb with a fresh breeze aft as they pass Lambeth Palace and St Thomas's Hospital, the Houses of Parliament and Big Ben. Nearing Westminster Bridge both man and boy are aft to keep *Jubilee* straight, and they take the middle of No. 4 arch. The buttresses of this bridge are sharp-edged like a ship's ram. A bundle of straw hangs under the centre arch to signify that repairs are being done. They see a painter in the staging under the arch watching them.

'What stinks worse than a painter?' shouts Harry.

'A dirty little boy,' comes the riposte.

Harry, but a boy himself, shows his mate how to handle an oar, carry it from end to end of the barge, blade in water, speedily and safely; how to throw it for'ard for steering. An oar can easily take charge of its owner, especially when craft has good head on, or entering slack water from the Tideway, like catching a crab. How to shift the oar from the rowing tack or crutch to the opposite side in one movement by walking smartly forward with the blade tilted and parallel with handle, placing the point of balance on the bitt head or fore post, weighing down on handle, and with semi-circular movement with hands, arms and feet in unison, flinging it from port to starboard.

During the lesson they are drifting sideways. They straighten up above Hungerford Bridge. A sailing barge, known to lightermen as a 'sailorman', passes them with its mast lowered on deck, sprit overhanging aft, mizzen set and drawing well. One man is rowing, and the skipper is at the wheel. No bridge sail or small lug is set, and she goes past quickly. She is called *Maldon*. There is not a hoveller in sight, which is unusual for an Essexman. 'They usually drop down with the tide, anchor dragging, which is termed "gilling",' Harry says.

The wind will shorten in the next reach, and Harry decides on No. 4 arch of Waterloo Bridge to be up windward for the long stretch to Blackfriars. The tide is hard set to north at all times of the ebb. The mate is aft and Harry for'ard to edge to the south buttress of No 4 when *Maldon*, ahead of them, suddenly drops anchor 'all standing'. She swings round head upon tide, sheering about and paying out fathoms of cable. *Jubilee* is in direct line astern. 'The skipper is trying to steady the sheering to avoid us, we shaping to try and avoid him.' There is a glancing blow along the starboard side. There is no damage, but *Jubilee* is transformed from live ship to drifting hulk. The boy loses his oar, the barge loses way, and Harry loses his temper.

But not his nut. They are drifting sideways, almost at the bridge, and he throws his oar over to starboard and rows hard for No. 3 arch, then reverses the oar to portside and takes a dozen hard pulls to straighten up. They are just clear of touching. The skipper of the sailorman is told exactly in what part of his body Harry would have the pleasure of seeing him wear his anchor. *Jubilee* heads up on the tide to recover the lost oar, but now the barge is on the lee shore by the embankment, and they have a hard slog to Blackfriars. By now, though, Harry and his mate are laughing and in good spirits, and Harry gives Bankside a whistle, before quizzing the boy on the height of St Paul's Cathedral and the name of the architect who designed it.

Three lamps mark the centre of middle arch of Southwark Bridge, and by passing to south'ard of these they will work into Cannon Street arch. The tide between Southwark and London bridges is like a mill race. At this time of ebb tide there is a tidal set to the south at the middle of London Bridge, but from half ebb to low water the direction changes from a straight shoot to one hard to the north buttress.

The Pool had a tremendous buzz about it in Harry's time. Near East cargoes were at Fresh Wharf, Dutch at Custom House and brewers; Ghent steamers at Mark Brown's, Gravesend traders at St. Olaf's. Dunkirk steamers and schooners used the tiers in the upper Pool; below Tower bridge in the lower Pool were shipping lines serving German and Belgian ports, Hull and Yarmouth, the Channel Islands and Danzig. Every ship moored to a tier had attendant craft offloading or loading. Watermen plied for hire to the ships at every set of stairs. Apart from a handful of steam launches – the Thames Conservancy's, the police launches *Chowdikar* and Watch, the dry dock company's *Tynesider* - oars were everywhere. There were beer boats, old ropies, drudger boats for recovering coal knocked overboard (or borrowed before it went overboard), under-watermen's boats for recovering anchors and jetsam. Every quay lighterage firm had at least one boat rowed by boys. Some foremen sat, some huddled, some never took an oar, while a few took a hand at the oar themselves. The colours of the firms were painted on blades, and each firm had a distinctive whistle, so everyone recognised everyone. The river police had row boats with white blades, visible at night, and they would ferry men after dark for a price when there were no watermen about. The Customs had two- or three-man boats. The port surveyor was smartly turned out in a four-oar cutter. The captain superintendent of the General Steam Navigation Company had a boat with two watermen. The labour master and the coal foremen also had their own boats.

Whenever they passed under Tower Bridge, Harry and his mates looked out for horse-drawn omnibuses whose box seats next to driver were occupied by the fair sex. 'We would whistle "Mary is young and fair, she rides upon my bus in dear old London", and the driver would salute by dipping his whip.'

Another Harry, Harry Gosling, was already a freeman when Harris was bound. Gosling was born into generations of Lambeth watermen in 1861, and when three weeks old accompanied his parents in their wherry to see the Hay's Wharf fire. Fat was streaming out of the warehouses and watermen were gathering it up to sell it.

Gosling's great grandfather had a sailing barge called *Effort* that plied the waters between Surrey Docks and the Kent ports of Ramsgate, Margate, Herne Bay, Chatham and Sheerness. None but freemen of the Company were allowed to own craft to work on the Thames. When the eighteenth turned to the nineteenth century Gosling's great granddad would be rowed from Lambeth to the Old Swan by London Bridge by his youngest apprentice to negotiate cargoes with merchants. He smoked a long pipe on the evening journey home. Gosling's grandfather and father worked as master lightermen towing rafts of timber from Scandinavian ships in Surrey Docks to builders' yards along what is now known as the South Bank.

Harry Gosling MP

Gosling himself was apprenticed into this work at the age of 14 when he was ushered into Watermen's Hall by a uniformed beadle on 13 June 1875 to be bound to his father.

'Everything conspired to give dignity and solemnity to the binding act. Under the flags of the Watermen's Company, in a high backed chair, sat the master of the court wearing a heavy chain of office, and with him were the wardens and assistants all grouped round a large, bare table. On the wall hung a great oil painting of the judgment of Solomon, giving a scriptural incentive, I suppose, to justice and fair play, though it has always seemed to me a more suitable subject might have been chosen for the purpose. In solemn tones the beadle first announced that William Gosling wished to bind his son apprentice for seven years, and after this announcement he solemnly withdrew. Next, the master of the court asked me whether I was willing to be bound, to which I, of course, assented.'

He and his father made the necessary declarations and the indentures were signed. He was thus pledged to dwell and serve upon the Thames for seven years and refrain from damage, waste, fornication, matrimony, cards, dice, tables, taverns or playhouses. In return, his master must teach and instruct him, feed, clothe and lodge him.

Gosling's work as an apprentice began by accompanying his grandfather in one towing skiff while his father worked the second one, moving timber from dock to river yard. His grandfather wore a top hat whatever the weather, and remained a top-hat man when pilot caps came into fashion. Harry was soon aware of custom and practice. During his apprenticeship he made a private income by selling old rope that he found round the river. This, he says in his memoirs, was close to pilfering, for which he gives two definitions. Pilfering was either stealing in small quantities, or helping yourself to things that you need. No waterman would consider that acquiring a piece of wood or a lump of coal was dishonest. Employers often thought higher of apprentices able to borrow somebody else's gear – oars, hitchers, tarpaulins - for the purposes of navigation. Axe handles, thole pins, sugar from the bottom of a cask, coconuts and other items had a tendency to fall overboard when unloading. Supervision was lax, flotsam and jetsam abounded, and what was useless to one was useful to another. Pilfering was thus well established.

There were also customs and practices that amounted to a black market. Gosling's parents had a circle of friends in Lambeth that included a glassblower and temperance preacher, the headmaster from Harry's school, and the mate of the General Steam Navigation Company's steamer *Orion*. When the tide was suitable they would row up from Lambeth to Richmond in two skiffs lashed together, singing all the way. This glee club was also a small cooperative society, largely through the offices of *Orion*'s mate, Tom Crump. Harry and his dad would row down to the Pool to meet the ship when she arrived from Antwerp or Holland to collect butter, cheese, eggs and poultry that would be distributed to the Lambeth circle. 'It was remarkable,' Gosling says in his memoir, 'how cheaply the goods could be obtained in this way.'

Gosling's keen observance of working the river was to take him into the labour movement and, eventually, to become the first lighterman elected to Parliament. Discrepancies between wage rates and methods of hiring labour inevitably led to hardship, disputes and restrictive practices. For example, loading was more skilful than unloading because the ship must be trimmed by the distribution of its cargo. Thus stevedores, the loaders of cargo and responsible for its stable distribution in holds, were the aristocrats of the dockside crafts. Dockers did the unloading, also a skilled task with its hard physical labour and variety of goods handled. Gradations of skill and exclusiveness developed long before wet docks, so that corn and deal porters, lightermen, coopers and riggers ranked above tallymen, warehousemen and dock labourers. Many thousands of dockworkers had no security of employment, with divisions between 'preference men' who had guarantee of some work each week and those who did not. The dangers of working unpleasant and dangerous cargoes – sugar, asbestos, sulphur, phosphate, animal stuffs - with accident-prone equipment such as cranes, winches and tractors encouraged specialisation on the basis that the more skill one possessed, the more value was one's work and the more security of employment one would get. Divisions led to demarcation, but also to a wider social cohesion and solidarity.

The arrival of the Royal Yacht off Gravesend 7 March 1863 (Watermen's Hall Collection)

Binding together in common cause was bound to happen. The first dockworkers to be unionised were the tea warehousemen of West India Docks, who conducted strikes in 1871 and 1872. In 1886 there was a dispute at Tilbury, led by Ben Tillett, who became a powerful spokesman. Three years later Tillett and John Burns were the leaders of the first major dock strike, a dispute that closed the docks for a month in demand of the 'docker's tanner', an hourly rate of six pence. Each day the dockers marched through the City supported by watermen, lightermen, sailors and shipwrights, and the employers eventually capitulated. They granted 6d, with an 8d an hour rate for night work and minimum total payment for any work of two shillings. The old rates were 4d to 5d per hour.

The first organisation that Gosling joined was the Lambeth Watermen's Turnway Society. Such societies were to be found at every stairs where watermen plied for hire, and were a throwback to the days when going by river was the only means of transport. They regulated turns at the plying place and numbers of passengers allowed in order to ensure that work was shared out between the men working the stairs. The Lambeth Turnway's headquarters was the Henry VIII in Lambeth High Street, where philanthropic work was organised.

According to Gosling, the 'quay lightermen' employed by general carriers were the first to be unionised. These men were mainly employed in the centre of the port and therefore had good communications among themselves and with other workers, and they remained the most important sector of transport workers after passenger carrying ceased in the 1920s.

But it was a dock strike in 1889 that had a profound effect on labour organisation. Gosling joined the Amalgamated Society of Watermen and Lightermen of the River Thames (ASWLRT), formed in 1872. The watermen and lightermen went to war over three issues – the wretched conditions of boy labour, the miserable cabin accommodation on lighters for boys and men, and the lack of union representation on the Company's court. The relationship between master and apprentice was breaking down because boys were increasingly apprenticed to large companies, where nobody was really in charge of them. The average binding age had risen to 16, barges had increased in size, and apprentices were often working 16-hour days with an average working week of six days and four nights.

In August the Company issued a proclamation setting out that withdrawal of labour 'without assigning any cause beyond their sympathy with the dock labourers' could result in freemen's disqualification from wholly or partially holding a licence to work as watermen or lightermen. It also hinted at intimidation to join the strike before urging an immediate return to work. Consequently the ASWLRT called a packed meeting at Bermondsey Town Hall chaired by W. F. Drew, Conservative candidate for West Southwark, at which R. Iles, chairman of the strike committee, moved that every licenced man had left his employment of his own free will. He said that they were agitating for a reduction in hours to twelve a day, not for an increase in pay, and that the watermen and lightermen were three hundred years behind the times. It was also suggested that there would never have been any conflict with the court of the Company if watermen and lightermen had the right of representation therein. Iles's motion was carried unanimously.

James A. Little gave a description of a lighterman's cabin in The Worker's Daily Round. Entrance was by dropping through a small hatchway to a fillet from which to step to the floor. The ceiling, the after part of the deck, is too low to enable one to stand. The area is about 14 by 4 feet, with a shelf for a bed in the after part. The smell of bilge water rises through a hole in the floor. A portable stove occupies the centre of the floor with a stovepipe rising from its top. On a cold morning frost fills the cabin and the ironwork gleams with ice. A lit stove fills the cabin with smoke and changes ice to water. Little concludes: 'A lighterman's cabin is the most dreary place imaginable.' A bill initiated by ASWLRT to improve conditions failed, but the Port of London Authority passed a byelaw aimed at improving cabins by 1920.

In his settlement of the 1889 strike, Lord Brassey reduced working hours to twelve for men and boys. Another 17-week strike in 1890 forced erring employers to implement Brassey's decision.

Gosling became general secretary of the watermen and lightermen's union in 1893. His offices were above the Billingsgate Christian Mission which offered soup and bread with hymn and prayer to the unemployed. Under Gosling's influence the mission changed its role to dispenser of medicine to injured workers. The third question of the 1889 dispute, that of union representation on the Company's court, was resolved fifteen years after Gosling became secretary of the union. The court had 26 co-opted members who were all freemen, most of them employers. In 1909 the Company was persuaded to co-opt three working freemen. In the same year the chairman of the Association of Master Lightermen and Barge Owners (AMLBO) tried to introduce a 14-hour day for his own apprentices. In August 183 apprentices went on strike, supported by a sixpenny levy in the pound by ASWLRT. Employers replaced apprentices with lightermen on full pay working 12-hour days. But after 14 weeks the union's position was vindicated.

The Dock, Wharf, Riverside and General Labourers Union (DWRGLU) was formed after the 1889 strike, with Ben Tillett, the leader of the 1886 Tilbury dispute, as secretary. The men now enjoyed industrial muscle to pursue grievances, hold local stoppages and organise go-slows. But in the face of unionisation, dock owners allowed shippers to hire their own labour. This increased the casual labour system.

The 1889 strike was important for encouraging gradual solidarity of objectives and organisation among the unions. There were strong unions such as the ASWLRT, the Stevedores' Protection League and the Crane Drivers' Union, but they were plagued by differences within themselves. Sailing barge and dumb barge operators had differing interests, and so did licensed men who navigated tidal waters and the unlicensed who navigated non-tidal waters. There were complications between kindred crafts and craft status, not to mention social status. The so-called unskilled labourers and dockers were at the bottom of the heap. One effect of the 1889 strike was a 20-year movement towards solidarity between waterside transport workers – dockers, coal porters, porters, carters, lightermen, carmen and crews. In 1900 the licensed and unlicensed watermen made a marriage of convenience, and then the Medway watermen joined them.

On 27 September 1910 the Dockers Union called a meeting at Compositors Hall to form the National Transport Workers Federation (NTWF). The watermen, sailors and firemen's unions were among those who joined, and Gosling was elected president. Next year, the watermen struck and negotiated a ten-hour day with employers' associations such as the Master Lightermen's Association, the Short Sea Traders, the Shipping Federation and the Wharfingers. A further strike occurred in 1912, started by the sailing bargemen of the Thames and the Medway because many owners refused to implement the 1911 agreement. The spark was the refusal to work with one James Thomas who was employed as a lighterman by Mercantile Lighterage Company but did not belong to the Transport Workers' Federation. When other companies took on Mercantile's work, solidarity spread among dockers, stevedores and carmen, and the port was brought to a standstill within a few days. There were other issues, too, such as the failure of tug crews to reduce their 12-hour day in the 1911 dispute. They did not get a reduction until 1921.

Herbert Asquith's government called a public inquiry to settle it – the first time in a labour dispute. Sir Edward Clarke was charged with investigating the causes and report. He concurred with Gosling's assertion that employers should not be allowed to brief counsel on the grounds that understanding could be achieved only by face-to-face negotiation. The unions put seven grievances on the table, and Gosling rated the result as five to two in favour of the workers. The government then invited both parties to a conference chaired by Sir George Askwith. The employers declined. After a week, the NTWF called a national strike. Bristol was the only port to come out in support of the London men, and the strike was a complete failure. Various of the great and the good tried to break down the employers' spokesman, Lord Devonport, who was implacably opposed to any proposal until there was a return to work. The unions could no longer afford the nine shillings a week strike pay, and they capitulated at the end of July – beaten, as Gosling says, by starvation. The watermen and lightermen were the last to return to work. Many who had had permanent jobs lost them.

On the employers' side, a significant change occurred in 1909 with the birth of the Port of London Authority to put all docks, quays and navigation under one management. Next year the Dockers Union was absorbed by the Transport Workers' Federation – the precursor of the formation of the Transport & General by amalgamation of fourteen unions, including the Amalgated Society of Watermen, Lightermen and Bargemen. This took place in 1922 and ended Gosling's term as secretary. Thus orgainised labour gathered strength as the port grew. By 1913 it was handling more than 20 million tons of cargo, one third of Britain's trade. It had quadrupled since the 1860s, and was ten times higher than in 1800.

In his memoir published in 1927, Gosling reflects that it was his lot to travel through an amazing period of trades union history. He knew the craft union and could remember the day when you told a man's trade by what he wore. He was involved in the first stages of union federation and its fruition. He had seen advances toward international cooperation. When he took up the post of general secretary of the Society of Watermen and Lightermen of the River Thames in 1893, the membership was 1,800 paying three pence a week. His own union lot was man-of-all-work – correspondent and typist, orator of reason while rising to rally angry members at public meetings, negotiator backed by thorough understanding of his trade and the hidden language of settlement. He attributes the success of the 1911 dispute to a negotiating body of transport workers confronting a similar employers' body over transport problems. He attributes the failure of the 1912 strike to attempting to settle several different grievances of different groups at the same time. Calling a strike was one thing, but selling it to thirty constituent parts of your federation was quite another. What a union needs for success, he says, is a simple issue like an eight hour day or the 'docker's tanner' of the 1889 strike. He also recognised that the great advantage of the Company system of licensing and training is that all the men so trained come to possess a common fund of knowledge and experience of the river, shared between watermen, lightermen, pilots, steam boat captains and other users of the Tideway.

THE LOSS OF THE

Sunk by the S.S. "Bywell Castle," off Woolwich, on the
600 men, wom

[ENTERED AT S

AH! brightly the sun shone out, happy were we,
As the swift glancing waters rolled under our lea;
No thought of the danger, no fear of the death
That hovered above us with cold, icy breath;
The song and the dance made our hearts light and gay,
And many a kiss sealed new hopes born that day;
No thought of the morrow, for gladness, I ween,
Shook her banner of joy o'er the beautiful scene.

Yes! proudly the "Alice" swept over the tide,
With her rich freight of beauty, and pleasure, and pride;
Old Age shook its silver locks out on the air—
The father and fond loving mother were there;
The youth and the maiden, like gentle-eyed doves,
Fluttered down side by side, happy, blest in their loves;
There too, little children with pattering feet,
Made many a parent's heart tender and sweet.

With a song, on from Sheerness we merrily go,
And the gallant ship ploughs through the waters below;
On, onward by Gravesend, till Rosherville's past,
And down in our wake Erith's shadows are cast;
The Creek of old Barking we leave in our flight,
And the Gas Works of Beckton loom large on our sight,
Till the lamps of North Woolwich, like stars o'er the foam,
Tell us soon we shall be with our loved ones at home.

On deck stood brave GRINSTEAD, the Helmsman anear,
By Port, or by Starboard, the vessel to steer;
The soft swell of music in dance or in song,
Made mirth in the hearts of the gay laughing throng;
And all were so happy, so full of dear life,
So loving together, child, husband, and wife,
So full of sweet thoughts, of the glad happy day
That had passed from their lives in so pleasant a way.

But hark to that shrill cry, "see!" "see!" "there ahead"

" PRINCESS ALICE."

evening of the 3rd of September, 1878, with a loss of over
, and children.

TIONERS' HALL.]

Then rang o'er the waters the shriek and the cry,
The sob of strong men in their great agony ;
The scream of the mother, who clasping her child
To her bosom, dashed past in her mad terror wild ;
The piteous pleading of young children there,
Rose upward to heaven, beseeching in prayer,
A rush, and the pitiless cold waters close
On the deck of the doomed ship, as downward she goes.

And ah ! what a harvest black death gathered then,
Of children, and women, and struggling men.
The river around them was strewn with their heads—
As an orchard, when Autumn her ripened fruit sheds—
Or a red battle field, when the fiery blast
Of the cannon, and charge of the horseman has passed—
Till clinging in masses, or faint, one by one,
She sank, and death's terrible labour was done.

But not all were lost on that black, fatal day,
Who sank in the ship, or who drifted away ;
No ! brave hearted toilers were near, and with boat,
And with cable, and wreckage kept many afloat ;
From Barge, Brig, and Schooner, came true hearted men,
And like heroes they toiled for the sufferers ; then—
When the voices were silent, the mad struggle o'er—
Went they with their priceless freight back to the shore.

Ah ! many a heart now is aching, and sad ;
And many for grief have gone hopelessly mad ;
And many have lost all, child, husband, and wife ;
And many a lone one has saved nought but life ;
And many a flood of salt tears have been shed
For the loved ones, who now are asleep with the dead ;
The swift rushing river within its cold breast,
Clasps six hundred " lost, but loved," in death's long rest.

But the heart of Old England hears Charity's call

On the evening of 3 September 1878 human error lost more lives in the Thames than ever before. A collision between the paddle steamer *Princess Alice* and the collier *Bywell Castle* in Galleons Reach drowned about 640 passengers and crew of the ferry bearing the name of Queen Victoria's daughter as the ship made her way home from Sheerness on a balmy night.

Galleons Reach is eleven miles below the *Alice*'s destination, Swan Pier by London Bridge. She had left her last stop, Rosherville Gardens at Gravesend, heading for Woolwich as the sun was sinking. Port [red to the left] and starboard [green to the right] lights and the white masthead light were set by a boy with a lucifer as the paddle steamer sailed up Erith Reach while the band on the main deck played 'We don't want to fight but, by Jingo, if we do'. Children played on deck, while at the forward end a group of elderly women was singing hymns. Twilight gathered on the Kent and Essex marshes and the lights of Woolwich twinkled across Tripcock Point – so named because it was here that vessels making for the Pool would 'trip' and 'cock' their anchors in preparation for reaching their destination. A couple by the port side paddle box were having an argument. A large screw steamer, the Spartan bound for Cardiff, passed close on the starboard beam.

After rounding the point, some passengers observed that the *Princess Alice* had moved further away from the southern shore. At about twenty-five to eight another screw steamer, similar to the *Spartan*, was advancing downstream. First class passengers on the upper deck and members of the crew realised that not only could they see her green starboard light, but her masthead light and red port light as well. Within minutes, the empty collier bound for Newcastle loomed like a cliff above the graceful sleek paddle steamer, and screaming and panic took hold as the bows of the *Bywell Castle* smashed into *Alice*'s starboard paddle box, splintering it like matchwood. Steam billowed from a gaping hole. The *Princess Alice* split in half, and in no time the bow was adrift while the stern rose high in the water before slipping into the deep.

The band on the foredeck had stopped playing as the point was rounded, and Robert Haines, the double bass player, was holding his instrument waiting to descend the stairs as the crash occurred. He rushed to the top of the saloon and passed Captain William Grinstead who was pulling the steam whistle lanyard until the sound was cut off by rushing water that put out the fires. Haynes said, 'the water rushed up to my whiskers and away I go.' A non-swimmer, he tumbled into the water and surfaced near a lifebuoy. His instrument floated away, while he himself was rescued by a boat and eventually re-united with his bow, which was picked up at Gravesend.

The master, Grinstead, went down with his ship. The water that claimed hundreds of lives was contaminated by 75 million imperial gallons of raw sewage discharged from outfalls at Barking and Crossness, close to the scene. Such discharges were made twice a day, and one occurred an hour before the *Alice* met the *Castle*.

An exhaustive inquest was presided over by Charles Joseph Carttar, the west Kent coroner, with a jury of nineteen. The business of identifying the dead took ages; some survivors scrambled aboard the *Bywell Castle*; others were picked up by watermen's boats and dispersed to Woolwich or Erith or Beckton on the Essex shore.

Previous page: Poem commemorating the *Princess Alice* disaster 1878

The *Alice* was owned by the London Steamboat Company, whose manager lost his wife and four children in the disaster. She was built at Greenock in 1865, 219 feet long and 20ft beam, and fitted to carry 936 passengers between London and Gravesend and 486 below Gravesend. Eight of her fourteen crew drowned. Carttar's task was, therefore, challenging to say the least; some would say too challenging, as evidenced by an anonymous rhyme to the tune of 'Lord Lovell' found in the coroner's papers:

The foreman stood at the Town Hall door
Smoking a twopenny weed,
When up came the jury and softly said:
'You naughty old man, take heed.'
You naughty old man, etc.

'Oh, when will you stop, old man,' they said.
'Oh, when will you stop,' said they.
'When I've asked 50,000 more
Of the silliest questions, hi, hi.'
Of the silliest questions, etc.

He talked and he jawed in his grizzling way
Till he couldn't jaw any more,
And then the jury boiled him down
And gave him away to the poor.
And gave him away, etc.

All the survivors among the *Princess Alice*'s crew gave evidence, but none could say with certainty where the ship was positioned immediately before the collision. Accounts of crew and passengers varied, but no crew member suggested that Captain Grinstead was unaware of the presence of the *Bywell Castle*. The first and second mates denied that lookouts had been formally posted, but the man and boy in the bows of the vessel were looking out, ordered to or not. The twenty-eight surviving passengers who gave evidence contributed no assistance to Carttar's quest to solve the cause of the collision.

Abraham Deness, waterman with thirty-six years experience on this part of the river, was called as an expert witness. He was sitting on the hatchway of his barge after discharging a cargo of bricks on the north bank near Beckton pier. He testified that he saw the three lights of the Alice as she passed Tripcock Point as close to the south shore as she could sail. Then he saw *Bywell Castle* with her red light showing plainly in good moonlit visibility, and saw the impact, whereupon he set off in his boat to rescue people. He testified that an ebb tide coming round Bull's Point (on the north shore upstream of Tripcock Point) will set off Tripcock Point northwards, making considerable difficulty for a vessel rounding the point in getting her starboard helm to act. A running tide would carry her toward midstream. At times, he said, the tide will take command of a vessel against her helm, even in his short barge. The longer the vessel, the more time required to get round. If this occurred, the vessel would be presenting her port light to a vessel proceeding down Galleon's Reach. When they got her straight in midstream she would spin like a top.

Peter Brown, waterman, was aboard a schooner at anchor above Beckton gas works. He saw the *Princess Alice* round the point close to the hulk *Talbot*, a permanently moored powder magazine before stopping abreast the schooner with her head pointing towards the south shore. He wondered aloud to his master if there was something amiss with the engine. He was than cross-examined under oath about statements he had made suggesting that the *Princess Alice* was stopped for five minutes before the collision. Brown denied that he had signed statements, and alleged that he had been offered bribes to do so. Evidence from examination of the engines was inconclusive on this point. Joseph Burnitt, master of the Goole schooner *Anne Elizabeth* at anchor 300 yards above Beckton pier, saw *Princess Alice*'s red light turn to green as she rounded the point. He heard the call of 'Hi, where are you coming to?" from the *Alice* to the *Castle* and saw the *Castle* cant to the shore before setting off in his boat. Henry Erb, master of the barge *Sarah* lying at the upper end of Beckton gasworks jetty, noticed that *Princess Alice* was stopped, and thought this strange. He judged that *Bywell Castle* would not have gone near the paddle steamer by three or four lengths had she held her course. But she suddenly hard a-ported and went athwart the reach. There was plenty of room, he said, so could not see any reason for the collision.

William Steer of the topsail barge *Benjamin Riddell* was under way off Tripcock Point, bound down with the tide. The *Alice* passed close inside him showing her starboard light and within a stone's throw of the bright red *Talbot* moored 100 yards off shore. 'Then I saw the screw,' Steer said, 'and the *Princess Alice* going up on her starboard helm to come the opposite side of him. The screw suddenly hard a-ported on top of him; that is the first time we saw his red light at all.' He thought that the paddle steamer was heading for the slack water between Beckton and Bull's Point towards the north side. The *Bywell Castle* would have seen her red light and correctly ported helm to pass under the *Alice*'s stern. If the *Alice* had then turned to port, she would have shown her green light to the *Castle* for too short a time to avoid a collision course.

Captain Thomas Harrison of the *Bywell Castle* was a master mariner with 37 years at sea behind him. His ship was under the charge of an experienced Trinity pilot, Christopher Dix, who was also of the opinion that the *Princess Alice* was following the common practice of heading for the north shore.

Harrison told the inquest: 'in the navigation of these screws, in steering them, in stopping and backing astern, they have certain peculiarities. I have no experience of paddle wheel vessels so as to be able to compare them… In a screw, after the orders "Ease her" and "Stop her" are given, her way through the water continues and, when she is stopped, her rudder has not that effect on her that one would wish – she is out of your control to a very great extent.' Harrison denied any intoxication on board, and accounted for her progress down the Thames at half speed until the *Princess Alice* came across the river. 'She straightened up and we got hold of her port light, her red light. I suppose she was all right making for the north shore when she came on and suddenly she starboarded and we hard a-ported immediately; she was about one hundred yards off when she starboarded. The orders were given "Stop the engines" and then "Reverse full speed" and the collision occurred immediately afterwards. The way of our vessel was stopped very little. The order to go astern, though given, was not carried out, as we found afterwards. The engineers say they never got it and the vessel in fact never went astern.'

Harrison lowered his three boats, threw lifebuoys over the side and wooden articles and ropes over the bows. The ship saved thirty-five souls and its boats a further twenty-eight. Discrepancies of Harrison's accounts to the Receiver of Wrecks and the Board of Trade were attributed to his agitation on the morning after.

The coroner heard expert opinion on the question of whether the *Princess Alice* was unsafe to proceed beyond Gravesend because she was built before watertight bulkheads were required in such vessels. The conclusion was that bulkheads would

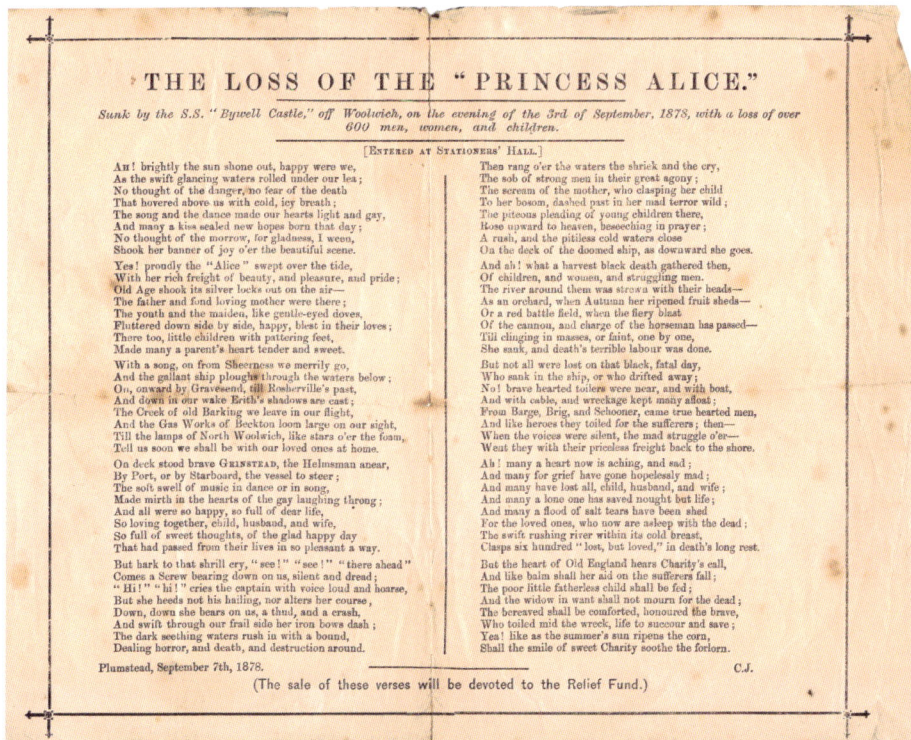

Poem commemorating the *Princess Alice* disaster 1878

at most have delayed her sinking for a short while and therefore saved more passengers. Stronger construction would, it was opined, not have made any difference to her fate given the angle at which she was struck.

The hearings brought out confusion and ignorance of two sets of navigation rules among seafarers – the Board of Trade's Rules of the Road relating to ships at sea and the Thames Conservancy's Rules of the River. Although broadly similar, they were open to different interpretations and practices. The Conservancy's 1872 by-laws mandated the 'port to port' rule without any provision for exceptions. Evidence at the Board of Trade inquiry revealed that most craft using the river around Tripcock Point followed no rules at all. It also emerged that the board's rules were given out free, whereas the conservancy's had to be paid for. What impact this had on those in charge of mentoring apprentices at the Company is unknown.

Coroner Carttar's summary stated that the condition of the *Princess Alice* was irrelevant but her manning was deplorable, and that the accusations of drunkenness aboard the *Bywell Castle* were false. He noted that the lookouts and the steersman on the Princess Alice were young and inexperienced but complimented the conduct of the *Bywell Castle*.

After fourteen and a half hours of deliberation on 14 November 1878, the coroner's jury reached a verdict of death by accident or misadventure by a majority of fifteen to four. They found that the collision was not wilful, that the *Bywell Castle* did not take the necessary precaution of easing, stopping and reversing her engines in time and that the *Princess Alice* contributed by not stopping and going astern. They

Contemporary engraving of Bywell Castle bearing down on *Princess Alice*

considered that the *Princess Alice* was seaworthy, undermanned, carrying more passengers than prudent and lacking in sufficient life-saving means.

The Board of Trade inquiry published its findings on 7 November, before the coroner's findings, and found that the *Princess Alice* had swung across in front of the *Bywell Castle* and, like the coroner's conclusion, that the *Alice* was poorly manned, carried too many passengers and not enough life-saving equipment.

There was a great deal of argument and argy-bargy at the Board of Trade and Court of Admiralty enquiries concerning navigation, seaworthiness, seamanship and safety. Eventually the Court of Admiralty concluded that had the ships remained on their parallel course, red to red, they would have passed safely; that the *Princess Alice* was going at full speed and the *Bywell Castle* at half; that the *Bywell Castle* was navigated with care and skill up to a very short time before collision, and that the *Bywell Castle* did wrong in ordering her helm hard a-port. The Court of Appeal then held the *Princess Alice* solely to blame.

The companies that owned the two craft sued each other at the Court of Admiralty, which found both partly to blame for the accident – the Alice for veering to starboard, the *Castle* for going hard to port and turning damage to sinking. This was at odds with the nautical assessors who both put the blame on the *Princess Alice*.

Locals had a different point of view: 'Many Thames watermen considered that, as all experienced Thames pilots were well aware that 'working the slack' on the south side of the river was a common and accepted practice of the day, the pilot of *Bywell Castle* should have realised the situation and acted accordingly, but no watermen were called to give evidence at the inquest or subsequent enquiry.'

Not every local blamed the *Bywell Castle*, however. One paper quoted a local, unnamed, official: 'These so-called saloon steamers are little better than floating platforms, egg-shells, that go down on the smallest contact with anything like iron or timber. The London Steamboat Company ought to be prosecuted. This vessel, with its boasted 30 feet beam, hasn't 20 feet; the breadth is pricked out by planking. It is a mere platform, planked in. The description given by the Captain of the *Bywell Castle* of its condition is quite true. Moreover, passenger steamers have no business on the Thames hereabouts after dark. The river is full of heavy shipping, masses of wood and iron, not easy of control at certain states of the tide.'

On 20 August 1989 the pleasure boat *Marchioness* was run down from the rear by the *Bowbelle* near Southwark Bridge in the early hours of the morning. This was the worst peacetime loss of life on the river since the *Princess Alice*. Both were moving in the same direction. The *Marchioness* with its 127 passengers, two crew members and two bar staff, was flipped over and sunk within seconds, 'like a toy boat' according to a witness. Five police boats were quickly on the scene and rescued fifty-three, while another pleasure boat, the *Hurlingham*, picked up thirty-four. None of the twenty-four people who were in the cabin of the *Marchioness* survived. The final tally of death was fifty-one, a shocking statistic and shocking occurrence on a summer night in central London.

There were similarities with the *Princess Alice* disaster, in that the *Marchioness* was sixty years old and constructed in such a way as to make keeping a rear lookout difficult, and she was struck by a much larger vessel with a rear wheelhouse that did not afford good visibility to the front. The *Bowbelle*, a dredger, was one of the largest ships to use the upper Tideway. A director of Tidal Cruises, owners of the *Marchioness*, likened the accident to a bus running over a cyclist.

Such an incident stands out because of the loss of life and changes in the safety precautions on the Thames that came about as a result. The first difficulty echoed the *Princess Alice* a hundred years before, namely that it took several days to determine how many passengers were on board the *Marchioness*. There was no requirement to count the number of people who boarded vessels. There was no mandatory emergency drill before sailing. The press pointed out the shortage of life-saving equipment on pleasure craft. One safety test concerned crews' competence in knowing the rules of the river, but there were exceptions to the rules. In this case, both vessels used the centre arch of Southwark Bridge. Captain Henderson of the *Bowbelle* was prosecuted for failure to keep a proper lookout, but two juries failed to come to a verdict, and the families of the victims were refused a public inquiry on the grounds that the recently set up marine accident investigation branch would investigate.

The Thames safety inquiry that followed heard witnesses claim that the *Marchioness* had veered across the path of the *Bowbelle*, and an expert witness explained that such a move could be the result of loss of steering control by the smaller vessel because of the larger's pressure field.

The inquiry found that the main cause was the lack of visibility from the wheelhouses of both craft. The chief inspector attributed much of the blame to the two captains. The inquiry suggested that numbers of passengers on pleasure boats should be recorded, that emergency procedures should be explained to passengers before setting out, that lookouts should be posted on craft more than 40ft long at all times, and that passenger boats should have lookouts at the stern who are in communication with the wheelhouse.

In 1997 the incoming Labour government announced a public inquiry under Lord Justice Clarke whose report largely echoed the above. He found that the basic cause was poor lookouts, that the *Bowbelle*'s owners had failed properly to instruct or monitor crews, that the *Marchioness*'s owners failed to issue proper instructions about keeping lookout, that the Department of Transport had known for years about the problem of limited visibility of steering positions on such vessels, and that the police had no contingency plan for dealing with a major river disaster.

The episode showed up the vulnerability of travelling on the Thames. In 1992 the PLA fitted a new system of automatic warning lights to nineteen bridges. Ten years after the disaster, the Thames safety inquiry report resulted in enhanced regulations on life-saving equipment in passenger boats and the introduction of lifeboat stations at Gravesend, Tower Pier, Chiswick Pier and one run by volunteers at Teddington. They opened in 2002.

All accidents are sobering, and the disasters of the *Princess Alice* and the *Marchioness* are stark reminders that the river is a dangerous place. The history of the working river is peppered with mishap major and minor, and this account of watermen's and lightermen's lives could have been draped round a frame of injury, death and misfortune through century upon century. Suffice it to say that *Princess Alice* and *Marchioness* represent catastrophe at its worst.

When the transatlantic steamship *Deutschland* ran aground on the Kentish Knock, a shoal near Harwich, in 1875, Gerard Manley Hopkins wrote a poem that encapsulates the estuary dangers, where deep-draughted shipping was endangered by being blown awry among shifting sand and meandering channels, and where local knowledge was at a premium:

Into the snows she sweeps,

Hurling the haven behind,

The Deutschland, on Sunday; and so the sky keeps,

For the infinite air is unkind,

And the sea flint-flake, black-backed in the regular blow,

Sitting Eastnortheast, in cursed quarter, the wind;

Wiry and white-fiery and whirlwind-swivellèd snow

Spins to the widow-making unchilding unfathering deeps.

She drove in the dark to leeward,

She struck—not a reef or a rock

But the combs of a smother of sand: night drew her

Dead to the Kentish Knock;

And she beat the bank down with her bows and the ride of her keel:

The breakers rolled on her beam with ruinous shock;

And canvass and compass, the whorl and the wheel

Idle for ever to waft her or wind her with, these she endured.

The Deutschland moved Hopkins because the North German Lloyd line vessel on route from Bremerhaven to Southampton (eventually bound for New York) had, among its passengers, a group of Franciscan nuns escaping persecution of Catholics in their homeland. The incident was controversial for a number of reasons, not least the accusation that the slow response of rescuers was deliberate. The English pilot on board was from Southampton, and the skipper had seriously miscalculated his position. When the *Deutschland* tried to float off the bank in reverse, the screw propeller fractured. A number of passing vessels ignored distress rockets, the authorities at Harwich appeared to react slowly, and no help came for thirty hours.

When help did come, the *Times* described, and the *Illustrated London News* depicted, corpses being ransacked for jewelry and wreckers from Harwich and Ramsgate pillaging the ship. There were even accusations that the *Deutschland* had been deliberately wrecked. The Harwich steam paddle tug *Liverpool* eventually rescued 135 of the 213 souls on board. The nuns, four of whom drowned and the fifth lost at sea, found peace at a friary of their order in Stratford, and are buried in Leytonstone. The Board of Trade inquiry into the accident exonerated everyone except Captain Eduard Brickenstein. Soon after the *Deutschland* affair, Harwich had its first lifeboat, the *Springwell.*

The estuary was short on navigation aids, and until purpose-built lifeboats and the Royal National Lifeboat Institution began to make their presence felt in the mid-nineteenth century, shallow-drafted fishing smacks that could sail where others could not acted as the main salvation boats for souls and the shadowy but lucrative business of wrecks. A wreck was defined as a vessel with no living thing on board, and the Receiver of Wrecks was entitled to cargoes. Cargo was auctioned and the proceeds went to the Lord Warden of the Cinque Ports after the salvagers' cut of about a third was paid.

In the ten years between 1840 and 1850 there were 170 vessels wrecked in the estuary, and many heroic deeds by the crews of fishing smacks. Master John Glover was credited with saving 300 people in his time and given a telescope by Kaiser Wilhelm for rescuing thirteen from the *Carl Agrell* in 1871. The King's Channel, frequented by the East coast colliers, has the reputation for the most wrecks.

Gravesend is the shipping point where estuary meets river. At Gravesend, customs officers boarded incoming vessels and outgoing vessels took on pilots. The first customs house was built there in 1816 with a lookout station on roof, replaced by another building in 1836. Incoming vessels were signalled to stop by a musket shot as they approached the town. If the captain had not responded after three shots, he ran the risk of the heavy guns of Tilbury Fort from the other side of the river. Pity the poor gunnery officer at Tilbury, challenged by range and speed of a moving target on a waterway crowded with steam and sail, large and small.

The basis for pilots was set with the founding of Trinity House in Henry VIII's reign as 'The Master, Wardens, and Assistants of the Guild, Fraternity, or Brotherhood of the most glorious and undivided Trinity, and of St. Clement in the Parish of Deptford-Strond in the County of Kent.' St. Clement adjoined Henry's new dockyard at Deptford. The Trinity carried responsibility for lights and buoys and assumed authority for licensing pilots to operate in northern European waters.

A third importance of Gravesend was that it was the last point before London where landing coal did not incur duty. Thus fuel was landed at Round Tree Point in great quantities, a spot marked by an obelisk.

Upriver from Gravesend, the main navigational hazard was congestion. There are countless accounts of tilt boats, wherries, skiffs, barges and ferries in difficulties with wind, fog and each other. The rule of thumb in strong winds or fog was to drop anchor or seek the nearest shelter, whether out in the estuary or on the river. The case of the *Albion* illustrates an unexpected hazard of a different kind. This occurred at Thames Ironworks, the enormous shipbuilding company by the entrance to Bow Creek and opposite the wharf where Trinity House maintained its lightships and buoys.

Thames Ironworks (whose football team became West Ham United) built ironclads and large warships, and the launch of such vessels was an East End event. On 21 June 1898 the 6,000-ton cruiser *HMS Albion* was scheduled to go down the slipway. Thirty thousand people, including school parties given the day off, gathered to watch in the presence of the Duke and Duchess of York. The future Queen Mary cut the cord, the champagne bottle refused to break, and the ship slid sideways into the river, sending a huge wave back towards the slipway.

Many people were washed into the river, and the noise and the enormous numbers in the vicinity hampered rescue. Debris from the cradle that had held the ship bobbed about in the water. It was another occasion, of course, when nobody knew who was there or who was where. Despite the efforts of the police and the yard's own rescue service, 32 bodies were washed up and a further six people died after rescue.

Intrigue arose from a collision in fog between the freighters *Magdeburg* and the *Yamashiro Maru* at Broadness Point near Gravesend, in October 1964. The *Magdeburg*, an East German ship, loaded 42 British Leyland buses at Dagenham and was bound for Cuba at a time when the United States was imposing a trade embargo on the Caribbean island in the wake of the Cuban missile crisis. The in-bound Japanese ship was empty, and she holed the *Magdeburg* amidships, sinking her and writing off most of her cargo. The incident was logged as an accident, but allegations arose later of CIA involvement with connivance of the British intelligence, despite the British Government's support for Leyland's export initiative. The *Magdeburg* was eventually floated and put under tow for Greece, only to sink to her grave in the Bay of Biscay with the fourteen buses that remained in the hold.

Wreck of the M V Magdeburg with cargo of buses bound for Cuba (www.tilburyandchadwellmemories.org.uk)

Foolhardiness in composition of cargo led to a spectacular accident on the Regent's Canal in 1874. On 2 October the little steam tug *Ready* was hauling three barges en route for Nottingham along the canal near London zoo at 5 a.m.. loaded with sugar, nuts, coffee and, in one barge, six barrels of petroleum and five of gunpowder. The crew had a fire going in *Ready*'s cabin, and as the string passed under Macclesfield Bridge a spark caught the petroleum vapour. The keel of the tug ended up embedded in a house 300 yards away. The bridge was demolished, and its replacement was known ever after as Blow-up Bridge.

From time immemorial, the Thames has commanded respect. The horrors recited above remind us why it continues to do so. The poet Andrew Motion was moved to write Fresh Water, a tribute to his friend Ruth Haddon who died on the *Marchioness*, from which this is taken:

One of the children asks if people drown in the river, and I think

of Ruth, who was on the Marchioness. After her death, I met

someone who had survived. He had been in the lavatory when the dredger hit,

and fumbled his way out along a flooded corridor, his shoes

and clothes miraculously slipping off him, so that when he at last

burst into the air he felt that he was a baby again

and knew nothing, was unable to help himself, aghast.

I touch my wife's arm and the children gather round us.

we are the picture of a family on an outing. I love the river

and the perky tour-boats with their banal chat. I love the snub barges.

I love the whole dazzling cross-hatchery of traffic and currents,

shadows and sun, standing still and moving forward.

the tangle of junk bumps the wall below me again and I look down.

There is Ruth swimming back upstream, her red velvet party dress

flickering round her heels as she twists through the locks

and dreams round the slow curves, slithering on for miles

until she had passed the ponderous diver at Folly Bridge

And the reed-forests at Lechlade, accelerating beneath bridges and willow
branches,

slinking easily among the plastic wrecks and weedy trolleys,

speeding and shrinking and silvering until finally she is sliding uphill

over bright green grass and into the small wet mound of earth,

where she vanishes.

26
PORT AUTHORITY

The twentieth century brought a new and powerful stakeholder to the Thames – the Port of London Authority (PLA). It was created in Parliament in 1909 to bring order to chaos. It was a logical development from a great river giving berth [sic] to a great city and spawning a powerful empire that transformed London into the world's greatest port. 'For centuries, the river almost seemed to manage itself, but imperial expansion, growth in trade, bigger ships and an increasing population all took their toll by the middle of the nineteenth century,' says Nigel Watson in his history of the PLA published in 2009. The stakes became huge and the stakeholders more numerous in a chaotic river-scape.

By the end of the 1800s there was commercial and administrative disarray. A joint docks committee took over the running of most docks in 1889, the year in which the docker's tanner strike brought some labour union recognition. During the same period, decline in India trade and drought in Australia caused difficult economic circumstances in the docks, while the riverside wharfingers enjoyed the lion's share of warehousing. Despite the success of the 1889 strike, the anarchic casual labour system would tax the minds of workers, trades unionists, management and government for decades.

There was a long list of complaints about the docks from bodies such as the London County Council and the London Chamber of Commerce. Shipping channels were restrictive, delivery was slow, lighterage was poor, rail links were inadequate, berthing and unloading was subject to delay, and charges were too high. Responsibilities were administered by a variety of bodies often at odds with one another. Trinity House regulated pilots, the Watermen's Company regulated lightermen, the Corporation of London was the sanitary authority, policing was divided between the Metropolitan, the Kent and Essex constabularies and dock companies' private forces, and the Thames Conservancy was in charge of navigation and conservation, having taken over navigation from the City Corporation in 1857.

In 1900 the wharfingers and lightermen were enraged by a private member's bill that attempted to end the free water clause that permitted lighters to use the enclosed docks without charge. A royal commission was appointed under Sir Joseph Broadbank in 1900 to inquire into administration and water access to the port, and this led to the creation of the PLA in 1909. The new authority took charge of docks and river, and under its brusque and energetic first chairman, Hudson Kearley (Lord Devonport), made an immediate impact. The wilful and assertive Kearley appointed a chief engineer, a docks and warehouse manager, a chief police officer and a secretary, and soon there were nine dredgers and more than twenty steam hoppers at work on the river. Forty-six wrecks were cleared in five years. Cargo grew to a record 20 millions tons by 1913, the PLA's permanent labour force doubled to 6,000 between 1913 and 1915, and the authority returned a profit each year.

The authority adopted the four-category labour structure of the old London and India Docks Company. Permanent labourers had regular work and were paid 24 shillings a week. The A list of registered labourers guaranteed regular work without

Previous page: TST&L's motor tug Irande at entrance to London Dock (Michael Wenban)

sick pay or disablement pensions; the B list gave preferential employment at six pence an hour with a daily minimum of two shillings except those engaged for the afternoon only; the C list comprised casuals without status. Although the Act bade the PLA to improve labour conditions in the port, the authority's powers were limited to persuasion, and it was thus hampered in this task by other employers. Disputes arose, and dockers and other workers struck in 1911 when one of the issues was recognition of unions. The men rejected the Devonport Agreement, the PLA resisted government pressure to negotiate, and it was the Board of Trade that eventually settled the dispute.

Lord Devonport
(National Portrait
Gallery, London)

The settlement saw provision of a docks ambulance service and the introduction of hospital care for injured dockers. But peace did not last long. In May 1912 the lightermen called a strike, soon joined by others, over the reluctance of employers to implement the 1911 settlement. The PLA pointed the finger at the National Transport Workers Federation for attempting a closed shop. Two of the strike leaders, Harry Gosling of the lightermen and James Anderson of the stevedores, had seats on the PLA board. The PLA chairman, Lord Devonport, threatened to starve the strikers out. The strike fizzled out in a drift back to work in August.

At the end of the First World War, trade was half the pre-war level, caused partially by a shift in shipping to west coast ports because of the U-boat presence in the Channel. By 1921, when the King George V Dock opened, the last and the largest of the Royal Dock group, there were more than 60,000 registered dockworkers but work for only 34,000 in an average week. Post-war wage increases were gradually eroded in the years that followed. The Shaw Inquiry recommended the adoption of registered labour, an early outline of the National Dock Labour Scheme that would not come in until 1947.

In 1924 four female students from East London College visited East India Dock as part of their studies. Enid Stokes wrote an account to a boyfriend in New York. 'We got some tea off a coffee stall and walked about until 7.45 when we watched the call of the men. Most of the labour is casual and about 75 per cent of the men were turned away.' They were shown round by a senior official who explained how the men worked. 'He hated the coloured men like poison and was pretty down on the ordinary docker because they were so slack.' Next day the students were met by two union officials. 'Both were very crude men but one you could see was a thinker, while the other was a soap box orator and gave it to us 'hot'. They told us all about the tally system and the payment of men on the PLA system and unemployment systems. They also waxed eloquent on the rats and beetles and things on board ship until one of them stopped the other and said the young ladies won't want to eat nothing no more if you tell 'em all about 'em.' The students were told about a ship just arrived from Sweden with a load of matches bearing the Bryant and May label with 'British trade for British workmen' on them.

The Royal Albert Dock 1932 (Michael Wenban)

While the PLA under its new chairman Lord Ritchie and its new general manager, David Owen, attended to dredging, decreasing pollution and providing oil terminals to encourage new cargoes and the health of the port, the world economy was not in tune with their aspirations. While oil companies moved in and Ford opened a huge factory on the north bank at Dagenham, colonial economies collapsed. Trade with India, for example, halved between 1925 and 1931. The PLA cut its rates, charges, dues and wages. It was the largest employer in the docks, with 12,000 employees, half of whom were dockers. But this represented less than ten per cent of the registered dock labour.

Dock workers, who had struck in 1923 and 1924, joined the General Strike in 1926. Two destroyers were sent up the Thames and army and police protection was provided for food convoys, loaded by volunteers, to leave Royal Albert Dock. Two submarines were stationed in George V Dock with their generators connected to cold stores containing three quarters of a million carcasses, a precaution against West

The barge *Wrekin* loading a vessel in Surrey Docks 1961 (Michael Wenban)

The barge *America* (Michael Wenban)

Ham council that held sympathetic views to the strike and threatened to cut off the electricity supply.

The 1930s saw a decline in the number of registered dockworkers to 37,000. There was terrible poverty and undernourishment in docklands. The PLA adopted a stand-off system whereby a quota of men were stood off in each dock day by day so that the little work available was shared around. The union favoured such a system and cooperated with a scheme to decasualise labour, but this foundered once more on the reluctance of other employers to join.

Despite the slump in export trade, London remained the country's biggest port, with a reputation for efficiency. It handled twice as much as the next largest port, Liverpool, and its import-export trade exceeded that of Liverpool, Manchester, Hull and Southampton in value. Export trade was half the 1914 level in the late 1930s, but imports were increasing as world prices fell. Pay and piece work rates in the docks were raised a bit in 1935 and 1937.

The Port of London was a prime target for enemy action during the Second World War. The first bombs fell on 7 September 1940. 'The whole bloody world's on fire,' said the brigade officer in charge as 375 German bombers swarmed overhead to incinerate timber, rubber, paint, flour and pepper, cause rum barrels to explode and enflame the river with liquid sugar. Fires at Surrey Docks burned for five days, and the bombers returned to the blitz for 76 nights. At the end of that, trade had been reduced by three-quarters, and the Home Guard was born to defend the docks, while food and raw materials were moved to other storage facilities.

PLA dockworkers discharged ships from 8 am to 7 pm six days a week, and until 5 pm on Sundays. Nothing deterred them, according to a Norwegian journalist who wrote: 'Before the war these dockworkers… would stop work for a drop of rain. Now… when I saw fly-bombs coming over, did they stop work? Why, the dockers didn't even look at them.' The government introduced compulsory registration for regular employment and a guaranteed wage in every port.

Hundreds of vessels of all varieties from the Thames took part in the Dunkirk evacuation, and the port played a major role in the D-Day landings including building and assembling many of the Mulberry harbours and laying Pluto, the 'pipeline under the ocean' to supply ships and armour at the landings. By the end of the war, a third of all warehousing and half of all storage capacity in the port had been lost.

As the war ended, ten years of repair and reconstruction began, as well as trends in the handling of cargo that would combine to bring hundreds of years of shipping and trade to an end in the docks and the Pool. Pallets and containers appeared, together with packaged timber and roll-on roll-off ferries. During the 20 years from 1947, trade doubled to over 60 million tons, almost a third of UK trade, a rise aided by rampant mechanisation long-favoured by the PLA top brass. Forklift trucks stacked pallets in purpose-built drive-in sheds; mobile cranes moved stuff around, and rail connections improved in the face of growing competition from road haulage. Ironically, though, larger ships, deeper channels and greater efficiency conspired to congest the port and fuel the call for a complete break. In 1964 Dudley Perkins, then the PLA's general manager, visited New York and saw the future. He put his authority's modernisation programme on hold, while opting to build a new container dock at Tilbury.

Industrial relations were fraught throughout the post-war period. During the first ten years after the war the port was hit by 37 strikes; in the two years from 1964 there were 93 strikes.

The National Dock Labour Scheme was introduced in 1947 in answer to a six-week unofficial dockers' strike over basic pay in 1945. Although this was an improvement in some ways, it loosened the bonds between casual workers and the port's four hundred employers. Dockers could not choose the employer to whom they were sent, nor could employers choose workers. By the time that decasualisation and a guaranteed minimum wage occurred in 1967, jobs were further threatened by looming mechanisation. As early as 1951, a mechanised export dock inside the West India had cut the number of men required by two-thirds.

Cleanaway barges under Tower Bridge by A N Blackman 1984 (Watermen's Hall Collection)

Many strikes were unofficial. Decasualisation recommended by the Devlin report in 1966 increased the permanent labour force of every employer and banned compulsory redundancies, burdens that played into the hands of ports outside the dock labour scheme. In 1967, the first major dock closures in the port of London took place. By 1980, Tilbury was the sole survivor, and it was privatised in 1992, leaving the port with no docks under its control. Pollution control was moved to Thames

Water in 1974, and the Greater London Council took over the piers (responsibility for which reverted to the PLA in 1989), leaving the PLA with 95 miles of the river from Teddington to a notional line running from Margate to Clacton as its remaining responsibility.

By 1989, the year that the National Dock Labour Scheme was abolished, the number of registered dockworkers had fallen from the 1966 total of 24,000 to 9,000, and the PLA's work force had dropped to 1,500. In 1976 a meeting of lighterage journeymen and shop stewards founded Transport on Water, a pressure group to promote the river as a commercial enterprise. And the London Docklands Development Corporation was created in 1981 to turn the docklands into a commercial and residential new world. Part of the Royal Docks became City Airport, where flights began in 1987.

A sidebar to the PLA story is the development and use of technology on the river since the Second World War. Short-wave radio was in use in 1948. Radar appeared on a PLA vessel in 1955. In 1959 the Thames Navigation Service began using VHF radio and harbour surveillance radar. By 1963, more than half of the ships entering the port were equipped with VHF. By 1965 the navigation service covered half the river. Weather report stations and tide gauges were set up in 1964, and an emergency traffic control system in 1966. The PLA began to require vessels to give advance notice of arrival and departure, anchorage and approach channel. In 1982 a river users' liaison group was set up as a safety discussion forum, followed in 1984 by the Port of London river information system (POLARIS) that comprises a vessel data management system. In 1986 traffic management went operational. Two years later

Thames Clipper *Tornado* by St. Paul's Cathedral (Thames Clippers)

the PLA took responsibility for navigation buoys, and in 1993 the global positioning system (GPS) came into play.

After a century and more since its inception, the PLA remains the chief stakeholder in the tidal Thames. It has presided over the 'gentrification' of the river from Greenwich upstream, a return not quite to its former glory as a royal river, but to a highway of leisure and living enjoyed by inhabitants and visitors alike. The PLA's three main roles are the safety of all river users, conservation of the marine environment and promotion of commercial use, particularly in the estuary. This encompasses river traffic, shipping lanes, pilotage and the supervision of sporting and other events. To these ends the harbour masters provide the visual presence of enforcement. They predate the PLA itself, having been given responsibility over navigation, mooring, movement, loading and discharge of shipping in 1799. They patrolled day and night in watermen's skiffs, and when in 1857 the City's river powers passed to the Thames Conservancy, the 'upper', 'middle' and 'lower' harbour masters held their responsibilities over the navigable channel and the control of speed by steam boats. The system, subject to examination by Trinity House, remained the same when the PLA succeeded the Conservancy on the Tideway in 1908.

27
THE MONSTROUS
JESTS OF WARS

'Before this monstrous jest of war, there was a certain raw gaiety about the place, brought thither by these same blond Vikings; but, since the frenetic agitations of certain timorous people against 'all aliens' – as though none but an alien can be a spy – these men are not now allowed to land from their boats, and Shadwell is the poorer of a touch of colour.'

Before the Great War, wrote Thomas Burke in his account of being out and about during it, one might often meet and fraternise with giant bearded Scandinavian seamen in the coffee bars, beer shops and pubs of Shadwell High Street. Burke, a pub-crawler from Fleet Street, recalled them as 'absurdly out of the picture in these tiny, saw-dusted rooms, against the hideous bedizenment of the London house of refreshment.' He noted that in the upper rooms on Saturday evenings one might have singing and dancing to a cracked piano and a superannuated banjo, and there the girls of the quarter would appear, and would do themselves well on seafarers' hospitality.

Burke found the environs of London Docks now all charged with gloom, broken only by the anaemic lights of a few miserable mission halls and coffee bars. 'The free and easy atmosphere is gone. Suspicion has been bred in all these docks men by the cheap press. The beer is filthy. The good Burton is gone, and in its place you have a foul concoction which has not the mellowing effect of honest British beer or the exhilarating effect of light continental brews.'

He found Shadwell High Street a dirty lane of poor lodging houses, foul courts, waste tracts of land, a mission hall exuding a stale air of diseased hospitality, and ships' chandlers, with their miscellanies of apparently useless lumber stored in a heap so you can't find anything.

But Burke found cheerier company on the Isle of Dogs amongst the ring of hammers and roar of furnaces at Cubitt's works, the scream of the siren and moan of the hooter, the voices of the island singing the accumulated agony of the East End. He found that under the arc lights of night loading and in the bars among sweaty engineers and grimy stokers it was still possible to stand silent on the peak of Darien, to travel the world in tales of Swatow, Rangoon, Manila and Mozambique, to wonder at yesteryear's cargoes of cornelian and jade, betelnut and bhang, malachite and onyx, ivory and coral. It was still possible to drink beer among men who could claim to have 'rolled down to Rio, and gone back to Mandalay, and seen the dawn come up like thunder out'er China 'crost the bay.'

For their part, the sweaty engineers and grimy stokers drinking in the Gun or the Star of the East ran the risk of running into Fleet Street bores slumming it on the Isle of Docks. But we can be grateful for the company that Burke kept. No doubt some of the misery he describes was caused by Lloyd George's government measures in 1915 to reduce the strength of beer and spirits and savagely cut opening hours to two and a half hours during the day and two to three hours in the evening. Until then, London's pubs were open from 5 a.m. and did not close until 12.30 a.m.

Previous page: (Major Edwin Hunt MVO)

When the Great War broke out in 1914 the young PLA ambitious expansion programme was well under way. In 1913 Tobacco Dock in the London Docks was being widened and deepened with the addition of a two-storey jetty and more sheds. Larger cranes were installed at Surrey docks, there were major works at West India Dock and the Royal Docks, Tilbury was being extended, and plans were announced to extend Royal Victoria. In 1916 East India Dock received a wider entrance. In April 1918 a bill proposed a deep-water port at Canvey Island.

This was all designed to cater for larger ships. By 1914 the largest vessel seen at Tilbury was the 675-ft *Ceramic*, with a laden draught of 34ft 6ins. The authority had spent £25 million in deepening and widening the channel from the Royal Albert Dock to the Nore, its intention being to allow ships the size of the *Mauretania* and *Lusitania* to dock at Tilbury (achieved in January1917 when White Star, Cunard and British India lines booked berths. *Lusitania* never made it, though, sunk in 1915).

Thames traffic increased almost overnight when the port of Southampton was made over to naval and military use. In September 1914 the Admiralty closed a number of channels in the Thames and required all ships entering the river from foreign ports to call at nominated pilot stations, and all ships leaving the river to obtain clearance. Some channels were mined in defence, some by the enemy. On 26 November the battleship *Bulwark* blew up at Sheerness, the cause being fire in its magazine rather than enemy action. On Christmas Day, German aircraft were seen over Sheerness, and on Boxing Day planes were sighted over the Thames, while German battle cruisers shelled Hartlepool, Whitby and Scarborough. In February 1915 Germany declared the waters round Britain a war zone for submarines. Patrol boats were assigned to protect barges and shipping in the Channel, the Company history noting that those in charge had little experience and often asked the impossible of barges. The U-boats took a heavy toll of Allied shipping.

In 1914 there was a critical shortage of barges after large numbers were requisitioned for transporting foodstuffs, coal and coke to France and Belgium. Tugs were also requisitioned to work the Channel ports and Continental waters, and more than a hundred shallow-draft landing craft known as X-lighters were deployed to land troops in the Dardanelles. The Royal Engineers was formed in 1915 to organise transportation on French and Belgian canals. Road and rail stock was also diverted from the docks to the war effort. Two sailing barges, the *Record Reign* and *Sarah Colebrooke*, were converted into Q ships to tackle U-boats in the Channel. They were fitted with twin engines and a 4-inch gun amidships concealed beneath a 'barge's boat', with two 12-pounders hidden behind collapsible screens fore and aft.

When 1915 dawned there was already extreme congestion in the Port of London. Ships were being diverted there from foreign Channel ports. Twenty-eight liners loaded with wheat, tea and sugar were waiting for berths off Gravesend, and there were 650,000 tons of goods stockpiled in warehouses. Demand from the military was great while flexibility in the docks was poor, and the 8,000 dockworkers were not numerous enough to handle the loading and unloading. Loading was speeded up and levies enforced on empty barges.

At the end of 1916 the new Ministry of Shipping requisitioned almost every British ship, and in April 1917 a convoy system was introduced with the effect of reducing U-boat inflicted losses dramatically. In July and August only five vessels were sunk among 800 that entered the English Channel. But convoys increased pressure on the docks because numerous ships arrived together, and loading became critical for joining outward-bound convoys.

Vital wartime traffic was fed into London via the inland waterways, too. Lucy Andrews brought gunstocks from the BSA factory in West Bromwich to Emanuel Smiths in Brentford. 'I've gone to sleep on the horse's back many a time as he towed the barge down. There was a 10-mile stretch without any locks,' she recalled years later. The empty barge would go to Surrey for timber or Millwall for grain before returning to the Midlands. Lightermen wearing big Melton overcoats, caps and scarfs came on board her barge. 'You were never allowed to go on the river unless you had a lighterman.'

A Zeppelin was first seen above the East End on 31 May 1915. The first bombs on the capital dropped on 8 September. Next March a Zeppelin bombed Winkley's Wharf near Millwall Dock. The anti-aircraft gun at Blackwall Point sometimes showered the nearby police station roof with shrapnel. By 1918 Gotha night bombers were attacking London.

But worse than air raids was the explosion at the Brunner Mond factory, between the Thames and North Woolwich Railway, on 19 January 1917. Its death toll was 69 with a thousand injured, 98 of them seriously. Brunner Mond was a TNT factory situated in a crowded area – TNT being classified as a safe explosive. The factory formerly produced caustic soda, and traces of it remained. Eighty-three tons of TNT went up, and the fire burned for 24 hours. Venesta Plywood and Silvertown Lubricants were destroyed, plus whole streets, a fire station, St Barnabas's church and hall, schools for girls and infants, and a gasholder on Greenwich peninsular. The damage extended to 17 acres and left 1,000 homeless.

All of the above contributed to difficult times in the port – difficult times for shipping and dock managers, difficult times for supply and demand, difficult times for workers and trades unions, and difficult times for reward, patriotism and making ends meet. The shifting sands of (bad) organisation and strife ran the full gamut. In 1915 dockers were on high enough wages to make them reluctant to work more than three days a week with overtime. In March stevedores struck, and sixpence a day war bonus was awarded to dock and warehouse workers to compensate for rapid price rises. Watermen and lightermen received a pay award of eight pence a day, reduced to seven for watchmen and three to four pence for apprentices. In July next year the PLA doubled its war bonus payments to quay and warehouse workers. Better organisation and facilities were producing dividends. In September a system was put into place to replace those fit to fight with older men, but also to protect skilled occupations from conscription introduced by the new Ministry of National Service. In October lightermen accepted a substantial increase in pay, though in November a new dispute over continuous overtime for night work was settled after arbitration, the award being an extra shilling for a long night's work (four to nine pence for apprentices). At the end of April 1917, two thousand labourers struck at Tilbury, but their dispute was settled in a day.

One general cause of irritation was that some employers were compensating for the shortage of skilled men by employing unskilled women at skilled rates of pay. Ben Tillett, the general secretary of the dockers' union, attacked the government's bad organisation for exacerbating the shortage of men, lighters, barges and tugs. He blamed officials from the shipping controller's department for acting in a 'disorganised and officious capacity'. He accused them of sometimes ordering ships to be unloaded, reloaded and then unloaded again, often departing half empty. He accused officials of contradicting each other, causing utter confusion.

In 1918 the Association of Master Lightermen and Bargeowners increased its rates for day, night and overtime work, at the cost of a 20 per cent rise in lighterage charges. The PLA raised its charges by 15 per cent. Turn-around times reduced. Wages in docklands had risen by about 65 per cent during the war, underlining inflation under the war effort.

The war ended on 11 November 1918, and the docks were never quite the same again. There were 7,000 lighters on the river, increasingly made of steel instead of wood. Towing gradually replaced driving by oars with the tide (at the end of April 1917 a Birmingham company issued a new challenge to lightermen by fitting a barge with a detachable engine capable of hauling two barges laden with 100 tons of coal to London). Driving a barge from Rotherhithe to Tilbury, a distance of 20 miles, required two ebb tides with the lighterman often staying on board in between. But tugs could tow six lighters at a time, two or three abreast. Lighters increased to 90ft long with a beam of 20ft able to carry 250 tons. And by 1919, seaplanes were landing on the Thames.

After the war a 'mystery' port was unveiled. This was a 2,200-acre site near Sandwich in Kent, alongside the River Stour, where could be found barge-building slips, machine shops, foundries, power stations, railway sidings, a church and 20,000 men. Military supplies to the tune of 1,200,000 tons, including artillery, aircraft and complete trains were taken to Calais and Dunkerque. Fifty tugs towed 9,654 barges across the Channel. More than 230 special steel barges of 200 tons deadweight operated in French and Belgian canals. Vessels were turned round in 25 minutes. Prefabricated barges were constructed for service in France and Mesopotamia.

No doubt much of the skill absent from the Port of London could be found in Sandwich. The port took a long time to readjust. But the wartime ventures of the watermen and lightermen were recognised by Sir John Eaglesome, an engineer and colonial administrator involved in wartime logistics. The bargees, he said, had braved 'the perils of the deep from the Murman coast to the Mediterranean, and laboured in the inland waters of Mesopotamia and Africa… In Asia they had visited the home of the first and greatest bargee Noah, and their lighters had been seen in the land of the Pharaohs… moored by the city when Sinbad the Sailor set out on his adventures.'

Not what most lightermen, raised on the scream of the siren and the moan of the hooter, had in mind in 1914, perhaps. But by 1918, Eaglesome's paean to bargees in the land of the Pharaohs echoed Burke's sonnet of salty seamen on the Isle of Dogs, rolling down to Rio, and back to Mandalay, with a dawn like thunder out'er China 'crost the bay.

Lightermen and watermen were caught up in the Second World War like everybody else, just as they had been in the First. The strategic importance of the Port of London and the vital work of the docks classified their work as restricted occupations, protecting many men from call up to the armed services. But as the war progressed, both army and navy recognized the need for the peculiar skills of those who could pilot vessels in tidal and shallow waters, and so many Company men were involved in events such as the evacuation from Dunkirk, the Dieppe raid, aid to Russia via the Persian Gulf, the D-Day landings, inland transport on the Rhine and other European rivers, and the war in the Far East.

One curious incident was the role of a small watermen's unit in the liberation of Venice. This came about when an irregular unit of the SAS known as Popski's Private Army, headed by Lieutenant Colonel Vladimir Peniakoff, took the sabotage skills it learned in North Africa to Italy.

Vladimir 'Popski' Peniakoff was an émigré Russian [Belgian] who had been brought up with English as his first language and was living in Cairo at the start of the war. He arrived in Italy as the British and Americans were fighting their way northwards. Popski set up mountain bases deep behind enemy lines and supplied his men by air.

After many adventures with other units and Italian partisans, Popski's Army headed for Venice, which entailed exploring and eventually crossing the Po estuary. In Popski's absence his second-in-command, Captain John Campbell, turned up in Pesaro at the base of the twenty-strong 945 Inland Water Transport Company and asked to try out the suitability of their landing craft for carrying Popski Jeeps. The beauty of it, said Lieutenant Brian Thomas who commanded the transport company, was that the top of a Jeep aligned with the gunwale of a ramped landing craft, obscuring everything from view except for the vehicle's armament that consisted of a Bren gun, a Browning and two mortars.

The transport unit moved to Rimini and Ravenna on the Adriatic coast. In Ravenna they assisted a specialized camouflage unit assemble a force of blow-up tanks and vehicles on the quay, aerial photographs of which were then leaked to the enemy. Eventually Thomas received orders to place five landing craft under the command of Popski's Army. Thomas and the lightermen were now styled as Popski's Navy and stayed with the army unit until the end of the war. They moved arms, supplies, casualties and prisoners around the estuary and the Adriatic, often behind enemy lines.

On 11 March 1945 the jeeps set sail for the Po estuary, escorted by two minesweepers. The fleet was manned by volunteer lightermen – Sergeant Jimmy Kinealy, warrant officer Tom Gillam and sappers Cawthorn, Frank Dobinson, Lou Foweraker and Butch Freeman. Gillam recalled that when he sought volunteers, the whole company raised their hands. 'You can't all bloody go,' he said.

The inshore end of the long flat approach with uprooted pitprops and a hedgehog.

Largest in the Ferry Fleet was the Rhino (7000 sq.ft. of deck space).

After the long gradual Approach the Beach rose up with a slope of 1 in 30. As a result the enemy were convinced that we would come with LSTs only at High Water. Instead landings were made at all states of tide by smaller Ferry Craft. When the Beach was no longer under fire LSTs could land where there were no defences on the Approach on a falling tide and wait more than an hour before their cargo could leave.

Right: An Allied air reconnaissance photograph of German beach defences around the *Gold* area. Notice the soldiers running for cover on the left. This defensive layout was typical of the obstacles emplaced along the French coast. Every assault force on D-Day had to clear a way through such defences before getting ashore; a task made no easier by the millions of mines that had also been sown (below right).

Publisher's Notes: All times given are on the 24-hour clock. Operations on D-Day were timed to double British Summer time: GMT plus two hours.

The photo was taken by a Spitfire with forward facing oblique cameras some weeks before D.Day. There were 70000 posts (similar to pit props in coal mines) eventually topped with mines. Some of the mines came adrift and it was on these that three of my Rhinos sat. Arthur Newcomb and I were on one of them about two hundred metres from the shore when it happened; we had been boat-boys together in 1935. Hedgehogs were two metal crosses joined together. These can be seen higher up on the shore.

They sailed ten miles up the coast, dodging a magnetic mine, and met up with Italian partisans to advise on navigation of the Po waters and the whereabouts of obstacles such as broken bridges and defensive cables that may have been booby trapped. Eventually they met up with Jean Caneri, a French officer under Popski's command, who planned to cross the Adige river to Chioggia under a white flag and talk the German garrison into surrender. When he landed close to Chioggia, Caneri found, to his surprise, a working public phone box. In perfect Italian he asked the operator for the German commander and was put through directly. In short, the Germans had lost their fight, and after Thomas and his men were given dinner in the garrison mess, Caneri secured the surrender of a well-equipped German force of 700 – no doubt assisted by the posed threat of blow-up tanks around Ravenna – several weeks before the German forces in Italy surrendered on 19 April. A few hours later Popski himself appeared, having just arrived from England with a beautiful chromium-plated hook to replace his left hand that had been blown off in a previous action.

Popski told the lighter crews that Canadian troops would be entering Venice from the north on the next morning, and they would enter by sea from the south. So after five years of adventure and action in North Africa, Sicily and Italy, Popski loaded his ten Jeeps into landing craft and sailed up the lagoon and round the island of San Giorgio Maggiore to moor on the gondola quay at Piazza San Marco. The Jeeps made seven circuits between the columns of the square, cheered by thousands of Venetians, and were in place to welcome the Canadians.

While Popski's Army flushed out a few remaining Germans round the lagoon, his Navy found a rusting coaster full of magnetic mines, and acquired an Aldis lamp and a 28-inch telescope from the German stockpile. Thomas remembers that, on the way into Venice, Popski said to him: 'Brian, thank you and your boys for what they've done for us. We will land all our boys in Venice, clear any, if any, Germans, and then it will all be over. There is only one way we will be going in the next few weeks and that is the Far East… now how about your unit coming with us?'

'Yes, we'll come,' Thomas said.

But Popski's Navy never went out east. After VE-Day on 8 May, 945 Inland Water Transport Company were sent to Venice, billeted on the island of San Giorgio and spent the next eighteen months running shipping on the lagoon. All finished up with military MBEs. As the war in Italy was drawing to a close, the Popski Army took 1,335 prisoners and captured sixteen field guns.

On 31 May 1940 the pleasure cruiser *Queen Boadicea II* set sail from Ramsgate for the Dunkirk beaches across the Channel with her 20-year-old skipper, Alan Spong, at the helm. The *Boadicea* was one of many 'little ships' from the Thames commandeered to rescue the British Expeditionary Force in the dark days of the Second World War. Spong, a waterman and specialist in shallow water navigation, sailed into Dunkirk harbour and was sent to the beach at La Panne to ferry troops to destroyers in deeper water. He and his crew shuttled from beach to warship for several days before returning to Sheerness in the first week of June after some narrow escapes. Once the

Alan Spong with his Dunkirk Medal

vessel next to the *Boadicea* was blown up by a direct hit, distributing body parts and wounded survivors in the surrounding water.

Sydney Ernest Albert 'Alan' Spong was the son of a ferryman in Twickenham who left school at 14 to sign on to an apprenticeship and a coastal sailing barge. He and his skipper plied the shallow harbours of the east coast with cargoes of coal or cement from the Medway. After his Dunkirk adventure he joined the Inland Water Transport Company of the Royal Engineers and was posted to the Indian Army. He learned Urdu and served in Egypt and Burma, where he was severely wounded. After the war he worked in insurance, but served in the Army Emergency Reserve and spent time removing wrecks from the Suez Canal after the 1956 fracas involving Egypt, Israel, France and Britain. He retired with the rank of major and was master of the Company in 1980. The *Queen Boadicea II* was cruising the Severn when the BBC made a documentary about Dunkirk in 2010.

Lightermen of 953 Inland Water Transport Company played a prominent part in the D-Day landings on 6 June 1944 by operating 'Rhino' ferries. These were self-propelled platforms designed to go where landing craft feared to tread. Rhinos could land tanks and vehicles on gently sloping beaches at any state of the tide. They derived their name from the conical post welded to the after deck of the rhino that docked into the outer skin of a tank landing craft's ramp. Rhinos were made by assembling 180 pontoon units in six rows, with the centre two projecting further aft to receive the landing craft's ramp. A rhino had two petrol engines mounted to allow its propellers to turn in any direction, while the prop and shaft could be raised manually in shallow water.

Once a landing craft had anchored in deep water, a rhino was attached and vehicles were driven aboard. When the rhino reached the beach, the vehicles were driven ashore via its forward ramp. A rhino could transport up to fifty tanks, Bren gun carriers or trucks at a time, and only two trips were required to empty a landing craft. Some landing craft were equipped with cots and a rudimentary operating theatre to tend to casualties brought from the beach during the return voyage across the Channel.

Major Ted Hunt was in charge of fifteen rhinos manned by 120 lightermen for the D-Day landings by British and Canadian forces on Gold beach. Each rhino was allotted eight Pioneer Corps soldiers to assist the crew, and on the outward voyage from the Solent some of the rhinos carried waterproofed bulldozers and crawler cranes whose jibs would not fit into a landing craft's hold. Hunt travelled on tank landing craft 504, an American vessel, and his crew soon learned to stick with the Americans at meal times if at all possible, since the 'Cheery oats' with maple syrup, white bread, ice cream and coffee on tap was better fare than their own 48-hour ration packs.

Another lighterman, M. F. Callen, was manning a pom-pom gun on board the destroyer *HMS Eglinton*. He described the last sight of Blighty, a huge V fashioned in lights on the fort at the tip of the Isle of Wight, and flashes of bombs at dawn in the southern sky when battleships and monitors – old warships with heavy guns – blasted away at Normandy as hundreds of paratroop gliders were towed over the coast and the sky was alight with tracers. The sea was rough for the landing craft, and he pitied the soldiers aboard them, and 'any poor sod in Havre or Cherbourg who was on the receiving end' of the 'bloody big battlewagon putting 15 inch shells ashore like there was no tomorrow'.

Major Edwin Ted Hunt MVO (Getty Images)

On D-Day, landing craft 504 anchored about a mile off shore as the rhino crew went down the scrambling nets to release the bridle and attach the 504's stern anchor and the horn to the rhino. The landing craft's ramp was already partially lowered, and the rhino was loaded in ten minutes. Beach defences consisted of rows of 'pit props', angled metal obstacles with mines attached. But sappers had cleared a hundred-feet pathway to allow rhinos to reach the shore. In six minutes – the time it took for the tide to drop six inches causing the water's edge to recede the length of a rhino – their cargo had driven up the beach.

Once the Mulberry harbour was functioning off the beach, the inland transport men also operated 'baby rhinos', half a dozen steam tugs known as TIDs. Hunt's commanding officer, Colonel Auriol Gaselee, told him that TID stood for 'tugs incredibly dirty'. Hunt said that they rolled so badly that their masts resembled the wand on a metronome. A storm that began on 19 June scattered the rhino fleet and caused a lot of damage along the beach. Lieutenant Royston was in charge of getting craft back afloat, and he constructed a causeway and floating pier from rhinos damaged beyond repair that became known as Rhino Alley. The alley enabled landing craft to dock during a three-hour period at high water, obviating the risk of ensnarement by 'pit props' and 'hedgehogs'.

The rhino squad had been asked to bivouac behind the beach at Ver-sur-Mer and survive for four days during the invasion. They stayed there, playing a vital rôle, for four months, after which they were sent to Belgium to work the canals and rivers ahead of the Second Army's advance toward Germany.

The invasion of Normandy on 6 June 1944, D-Day, involved a unit that became known as the Millionaires' Navy, recruited mainly from fishermen and Thames lightermen. The Millionaires' navy came about because Admiral Lord Louis Mountbatten, chief of combined operations for the invasion of German-occupied Europe, realised that he needed men experienced in the navigation of shallow tidal water if he was to land an army and armour on French beaches. He appealed to Ernest Bevin who, having been general secretary of the Transport and General Workers' Union until 1940, was minister of labour in the wartime coalition government. Bevin identified lightermen and fishermen as having the required skills. They were volunteers on six-month contracts, spending the first eight weeks training as able seamen with the navy, paid at the AB's generous rate of £6 per week, and promoted to petty officer or officer on completion at higher rates of pay – hence their dubbing as 'millionaires'.

Among them was Jack Gaster, an apprentice who moved up the ranks to become a navigation officer in the navy and wrote an entertaining account of his life in the millionaires' and thereafter, entitled Time and Tide. Also among them was Alfred Williams, an experienced lighterman, tug master, foreman and labour master for the firm of Mitchells who had seen service in the Dardanelles and the Somme during the First World War. He was also the father of identical twin boys, Geoffrey and Alan, born in 1930 and keenly observing what was happening around the docks from the family home at Blackheath, their school in Greenwich and their activities in the army cadets.

rhino at gold (958x458x256 jpeg)

Rhino F22 runs in to beach Jig Green to King Red at Ver sur Mer. This must have been her first run as she still has her RB 19 Crawl;er Crane aboard. Her skipper has taken up a position on top of the crane so that the two coxswains can read his hand signals.

(Major Edwin Hunt MVO)

The idea of such a unit as the Millionaires' navy was floated for the ill-fated Dieppe raid in August 1942, which itself served as a test for invading France. The aim was to capture a German-occupied French port for a short while and wreak havoc by destroying port, defence and strategic buildings, capturing equipment and gathering intelligence from prisoners. It was also designed to provide a morale boost to the French resistance and assure the Soviet Union of their allies' serious intentions of action on the western front. In the event a force of 6,000 Canadians with backup from a Canadian armoured regiment and units from the Royal Navy, Royal Air Force, Polish, American and Free French forces were routed with heavy casualties by a much smaller German defence force. Three and a half thousand Allied troops were killed, wounded or captured, 96 aircraft and 33 landing craft and a destroyer were lost. The Dieppe disaster knocked a big dent in Admiral Mountbatten's reputation.

Lightermen, many of them trained by Williams, put landing craft onto Dieppe beaches. The Dieppe raid succeeded in one thing, albeit at a heavy price. It taught lessons for Operation Overlord two years later, which was a different kettle of fish entirely. Like everyone else involved in the invasion of Normandy, the Millionaires' Navy were told nothing and required to sign the Official Secrets Act. But it was pretty plain to the tug and barge men and stevedores and dockers on the Thames that something abnormal was afoot. Apart from offloading food for the nation and victualing war ships with arms and supplies, they were towing newly-constructed concrete barges about, particularly on the Essex coast around Dagenham and Hornchurch. Alfred Williams's sons Geoffrey and Alan cycled along the Kent bank of the estuary one day wearing their cadet uniforms and came upon a vast encampment of armour, only to discover that the vast tents were empty, the tanks were mock-ups, the field guns and trucks were cardboard cut-outs. Don't talk about it to anyone, warned their father when they told of their discovery at supper that night.

Alfred Williams had resigned his commission when he was told that he was not going on the Dieppe raid because, as a veteran of the Somme, he had 'done his bit'. But in 1944 he volunteered for the Millionaires' Navy, realising from the activity in the docks that something momentous was going to happen. The millionaires' were sent to Ventnor on the Isle of Wight for training. To the initial annoyance of the Royal Navy personnel, the millionaires all knew each other and addressed each other by first names. Their job was to navigate landing craft carrying troops and armour to the French beaches, to operate 'TID tugs' that were spacious sea-worthy Admiralty vessels designed to tow steel and concrete sections of the Mulberry harbour, and to assist with the laying of another well-kept secret, the Pluto pipeline, to pump fuel over the bed of the Channel for the invasion force.

The D-Day landings were dogged by bad weather, but on the whole they went according to plan, although such a complex operation inevitably had hitches. The Mulberry harbour at Arromanches consisted of 600,000 tons of concrete between 33 jetties with 10 miles of floating roadways. While the harbour at Omaha Beach was destroyed by a storm, Arromanches landed two and a half million men, 500,000 vehicles and four million tons of supplies from deep-water vessels across the shallows in the first ten days, and remained operational for eight months. By 1945 the Pluto pipelines were supplying almost a million imperial gallons of fuel per day to the Continent, one effect being to release oil tankers from the Atlantic to the war in the Far East.

Bad weather sent Williams's friend Nobby Cruise, another Mitchells tug master, off on a near-disastrous adventure. On D-Day he opened his brown envelope and set off at the helm of his troop carrier, only to lose sight of the navy corvette escorting him. He disgorged his men onto a beach where they were alone until hundreds of German troops emerged from the dunes and began laying down their arms. Cruise had the presence of mind to agree with the German commanding officer that the allied force would withdraw, after which the Germans could recover their weapons. He sailed back to Wight, where a policeman called the Home Guard under the impression that a German force was landing. Cruise and his men landed in France a day or two later, this time where they were meant to be.

Once the Mulberry harbours were operational and the pipelines connected, most of the millionaires' work was done. The Germans, however, created a stumbling block for supreme commander Dwight Eisenhower and ground forces commander Montgomery of Alamein by blowing all the bridges of the Rhine. Thanks to that, many of the millionaire sailors saw service on the Rhine, building floating bridges and operating barges to open the Allied armies' approach to Berlin from the west.

28

FAREWELL TO
DOCKOLOGY

Business boomed on the river before and after the Second World War. With the PLA at the helm, the port and the docks remained in business until the last quarter of the twentieth century. The skills of watermen and lightermen were guarded jealously through decades of labour turbulence and the continuing struggle for a better living. High labour costs, bulk carriers, containers, floating containers, lighters berthed on ships, trains and lorries would put countless watermen, lightermen and others on the defensive, and would eventually cause trade to abandon the Pool and the Tideway and bury dockology. Oars would become redundant save for sport or ceremonial. But the skills of watermanship cling on so long as there are barges to move, tugs to move them, ferries and pleasure boats to operate and pilots to navigate the estuary.

Charles Phelps and his sons had limited formal education, but watermanship was bred into them from babyhood. Charlie's sons Edwin, Harry, Tom, Dick, Jack, Charlie and Bill were all literate and attractive men with the gift of public speaking and insight that impressed all who met them. The centre of their universe was the Putney waterfront. They were raised at a time when ferrying passengers was virtually dead, professional racing was spasmodic, and coaching work, for which many were ideally suited, was denied to them in Britain because of the caste system that separated professionals from amateurs. One of the ironies of rowing's pro-am divide and its social layers was that professional rowers and scullers travelled the world as coaches to the rivals of British amateurs.

An example is Dan Cordery, born in 1885 to a lighterman. Cordery was working on the Thames from the age of about six, claiming in later years that arthritis in his legs was caused by working on his father's barges in the rough winter months when he was a child. He became a formidable world rowing coach, spending most of his time in Germany while nurturing some of the successful German crews of the 1930s, including many Olympic champions in 1936. In 1918, however, Sergeant Cordery was skipper of the tug *Daisy*, with Charlie's son Harry of the Royal Engineers (Inland Water Transport Division) as his first mate. Together they navigated *Daisy* through the waterways of northern France while assisting in bridge building and transporting stores, mail and injured soldiers.

When Cordery returned to coaching in 1919, Harry Phelps virtually re-started his apprenticeship to his father Charlie, who was a journeyman boat builder, moving from yard to yard with the work. Charlie's long apprenticeship began with Sims, another Putney builder, and continued for five years under his elder brother, John Thomas 'Old Bossie' Phelps. Old Bossie founded his racing boat business in 1877 after beginning his working life as boatman to Leander Club. From Leander he moved along the shore to work for the renowned firm of Clasper that originated on the Tyne and migrated to Putney in pursuance of the flourishing market of amateur clubs and pleasure seekers on the Thames. Charlie won Doggett's in 1884.

Maurice Phelps, the chronicler of his family's dynasty, says that apprenticeships were notoriously poorly organised. 'The indenture documentation might have been

Previous page: The Big Freeze January 1963 (Michael Wenban)

highly formalised, but the training itself was often chaotic. Most apprentices were treated as cheap labour and were often kept as an apprentice for as long as possible. Apprenticeships were of five or even seven years duration, but often with a change of master an apprentice could remain bound for some ten years. It didn't really matter, for most young men just valued a job, and the promise of an eventual trade was everything. If you were a freeman waterman, you had a better chance of work than a labourer, and if you had to wait for the qualification it was worth it.'

Harry Phelps (centre) with the crew of the *Gull* (The Phelps Dynasty)

Years of meagre earnings encouraged the taking up of rowing wagers by those skilled in the science, and several Phelpses profited from such activity during the declining years of professional racing from the 1870s to the First World War. Old Bossie's grandsons Ted and Eric became the World and European professional sculling champions respectively. Ted became a tug skipper and Eric was employed as chauffer, handyman and sculling coach to Georg Opel of motor manufacturing fame. Several of Charlie's sons won Doggett's, and most found employment in the amateur clubs along the river.

Harry Phelps, although involved in the rowing side of things in his youth and winning Doggett's in 1919, used his strength, skill and stamina to sweep barges up and down the Thames on the tide. His long irregular hours were spent in Wapping and Bermondsey. In the 1920s and 1930s world of casual labour, favouritism was high and families often depended upon their men catching the eye of a foreman or a gang leader. Bribery, theft and violence became a normal feature of life. The dockers and their compatriots were a formidable force, independent, piratical, embittered and opportunistic when it came to opening a cargo or rifling the contents of a barge.

Harry was part of this environment, and his son Maurice took away a lasting impression of East London morality from Sunday morning outings with his father as a seven-year-old in 1943. Harry would take him to the 'roads' where the barges were moored on the Wapping side of the river below Tower Bridge. They would walk from Mark Lane station (now named Tower Hill) to St. Katharine's Way among the warehouses, and take a dinghy from the foreshore to the barges. The dinghy was usually bombarded by bricks and stones launched by small boys. 'Keep down son!' Harry would shout, then shake his fist at the ten or so boys on the wall. 'Clear off, yer little buggers!' he would shout, but the hail continued until the dinghy was out of range. After a couple of hours of pottering on the barges, Harry and Maurice set off home, stopping for a lemonade at the Tiger Tavern near the station. When they encountered their attackers, the lad who threw the first brick would greet them with 'See yer, 'Arry.'

Harry's typical response was 'Look after yerself, Tony!'

'Muvver said thanks for the wood 'Arry,' said Tony.

'That's alright son, tell 'er to keep warm!'

Harry knew everyone they met between the station and the roads. In the East End, most people were chancers, looking for a quick penny or a bit of fun, but living too close to each other to bear grudges.

Theft was rife, and Harry joined the seemingly accepted practice of lifting small gifts from cargo. One of his cargoes was fine wines from Bordeaux, and news of such travelled fast on the Thames. His barges became a popular stopping off point for lightermen and watermen when liquor was in the holds. Canvasses were skillfully laid aside, lithe men would descend to the bowels of the barge, and bottles would be handed out to eager hands. Things habitually fell overboard from barges long before they fell off the backs of lorries.

In 1927 Harry was made bargemaster of the Fishmongers' Company for a salary of £21 per year. His duties involved attending state occasions and events on the river, but his main task was to supervise and umpire the Doggett's Coat and Badge. During his term of office he witnessed four more members of his family win the one-shot race – his brother Jack, Young Bossie's sons Ted and Eric, and his nephew 'Shaking' Ted.

Late in the Second World War, Alan Lee Williams and his twin Geoffrey were apprenticed abruptly to their father Alfred at the age of 14 because they were expelled from the John Roan School in Greenwich for organising a homework strike. They began their new lives on tugs operated by the Union Lighterage Company, Alan on the *Banco* and Geoffrey on the Rio. One day both tugs were approaching Folly House when the jetty was struck by a V2 rocket. After the explosion, Geoffrey yelled: 'Is everything all right?'

'Yes, everything is,' Alan replied.

'Well, that will be the last of the rockets,' Geoffrey called.

'No, it's not, it's only just the beginning,' riposted, commenting sixty years later that his was a very perspicacious remark for a 14-15-year-old at the dawn of the new rocket era.

Alan was destined to become the second lighterman to enter Parliament, but meanwhile, the river was very busy and short of men. He spent his first two years on tugs and barges, including 'quay lighterage' to deliver consumer and bonded goods and 'rough goods lighterage' to move coal and rubbish. He also did some wreck and salvage work with the PLA. Once equipped with his two-year licence, he went to work carrying explosives from Tea Pier to Chatham for H. R. Mitchell and Sons, a small firm at Royal Arsenal. His father worked for Mitchells also. Alan always carried bread and a lump of cheese in his pocket, and a penknife, an indispensable tool for working on lighters, not only to cut the bread and cheese. 'If a sheet of a barge [the cover] blew up in your face, you may need to cut the lashing to get free.' The days were long because the tugs were underpowered, but the overtime was good, and the 16-year-old wore smart suits and hired a box for his friends for weekend shows at the Garrison Theatre, Woolwich.

Alan walked into what is now a familiar problem when he switched to Humphrey and Grey who dealt in bonded goods in the upper and lower Pool. 'It was very tricky because you tally your load in to find it inaccurate when you unloaded because of pilfering,' he says. The tally clerk would sign 'cargo said to be' to protect the lightermen. Alan was questioned by the chairman of the company about whether he took a cut. The incident gave him important lessons in dockology: don't tally from a position where you can't see, and avoid involving the police. His father told him ways of keeping the cops out of it. H R Mitchell & Sons once had a cargo of Royal Navy officers' raincoats, a fine garment subsequently adopted by most of the company's workers.

Alan was soon to learn more about dockology. In 1946-47 a political strike organised by the Canadian longshoremen's union, known as the Beaver Brae strike, spread quickly to New York and London under the rubric of solidarity. Dockers and stevedores joined in, but at first, members of the Watermen, Lightermen, Tugmen and Carmen's Union stayed at work, although some stopped unofficially. They were not necessarily against the strike, but procedures were elaborate and slow. One day Alan was putting a barge alongside a ship to jeering from strikers when soldiers appeared on board the vessel to unload it. He immediately pulled away. 'You don't necessarily have to support every strike, but you certainly don't work with troops,' he says. The big lesson was also a contradiction to him at the time. Why had he been forced to support a strike fuelled by strong unions in which communism was popular against a Labour Government that he was very keen to support? He learned that solidarity was everything in the understanding of dockology.

Despite his opposition to homework at school, was brought up listening to the BBC Home Service. He thus spoke more like a BBC announcer of the period than a river worker, and he did not swear. This, and his habit of never being without a book, anointed him with the nickname 'Shakespeare'. If it wasn't Shakespeare, it was The Professor. His experiences as an apprentice and a National Service man in the RAF (which counted towards his time on the river) sharpened his interest in socialism and nurtured a belief in a more equal society. He began to make speeches for the Labour Party outside Barclays Bank and the Railway Tavern in Blackheath, describing himself as an evangelist addressing 'four people and a dog'. A tug man in the firm's cricket team told him he'd been brainwashed.

(Michael Wenban)

In 1952 Alan became a freeman at the age of 21, was elected to Greenwich Council for a three-year term, and was offered a place at Ruskin College, Oxford. After Oxford he was successively national youth officer of the Labour Party and the United Nations Association, and in 1966 was elected Member of Parliament for Hornchurch, a marginal seat he lost in 1970 but regained in the first 1974 election and retained in the second. He was parliamentary private secretary to Denis Healey and Roy Mason during their tenures as ministers of defence. He defected to the Social Democrats in the 1980s but returned to Labour and held a number of academic and administrative posts with such bodies as the European movement, NATO and the Atlantic Council. At the time of writing he is visiting professor of politics at Queen Mary College, University of London.

Through this life of political engagement, it is evident that Alan's opinions were steeped in the left before shifting rightwards, if not to the right. His personal voyage was through the labour movement's sometimes fragile and fractious relationship with the Labour Party, intense post-war flirtation with Soviet communism and the Communist Party, inter-union strife, disillusionment, and the pull of solidarity along the quays and within the dock walls.

He observed the lighterage industry becoming much more regulated because of the way the National Dock Labour Board (NDLB) allocated labour. He realised that survival in a declining industry was only for the large, the efficient and the diverse.

Herbert Clark began working on tugs at the beginning of the Second World War. On his first morning, he gingerly descended the iron ladder down to the boat and noted that none of the tug captains wore uniform. They all wore suits. He thought it must be because they were lightermen and, by definition, rebels of society. His new skipper looked like the film star Errol Flynn. He was sent down to the cabin, via a companion way in the stern and found himself in a space 16 by 12 feet square, with lockers, a stove, table and shelves. The atmosphere was smoky, yellow poison continuously curling upwards from a crack in the top of the range. (Tea on tugs was often a pungent blend of fallout from many cargos; the stock pot might contain contributions that would confound analysis). The skylight was broken. Men in oilskins and canvas leggings were chatting, and friendly to the newcomer. He was introduced to Bert, another boy who was dressed in bib-and-brace dungarees, a railway jacket and an enormous cloth cap. Bert was to show him the ropes. He started at £1 a week.

(Michael Wenban)

The tug was the firm's day boat, its job being to hang around and undertake unexpected requirements, so they could find themselves at Tilbury Dock or Higham or Deptford or Bow Creek. The crew were young and tough, and they skylarked and fought. They all went by nicknames, and many were related. The tug mostly towed flat-bottomed barges, barges that had no point at the bow and no steering at the budget or stern, and carried 150-250 tons. Coal, sand and soap-ash were the main cargoes, and the rule specified one hand aboard the tug for every lighter under tow, with a maximum of six. They voyaged from Canvey Island to Dagenham, Silvertown and Hammersmith.

The firm employed about 80 men and ran four tugs - day boat, lift boat, London boat and creek boat - each with three crews. In addition there was a Lea crew, three molasses barges and a motor vessel, plus quay hands, roads men and a coaling station controlled by the foreman who was God Almighty. The yard had a bay for barges, three jetties and a heavy lift crane. The tugs were moored to an old wooden naval hulk, manned by three men who rotated 24 hours on and 48 hours off 'on pay'. The men went ashore in 18ft rowing boats, all standing while one man sculled over the stern - always sculled ashore, never pulled. There was a beer shop at the yard, and a tin shack 'corner shop' that sold everything. Early in the morning there was a warm smoky atmosphere in the canteen.

Clark's ship was built in King's Lynn, 100ft long in the shape of a trawler. There was a chain locker at the stem, a wheel box, boiler and engine room, aft cabin, water tank and small compartment. There were two dollies on the foredeck with a coil of three-inch sisal rope between them. The line had a loop the size of a bicycle wheel secured by a bowline and was 250 feet long. 'We would cast the eye of the line on a bollard that was quite a skill, then haul the line in,' Clark says. 'The rope was greasy and sometimes had little bits of coal in it. Milky liquid came out when it was tightened by the dolly.' The men had to know their ropes. Manila and hemp ropes absorb water and sink, but can also freeze solid when they are wet. Nylon rope was found to stretch too much and float, with danger of entanglement with propellors. The foredeck had the fore cabin scuttle, coiled line and spare ropes. There was a windlass with an anchor lashed to bulwarks behind the stem. Clark only saw the anchor used once in his time on tugs.

Tom Gillam in his memoir describes communication by bells between bridge and engine room. A double ring on a tug's telegraph, with the handle being thrown full over one way and then the other, calls for immediate maximum power, an instruction used in emergency only. Three short blasts on the siren means about to go astern; one blast, moving to starboard; two blasts to port; four short blasts followed by two long means about to turn round to port, one continuous blast means about to leave a dock. He recalls being sent forward on a foggy morning to operate the radar. What radar? The mate handed him a bag of stones.

The boys' job when picking up a craft was to put the line on, hang the fend-off between barge and tug, hand out 'spare' ropes, and give out towropes. The tugs went alongside a hulk to get coal for their boilers. The fuel came over the side in steel buckets, tipped into the bunker by a collier on the pontoon through two 16-

inch manhole covers on deck. Thus dust penetrated everywhere, and the crew prepared for this by taking the funnel down and closing down and covering all fanlights and openings. While the stoker opened the bunker doors below decks, the boy's job was to help the coal on its way by keeping the scuppers clear and washing the dust away.

Clark worked on different boats. The jetty boat was at work round the clock, and the men worked 12 hours on and 24 off. The skipper wore a bowler hat and the female cook no drawers. One of his jobs was to clean the lamp glass with cotton waste. He also spent some time on the creek boat that operated up the Lea to Bromley lock, and under the quay system, where all labour was employed on a daily basis. Under the 'rough goods' system, master colliers offered guaranteed work for a week if certain conditions were met. The shifts in the 'quay trade' were 8 a.m. – 5 p.m., with overtime rates paid for 6 - 8 a.m. and 5 - 8 p.m. 8 p.m. to 1 a.m. constituted a short night, 8 p.m. – 6 a.m. a long night.

Herbert Clark was keen to learn how to drive barges, how to 'weight' and move an oar. He was hired by a firm below Tower Bridge on the Rotherhithe side - St. George's Tier by way of St George's Stairs at Butler's Wharf - where most of the work was moving cereals from ship to wharf. There was deep water at any state of the tide in the lower Pool, and room to moor four lengths of craft about five wide. Clark's first job was to take an empty barge from Carr's bargeyard to adjacent Archers wharf. The firm's craft were in good nick and well fitted out with oars, rowing crutches, fendoffs and ropes. A 50-ton barge, called a punt, was operated by one man, while larger boats required two or three. A barge's bow is known as 'the head', stern as 'the arse', bilge pump as 'the organ', and an empty barge as a 'light'. Tarpaulins are called 'sheets' or 'cloths', and lightermen would sometimes sail barges by raising the sheet to pick up a breeze. Oars are known as 'paddles'.

There were, of course, practices and hazards peculiar to cargoes. Tom Gillam recalls the special skills required for handling logs. When a barge sinks, he says, it normally takes its cargo with it to the bottom, but this is not so with logs. Those at the top of the stowage float away. Those lower down in the hold go down with the barge until the forces of buoyancy take over, when a pole weighing several tons arises like a Polaris missile without a guidance system. Logs have their weight and length written on them, but these figures were not to be trusted because the markers often under-represented their weight to reduce dock fees. A three-ton log might actually weigh five tons. Another risky cargo, Gillam says, was rubber. If a sling was overloaded with bales and one broke free to cries of 'Greenacre', those below would witness a 'three hundredweight ball bouncing around the barges like a tennis player returning a forearm smash'.

Shooting a barge was a risky procedure whereby a lighter was delivered to a wharf where the water was too shallow for a tug. The barge was secured alongside the tug, the skipper aimed the tug at the wharf, gained speed, released the barge and went full astern. The lighterman aboard the barge cannot steer it because it has a fixed budget plate or rudder, so he must contrive to arrive at the wharf broadside on, not head on. Gillam witnessed a near disaster when his tug was shooting a barge to the wharf next door to the Prospect of Whitby, where drinkers crowded the veranda that projects from the back of the pub. The tug released a 200-ton lighter which unbeknown to the crew had a bent budget plate. It turned towards the pub and threatened to smash the piles under the veranda like skittles. The tug managed to get a line on board at the last minute and avoided disaster by a few feet. It was like a Carry On film, Gillam says.

Alan Lee Williams, tug master

Another risk was that of loaded barges being held down in deep mud by suction on an incoming tide. To avoid this, a raised shelf constructed of chalk, gravel or stones and called a campshed was constructed to extend from the shore, enabling a barge to sit level instead of sloping with the river bed.

Another specialist cargo was hay brought on spritsail barges, stacked 20ft high on the hatches. These 'stackies' required a lookout atop the hay stack to guide the blind steersman in the stern. The cargo was the food for London's thousands of horses. The sailormen, as the stackies were also known, returned with manure from London's stables to grow more hay in Kent and Essex. The mooring buoys off Woolwich were known as 'starvation buoys' because no wages were payable for sailormen crews while they waited for cargo. A skipper would row ashore in his jolly boat to receive instructions when he heard the name of his barge called out from the shore.

When Clark satisfied the semi-circle of examiners at Watermen's Hall for his two year licence, he celebrated by rowing to a pub in Wapping for lunch. In the course of his first two years, he had observed that winners of Doggett's were always kept in work. He determined to try and win it, and joined Poplar and Blackwall Rowing Club on Good Friday in 1946, the fifth year of his apprenticeship. The club contained barge-builders and shipwrights as well as lightermen, and its headquarters was an old railway station on the Isle of Dogs, with changing facilities in the former waiting room. His first outing was in an outrigger sculling whiff known as a rumtum. Smaller lads than him were faster, and he realised there was a lot to this rowing lark. He bought himself a boat, found a trainer and joined a small group of scullers who kept their boats in the yard of the White Swan at Blackwall Stairs. Despite his intentions, Clark made little progress in sculling, but he found success as an oarsman and stroke. His first win was at Barnes Regatta.

Clark described the great day when he obtained his freedom – although he was the only one who seemed to be excited. 'My master did not come with me, so I had no moral support. I went by Underground train to Monument station. It was a beautiful autumn morning as I walked through the fish market. I enjoyed dodging the fish porters' barrows as they pushed them in their tarred straw boaters and white coats. Even the smell of fish did not seem to offend.'

At the Hall he was taken upstairs by the clerk. 'I was then presented to the master and I made my petition for my freedom. When this had been granted I made my way down the stairs and pushed my way through the passage that was full of applicants for binding. When I stepped out on the pavement from Watermen's Hall, I was a fully licensed Freeman of the Company of Watermen and Lightermen of the River Thames.'

Alan Lee Williams (right), MP for Hornchurch, with Ron Ledger, MP for Romford, on his first day at Parliament, 1966

Freedom granted, Clark went to the National Dock Labour Board in the Minories to register for work in the port, for without registration he could not go to work.

The National Dock Labour Board came into existence in 1947 as an attempt to improve labour conditions. It was in charge of registering, paying and allocating jobs in the port and providing medical care for the workers, but it did not do away entirely with the call-on system of casual labour. Even though Ernest Bevin, the general secretary of the National Transport Federation, had secured a 16-shillings-a-day 44-hour week in 1920 and earned himself the title of 'Dockers' KC', industrial strife continued unabated over wages, conditions and demarcation. When the government decided to end decasualisation in 1967 – a time when the docks of St. Katharine's, London, East India and the Regents Canal were already closed for business – there was widespread opposition from the rank and file and a massive strike, followed by a hundred industrial disputes in the docks over the next two years. Pallets, containers, roll-on-roll-off took their toll, and the numbers of registered workers dropped to 12,000.

Fewer and fewer vessels were 'bound up' on the flood tide or 'bound down' on the ebb through the 'bridge holes' (arches). The business of locking in was no more (imagine the dialogue when a lockmaster inquired the names of Messrs. Whitehair's tug *Weno* pulling the barges *Ino* and *Uno*). The skills of handling bales, bags, casks

The Royal Victoria Dock (Michael Wenban)

and barrels ebbed with the tides, and with them the traditions and the language of dockology. No longer would men talk of garbling (sorting and grading of spices), nor of sucking the monkey (siphoning off a 'waxer' or illicit taster from a barrel of spirit or wine), nor yell 'Greenacre' (a warning when cargo shot from a strop or sling to the quay). Soon even the Bovril boats (sludge waste, i.e. sewage) would go to the breaker's yard.

No longer would men chase bunnies (rats) or stand hard (a warning to hold on to something when another vessel came alongside), nor deal in briefs (the return half of a return rail ticket). Dockology, and the worlds of Charlie and Harry Phelps, of Alan Lee Williams, of Herbert Clark, of Tom Gillam floated off like a Thames trout (used condom), seeping into the great container of folk memory.

PART 3
THE COMPANY IT KEEPS

29
DOGGETT HAS HIS DAY?

The question facing the Watermen and Lightermen's Company of the River Thames in the twenty-first century is whether, from its hall that harbours traditional interests and influences in the heart of the City at St Mary-at-Hill, it remains fit for purpose. Is there a future in the Company's time-honoured apprenticeship scheme if the scheme is no longer a compulsory passport to working the Thames? Can its charities be tailored to the diminished needs of its shrinking number of parishioners? Does Doggett's Coat and Badge have a future life in the worlds of watermen and rowing?

Doggett's reached its fourth century in 2015. It is owned by the Worshipful Company of Fishmongers, but it belongs to the watermen who work the river and row the race. It remains the oldest continuous sporting event in Britain, having been contested by men in their first year of freedom every year since 1715. The switch to racing with the tide and the introduction of heats to enable the best to contest the final in 1873 gave the race its modern form, together with the move from heavy wherries to fine racing boats by 1907.

Measures have been taken to ensure the continuation of Doggett's in the face of the declining number of apprentices and freemen of the Company. Since 1988 the race has been open to unsuccessful prior competitors for a second, and if again unsuccessful, third shot. Amateur status is safeguarded, and Claire Burran became the first woman to compete in Doggett's in 1992. The fastest time to date from London Bridge to Chelsea is 23 minutes 22 seconds, set by Bobby Prentice when he won the race in 1973. At the time of writing, Prentice is umpire of the race in his capacity as barge master to the Fishmongers' Company, and he was also master of the Watermen's Company for 2013-14.

Doggett's marked its place in the rowing world during the twentieth century by producing a succession of internationals. The professional sculling champions Ernest Barry and Bert Barry won their coats and badges in 1903 and 1925 respectively, the former narrowly avoiding interference by coal barges floating on the turning tide. Martin Spencer (1970), Ken Dwan (1971), Chris Drury (1975), Simon McCarthy (1984) and Ross Hunter (2006) became internationals, and other competitors have rowed for their clubs at a high level. Winners have also made their mark in other ways. William East (1887) became King's Bargemaster to Edward VII and George V. Bob Crouch, who won in 1958, is one of five Doggett's winners in the past hundred years to become bargemaster to the royal watermen, the others being Tom Phelps, Ernie Barry, Bert Barry and Ken Dwan. Dick Pocock of Eton (1910) emigrated to Vancouver with his younger brother George and eventually became boatman to Yale University, while George founded the Pocock boatbuilding business at the University of Washington in Seattle. The brothers learned their trade under their father Aaron at Eton. Dick built the eight that Yale used to win the 1924 Olympics in Paris, and George the eight in which Washington University won the 1936 Olympics in Berlin.

Doggett's continued to be dogged by interference. In 1890 Bates got stuck under Victoria Pier at Battersea after 'a most unsportsmanlike course' by sculling directly

Previous page: 296th Doggett's winner (Daniel Arnold) by Jonathan Parker (Private Collection)

in front of the eventual winner, Sanson. In 1891 William Barry of Victoria Docks won the race while Crawley of Limehouse had his boat broken in two before being rescued by the spectator craft which were responsible for his fate. In 1898 Arthur Carter of Greenwich won amongst interference by tugs 'including one of the Thames Conservancy's.' At one stage he suffered a crest of water breaking over his head.

In 1901 Alfred Brewer of Putney won after almost hitting the pier of Cannon Street Railway Bridge. The second and third men collided two or three times, early in the race: 'Henry Webb narrowly avoided Hungerford Bridge, while James Bowering capsized by turbulence near tunnelling works near Waterloo and finished sixth,' said the report.

The usual complaint of spectator boats interfering with the stragglers took place after Dick Pocock's race in 1910: 'Such lack of consideration was unfortunate and irresponsible and one can only admire the courage, skill and determination of the scullers who had also to contend with the everyday commercial traffic of the river which made no concessions to the competitors,' said the report.

James Bone, soon to become London editor of the *Manchester Guardian*, wrote an account of Pocock's race for his paper that captures the spirit of Doggett's:

'Our compliment on the good steamer *Pepys* was partly made up by coalmen from Erith, bargees from Limehouse, rough riderhoods, and other riverside characters. Five aquatic bookmakers were in attendance, and on the inviolate Thames fearlessly shouted the odds in the beard of a pier policeman. Pocock of Eton, Joe Becket of Lime'us, Young Jeffries of Erith, and Rough of Putney were the fancied ones, and Gibson and Bland were the odds you liked. Pocock, however, was the big favourite, and he showed himself the winner from the first, his big long body in dark green getting clean away at the start.'

Pocock had indeed taken the race seriously, sculling ten miles a day at Eton with his brother George. Two weeks before the race they sculled down to London Bridge, stored their boats in a shack near the bridge, and tackled the Doggett's course every day.

'Everyone agreed that no man could wish for to see a better race till the day he died,' Bone continued. 'Off went Pocock in the centre of the river, tossing the spray as high as his head before he steadied to it. Becket, in white, was close behind, and Rough next. Pocock shot Southwark Bridge well ahead, with the river fairly clear before him, the steamers hurrying well behind, and dodging round a couple of dumb barges with sweeps out, he went through Blackfriars easily. In the long stretch to Waterloo the race came on a fleet of seven sail of compressed hay well in the fairway, and just at Waterloo we saw that Rough had slipped inside of them, and in smoother water was shooting the south-most arch of the bridge at the same time as Pocock.

'High on the bridge of the *Queen Elizabeth*, which carried a worshipful of Fishmongers, stood a man in a cocked hat with a port-wine coat and light blue trousers and a gold badge like a tray on his arm. He was the bargemaster of the company and the father of Pocock, yet never once did he run down any of his son's rivals, nor give them his wash more than is customary. Pocock won by half a dozen lengths in 33 minutes, and he could turn up a river before he lifted his 6 feet 3 inches of young manhood into the launch. Jeffries and Gibson, who had kept within three lengths of one another for half the course, making spurt after spurt and reducing even the coalmen to speechlessness, so that they couldn't in the end say, *Dig, it, boy – dig it – dig it, my bully boy – hoorah*, had to be taken from their boats. The giant young waterman had rowed them out.'

A hundred years on, Richard Williams in reporting the 2013 race in the Guardian remarked that it is typical that one competitor, 21-year-old Harry McCarthy, should be the son of a previous winner. His father Simon triumphed in 1984 and his uncle Jeremy won in 1992. Harry was successful in 2014, taking an early lead in a well-judged race. The winner in 2012 was Merlin Dwan whose father, uncle and cousin have won during the past forty years. The Barrys have notched up four winners, and the Phelpses ten.

McCarthy is the Company's rowing officer, responsible for promoting and commending sculling and rowing to apprentices. Basically, his job is to preserve Doggett's and save it from changes that would alter its nature. He says: 'It's the hardest race I've ever rowed in, and that just comes from the pressure that's put on by the river fraternity. I've rowed harder races internationally, physically. But mentally, Doggett's was the hardest race. People race it for their family, and you're winning it for the family name. I was more scared on the start than at the world championships - confident, but scared of losing. '

He advises people contemplating Doggett's to go and talk to the people who haven't won. 'The losers have had to live with it all the days of their lives. They have to go to work every day alongside people who have raced against them. I raced my cousin and my best mates. It's all family-orientated, very incestuous.'

There is, however, more to Doggett's than that. It has several problems. One is that, despite its procession through central London and the pageantry of the launches and steamers following the scullers, it is unexciting for casual spectators. To the rowing fraternity it is exciting, but it is merely a footnote of sporting history to those outside it. A sculling race over five miles has none of the cachet of the Oxford and Cambridge Boat Race. It is usually done and dusted in the first five minutes of a struggle that you are lucky to glimpse unless you are following it afloat.

Secondly, its relevance to the art and science of watermanship can be questioned in a century when the only oars seen on the river are competitive or ceremonial. Thirdly, Thomas Doggett's will long ago ceased to cover the Fishmongers' considerable costs in running the race. The costs are considerable. The scarlet uniform and silver badge account for several thousand pounds, and the steamers and lunch for guests is a generous provision, not to mention the dinner later in the year to acclaim the winner.

Thus the working group on Doggett's, chaired by McCarthy, faces awkward questions. The race was a good investment for the Fishmongers' Company when they bought into it. It became part of their heritage. They don't want to lose it, but

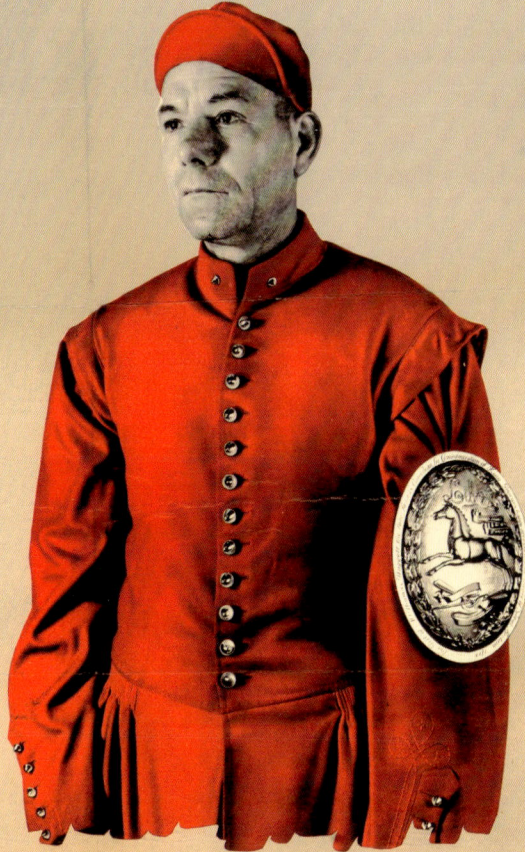

MAY 9·
SEPT 29
1951

DAILY
10 to 8

SOUTH BANK
PAST AND PRESENT
— EXHIBITION —

The County Hall·Westminster Bridge

Admission 1s. · Children 6d.

Poster for South Bank Past and Present Exhibition in 1951 featuring Thomas James Phelps, the 1922 winner of Doggett's Coat and Badge (London Rowing Club) Thomas James Phelps was Bargemaster to the Watermen's Company from 1962 to 1968.

they would like to find partners to help pay for it. One of their proposals was to turn it around, starting in Chelsea and running with the tide to Fishmongers' Hall beside London Bridge, where guests could watch the finish. McCarthy had to point out that the most exciting part of the race, almost without exception, is the start.

Jostling for a good start under London Bridge and powering off towards Southwark Bridge is a lot more exciting than waiting at Chelsea for scullers to cross the line several minutes apart. By turning the race round, spectators would miss the excitement of the start.

Five members of the Dwan family, all winners of Doggett's Coat and Badge Wager, on duty at Fishmongers' Hall.
From Left: Nicholas (2002), Ken (1971), Merlin (2012), John (1977) and Robert (2004)
(Photograph by Phil Bourguignon)

'If you turn it round, it's not the Doggett's Coat and Badge,' McCarthy says. 'It is something brand new. What is it that we are selling? The thing about Doggett's is that it's the oldest annual sporting event. Someone in the City may like to buy into a 300-year old tradition, so why change it?' The watermen are not opposed to sponsors, but they would not like to see a sponsor's name hyphenated to the name Doggett. There are other ways of acknowledging sponsors, like naming boats after them.

Happily, over the months in which this book was written, the Fishmongers have taken on board the watermen's view of the nature of the race, and are working towards giving it a higher profile. In 2013 they began a three-year sponsorship with Thames Water, the water supply company that is about to construct an enormous Thames Tideway tunnel to upgrade the nineteenth century sewage system built by Sir Joseph Bazalgette. The project will also create employment on the river in construction and transport of materials. The Fishmongers have also teamed up with the charity London Youth Rowing to run a competition on rowing machines outside Fishmongers' Hall on Doggett's day. Competitors are teams from boroughs that flank the course.

So as Thomas Doggett's race reaches its 300th birthday, Simon McCarthy and the men in red coats express optimism about the future. But McCarthy is also a realist. He says that the race would survive if financial support floundered because the Doggett's winners themselves would find enough money for the annual coat and badge.

Even this riches-to-rags scenario would fail if it fell below the bottom line. 'The bottom line,' he says, 'is that we must go on producing apprentices. If the flow of apprentices dries up, so will Doggett's.'

GEORGE·S·ELGOOD

30

ALMS AND THE
WATERMEN

The Company has been involved in a mesh of charitable work since the seventeenth century. In the late 1900s it set about rationalising its charities, a move that led to the creation of the Royal Benevolent and Educational Fund for Watermen and Lightermen of the River Thames that attends to three interests – the old, the young, and Watermen's Hall.

Provision for watermen in straightened circumstances began with Henry VIII who erected almshouses at St Stephen's, Westminster, in 1545, close by the royal wool staple where watermen were employed as porters. The eight houses were close to the spot where William Caxton set up his printing press. They were rebuilt in 1735 when Westminster Bridge was constructed, and by 1824 had been replaced by baths and washhouses for inhabitants of the parish. Evidence suggests that watermen acted as vergers at Westminster Abbey in the sixteenth century. The dean and chapter gave a dozen watermen a purple robe every second year and paid them an annual stipend of £7:2s:4d, plus other amounts on burial of dukes, marquesses, earls and barons or their ladies.

In 1626 the Lord Mayor prescribed that any person of the Company who fell into extreme poverty, age or disability or was maimed in military service shall receive a weekly sum of 18 pence, to be paid by the Company. This was extended to widows in 1662. In January 1684 a large sum was distributed to poor watermen to alleviate frost distress, and money was given to poor freemen whose houses were destroyed in the great fire at Wapping on 19 November 1682. Payments are recorded after many occasions when the Thames was frozen for extended periods.

In 1684 Thomas Martyn left his estate in Putney for a school for sons of free watermen in the area. It catered for twenty boys aged 7 to 16. who were given a complete suit of clothing and an extra pair of trousers each year. In 1888 the Company agreed to supply two governors. The school was eventually demolished to make way for the District Railway's branch line from Putney Bridge to Wimbledon.

In 1608 there is reference to a ferry being set up by watermen between Cold Harbour and Bankside, but such ferries appear to have been roads on ice when the river froze. A milestone in poor law was passed in 1705 when an Act of Parliament established Sunday ferries to finance the relief of 'those miserable subjects, hundreds of whose fathers, husbands or children had been either killed or maimed in the Royal Navy.' A small number of watermen were appointed 'to convey persons across the river on Sundays, applying the profits arising thereby to the maintenance of the aged and decayed watermen and widows of watermen.'

The Sunday ferries, which long enjoyed a monopoly of movement on the Sabbath, were the subject of immunity from navy press gangs, recompense for loss of livelihood whenever a bridge was built and frequent disputes over who could rightfully operate them. One such argument took place in 1729 when agreement was reached that the manning of the ferry from Westminster to Stangate was agreed to alternate between Westminster chestmen and Company watermen. A similar agreement was made in 1742 between the Company and the Westminster Society for the Horseferry.

Previous page: Watermen's and Lightermen's almshouses at Penge by George Samuel Elgood 1851 – 1943 (Watermen's Hall Collection)

Mrs Grimmett, headmistress of the Watermen's School of the Thomas Martyn Foundation, entertained by her former pupils. (The Phelps Dynasty)

The Company history records that the rector of Poplar possessed a paper stating that John Fell willed four houses for poor watermen in Blackwall in 1742, but no further information was found. Another mystery occurred in 1826 when the search for the will of Sir Martin Bowers, a sixteenth century Lord Mayor, was unsuccessful. It was thought to bequeath alms houses in Woolwich to the Company.

The Company came around to consider providing an asylum for its poor in 1808. Donations and land were sought, and in 1839 John Dudin Brown gave two acres of land in Penge for the erection of thirty almshouses. By 1851 there were terraced houses, an asylum endowed by Queen Adelaide, and a church dedicated to St. John had been constructed. Queen Victoria and Prince Albert, together with the Duke of Northumberland, were patrons. More houses were added in 1895 at what was now known as Watermen's Square. The square has a retaining wall with three entrances, each having pillars surmounted by a pair of griffins. There are sixteen houses with the chapel adorned by arms and the inscription TREU UND FEST (Faithfully and Firmly) as centrepiece. The left hand castellated tower has a sundial and the right a clock. There are a dozen houses on a second plot across the street from St. John's church that stands on the corner of Penge High Street and St. John's Road and was enlarged in 1866.

The Company's tenure of the almshouses – the latest thing in modernity when they opened – lasted until 1973 when the residents were transferred to a new campus at Hastings. A granite obelisk still marks the foundation at Penge, its inscription stating:

Monument erected by the Worshipful Company of Watermen and Lightermen of the River Thames in memory of the late JOHN DUDIN BROWN Esq

Many years a member of their court
And president of this asylum
In recognition of his magnificence in
Giving the land on which it is erected
… his liberality in aiding
this establishment and endowment
and of the constant care and nurturing
zeal with which he watched over and
promoted its interest and welfare
and of the great regard evinced by
many… occasions for the comfort
and happiness of its inmates
1855

This unique reference, set in stone, to the Company being 'Worshipful', is presumed to be either poetic licence on behalf of the mason, or a subtle attempt to award the Company livery status. The Penge site, listed but no longer fit for purpose, was sold to London County Council when the Company moved to its present site in the St. Leonard's Park area of Hastings in 1972. The estate at Hastings was acquired from the Anderson family who had connections with the Peninsular & Orient company, and is set in lovely gardens on the rise of a hill overlooking the old town and the English Channel. Twenty-six bungalows and a community hall and chapel were erected there for retired watermen and lightermen. By 2013 demographic change meant that fewer than half of the tenants are watermen, so bugaloes are let to outsiders on six-month tenancies through Hastings Borough Council. Their rates go towards maintenance costs of the dwellings.

Martin Hackett, whose father was warden in Penge, fulfils the rôle at Hastings. He supervises two full-time gardeners and is responsible for maintenance and modifications of the bungalows that have good-sized kitchens, living rooms, bedrooms, bathrooms and a terrace, and low windows so that residents can sit and look out on the grounds. There is a green that doubles for bowling or putting, mature trees, garden benches – one of which sports the legend 'Nobody's perfect except the captain' – and extensive badger runs and setts. There are wild flowers, multiple vegetable patches, bird tables and bird baths, and an aviary containing a European eagle owl that can raise an alarm when required.

Hackett sees his job as keeping an eye out for people in trouble, and making sure they seek or get help when necessary. Social life is run by a committee of residents and comprises classes in painting and line dancing, bingo and Sunday morning drinks-with-argument, and visits to places of interest and entertainment. The chapel has services on high days and festivals and – a nice touch this – doubles as games and snooker room. There is a good library with books supplied by residents. There is also a weekly minibus to a supermarket.

In 1897 a bequest from the Vokins family gave the Company twelve cottages at Ditchling, Sussex. Vokins & Co. was a large lighterage company with additional business interests in nearby Brighton. The benefactor requested his widow to pick up maintenance costs, but she 'was far from receptive to the idea,' saying that she had 'not any intention of taking any interest in the Ditchling cottages'. The Company nevertheless accepted the terms of the will in 1890. The problem with the imposing terrace at Ditchling is that the units are large, with high ceilings and big windows and lots of awkward stairs. They were not designed as almshouses and there are no extra facilities on site. When Hastings opened, watermen residents of Ditchling were gradually relocated there, and so by 2013 the Ditchling houses were all occupied by third parties. When the time is thought to be right to sell them, the proceeds will go into the Company's charity coffers.

Almshouses Benevolent Fund for Watermen and Lightermen banner made by George Tutill c1817–1887 (photo taken after restoration)

The Royal Benevolent and Educational Fund for Watermen and Lightermen of the River Thames was born on 1 July 2011. The date marks the rationalisation of purpose and re-packaging of all the Company's charities. Together with the Watermen's Hall Preservation Trust, it is known as the Watermen and Lightermen Charities. The Company is trustee of the combined charities, the Charity Commission scheme of 1 July 2011 governs the benevolent and educational fund, whilst the hall trust continues under its original declaration of trust of 10 November 2003.

The object is relief to persons in need due to age, ill health, disability or financial hardship by provision of financial assistance, advice, guidance, counselling, provision or assistance with accommodation, nursing care etc.; education and training, including skills associated with use of inland and estuarial waterways and in the history and traditions of the Company; provision of alms house accommodation for beneficiaries in need, hardship or distress.

The beneficiaries, in order of priority, are freemen and widows, widowers, children, other dependants, others working as watermen or who have worked as watermen or lightermen or in associated trades on or near the Thames; others in associated trade or occupation on inland and estuarial waterways in England; persons intending to work on or near the River Thames as watermen, lightermen or associated occupations.

Several steps led to this rationalisation. In May 2000 three separate charities concerned with the alms houses – Home Cottages, Henry Barry and Royal Watermen's and Lightermen's Asylum - were amalgamated to form the Royal Cottage Homes for

Almshouse cottages at Hastings (Martin Hackett)

Watermen and Lightermen. The scheme provides that almshouses at Ditchling and Hastings are used for accommodation for poor, aged freemen of the Company of good character, or their widows or widowers. The amalgamation also provided that proceeds of the future sale of the Ditchling cottages will be invested in trust for the charity unless otherwise directed by the Charity Commission. No such power of sale applies to the Hastings cottages.

Other amalgamations also took place in 2000. The Charles Willis charity and the Company's general benevolent fund formed the Benevolent Fund of the Company, income and some capital being applied for relief of 'freemen, widows, widowers and children who are in conditions of need, hardship or distress by making grants of money or providing or paying for items, services or facilities calculated to reduce need, hardship or distress.'

The Benevolent Fund is administered with the Company's Poor's Fund, set up in 1700 by Act of Parliament. An 1845 Act says that funds are to be applied to use of the poor, aged, decayed and maimed watermen and lightermen of the Company and their widows, and both capital and income can be expended for purposes of the charity.

Philip Henman
(Watermen's Hall
Collection)

The Philip Henman Foundation, under a declaration of trust in 1995, provides income and capital for education and training of persons who are making or intend to make a career in business or activity on or beside the Thames, or for encouragement of after-school education and training for persons, freemen or apprentices of the Company engaged or intending to be engaged in the Port of London lighterage industry. It also provides for other such charitable purposes in relation to the Thames or any other river in the UK where the aforesaid objects are deemed to be compatible.

Philip Henman began his career as a clerk in a City office before acquiring a barge in the early 1960s. His company grew into the Transport Development Group with twenty tugs, eight hundred barges and farming interests in Surrey. The foundation's assets were transferred to the Benevolent Fund in July 2011.

In 2000 two of the Company's past masters, James Johnson and John Allan, formed a working party to set up the Watermen's Hall Preservation Trust, which came into being four years later. The trust raises funds to keep the hall in the manner to which it is accustomed, encourages public access to the hall and advances knowledge of its history, art, furniture, artefacts and collections to the world at large (see Chapter 32).

31
FIT FOR PURPOSE?

If Doggett's cannot survive without a steady supply of apprentices, can the Company survive without Doggett's? The question is unthinkable. Doggett's men will fight to preserve their race by hook or by crook. But the really important question facing the Company is: would you invent it if it didn't exist? Can it assert and adapt the apprenticeship system that it was born to run so that it is fit for a further five centuries of purpose?

The hands-on approach to acquiring the 'local knowledge' requirement for the Tideway through central London has been under threat ever since a European Union directive transferred the granting of boatmasters' licences from the Company on behalf of the PLA to the Maritime and Coastguard Agency (MCA) in 2007. Yet traffic, although far from the glory days before the closure of the docks, is buoyant at a time when London has rediscovered its waterway as a commuter route and a tourists' channel.

It is easy to forget that he death of the docks did not result in complete closure of the Thames as a working waterway. The inevitable departure of big ships and strings of lighters wrecked thousands of jobs and tolled the death of bad labour relations. But in the interregnum between abandonment of the port and transformation of the river to a commercial, residential and tourism artery, lightermen's work continued in waste and construction industries, whilst passenger traffic for tourists and commuters increased. The Thames is transforming itself from the foggy bustling backwater of empire towards the misty, Grand Canal of dappled water and City palaces that it once was. Forty years after the demise of dockology, London enjoys millennium bridges, Thames festivals, Jubilee pageants and the Lord Mayor back on the water for his annual charity show. We have the Tate Modern, the South Bank halls, the O2 arena, the London Eye Ferris wheel, the Docklands Museum and the Thames Walk. We have the Docklands Light Railway and new piers linked by Thames Clippers. A cable gondola service floats in the air between Greenwich peninsular and the Royal Docks, and Blackfriars railway station now spans the river, giving access to both banks.

While the London Docklands Development Corporation (1981-1999) was bringing a new life and new look to Docklands, the folk of Watermen's Hall and stakeholders of the river agitated for workable commercial schemes.

Transport on Water (TOW) was set up as a campaign group in 1974 when seven shop stewards met in the Aberfeldy pub in Poplar. The meeting was called when the secretary of the Transport and General Workers' Union's waterways trade group, Bill Lindley, suggested that the modernised 24-hour shift system in the docks created an opportunity for the work force to sell the advantages of the river and canals for commercial transport, and an opportunity to educate the public and the media about existing skills that could be used. At the same time John McSweeney, one of the founders, organised a barge-driving race from Tower Pier to Greenwich that pioneered the annual race from Greenwich to Westminster.

The aims were to reverse the decline in commercial water-borne traffic on the nation's rivers and canals, promote the advantages of water-borne transport, encourage retention of old skills and adapt them to improved technology, to press for a national

Previous page: Court of Bindings ceremony c1960 (Watermen's Hall Collection)

coordinated transport plan, to obtain financial support and promote water-borne transport in the regeneration of London.

TOW took off. People and organisations with an interest in the river and its potential signed up, including academics, lawyers and environmentalists. Donations from watermen covered administrative costs. The Transport and General, whose general secretary was Jack Jones, made a contribution, and the PLA offered office accommodation. In 1975 a meeting at Watermen's Hall officially inaugurated TOW, with Alan Lee Williams, then MP for Upminster and Hornchurch and a freeman of the Company, elected chairman.

Williams had called for an inquiry into the lighterage industry in his maiden speech in the Commons in 1966, and the new organisation set out to allay fears that TOW would attempt to usurp the role of unionists, employers or the Company. Williams and the council, which included Nigel Spearing, MP for Newham South, John Wells, MP for Maidstone, marine barrister Laszlo Kovats and Bill Lindley, the former general secretary of the watermen and lightermen's union, set out on a course of cooperation with other parties to promote commercial opportunities. Jack Jones and Lord Aldington, chairman of the PLA, were invited to be presidents.

The PLA shared TOW's strong belief that use of the river should be maintained, and good relations were formed through this common purpose. TOW proved to be an effective pressure group. Jack Faram galvanised parties interested in the construction of the enormous One Canada Square skyscraper at Canary Wharf on the Isle of Dogs, designed by the architect Cesar Pelli. Negotiations to use barges for removal of spoil and supply of building materials with owners Olympia & York and its chairman Paul Reichmann took place on Sundays to satisfy religious considerations. The tower opened in 1991, the tallest building in Britain then at 235 metres, but it was not fully tenanted for fifteen years. TOW realised the importance of City Airport (whose flight path caused five floors to be deducted from One Canada Square) and supported it when many local people opposed its development. The Ford Motor Company was persuaded to keep its jetty at Dagenham functioning, and TOW ensured that the lock entrances to the main docks remained open. The Royal Docks are thus still accessible to large ships. TOW also backed the PLA's efforts to continue use of the lower reaches, the current manifestation of which is the 1,500-acre London Gateway container port under construction at the Shell refinery site, with a two-mile container quay. The animosities between craft-owning freemen and journeymen freemen which existed before TOW, evaporated, and the Company welcomed two members of TOW – John Potter and Alan Lee Williams – as honorary court assistants.

The barge race was a footnote to the aims of TOW, but was nevertheless an inspired idea, keeping lightermen's traditional skills in the limelight as Doggett's does for watermen. It showcases the traditional skills of moving lighters under oars. Five-man crews of freemen and apprentices of the Company use their strength, experience and the tide to navigate lighters with 20-feet sweep oars. No more than three crewmembers can row at any time, two at the forward end manning the sweeps and one in the stern steering by oar. To complete the course from Greenwich to Westminster successfully, each crew must collect a pennant from barges anchored along the course. This tests manoeuvrability and sometimes leads to a ducking as barges jostle for position. Prizes are awarded for the overall winner, the fastest small and large barges, the various stages and the best-dressed crew and decorated barge. A flotilla of pleasure boats gives chase, and hundreds watch the race from banks and bridges.

Tim Keech, the Company's training officer in 2013 responsible for the apprentice programme, points out that the 1555 Act that set up the Company refers to watermen having to work for a year with another before taking passengers on their own. 'We are still using peer training, an apprentice working with a practitioner to develop practical skills, strongly weighted towards individual ability to manage a vessel.' Vessels are getting larger and carrying out more diverse tasks. Training has to keep pace with new navigation systems, new technology and new propulsion systems, so that simulation on computers is now part and parcel of learning skills.

Passenger-carrying is growing, accounting for around 85 per cent of the work on the Tideway. The Thames clippers and tourist boats carry six million people a year between them, and the aim is to double that figure. Towing and civil engineering accounts for the rest, with the latter also on the increase. Recent developments that bring work to the river include the reconstruction of Blackfriars Railway Bridge. Earth from Crossrail's tunnels is transported by water to a bird sanctuary on the River Crouch. Work will start on excavating a massive new sewage tunnel, the Thames Tideway Tunnel, from Acton to outfalls at Beckford and Crossness in 2016.

All this means that there is opportunity to maintain the Company's training scheme and take it further. 'The realistic goal for us is to continue to do what we are doing. We would like to see the MCA share our examiners for passenger vessels and towing, where we are market leaders,' Keech says. Accident statistics say that our training is really working. Incidents are very small in number.' He also points out that the Company courses are recognised by the Royal Yachting Association and the merchant navy, and represent 'a fairly seamless route through to master of the *Queen Mary*'.

The current scheme awards a boatmasters' licence after two years, enabling an apprentice to drive a small workboat or a launch carrying up to twelve passengers. A further three years (and reaching the age of 21) qualifies a boatmaster for a full licence that allows him or her to take charge of tugs and barges, general and dangerous cargos and passenger vessels, and applies to 19 miles of the Tideway between the Thames Barrier and Putney Bridge.

Keech is a firm believer in the value of traditional skills. 'I learned more about the river from the seat of a sculling boat than at the wheel of a tug or passenger boat. It's still the best place to learn. Close to the surface.' Barge driving is also recognised as giving a feel for tides. 'On a daily basis people get into difficult situations where training in an unpowered vessel would be helpful.' he says. He says that for apprentices, rowing is almost compulsory. 'Very few don't give it a shot, whether it's the Great River Race, the Tudor Pull, and then Doggett's. We are proud of the heritage of Doggett's; it's at the centre of what we do to preserve a race for young watermen in their first year of freedom. It needs them to survive. All these things – Doggett's and sculling, barge driving, charities, apprenticeship and education are component

Her Majesty's Bargemaster, Paul Ludwig, and royal waterman, Robert Prentice, accompany the crown coach at the State Opening of Parliament 25 May 2010. (Photograph by Stephen Worsfold)

parts of a bigger deal.' Thus speaks the Company's training officer, in tune with the Company's rowing officer.

John Redmond, who was master in 2012-2013 and who worked for the Thames Conservancy before becoming chairman of Thames Clippers (Transport for London's passenger ferry contractor) says that the challenge is to keep the Company focussed on a clear objective. 'I always put the river first; what's good for the river is good for the Company.' This is reflected in its aims, which can be summarised as to maintain the Company's place at the forefront of the working life of the River Thames and to bring to bear its skill, knowledge and experience towards assuring the safe and healthy future of the river; to develop its activities and use its assets to ensure that best use is made of the opportunities presented by the changing needs of the river; to undertake its duties as required by its statutes and other legislation and to ensure that it has the powers needed to fulfil its aims; and to encourage active participation in and recognition of the work of the Company.

In addition, the Company's key objectives include the management of an apprenticeship and training scheme for those wishing to work on the Thames or inland waterways, to encourage rowing, barge driving and other skills and to maintain a flow of qualified competitors for the Doggett's Coat and Badge wager.

'Broadly, safety is number one,' Redmond says, 'ensuring a safe and healthy future for the river. The old system was that the Company licensed watermen and was paid a fee by the PLA. It wasn't a closed shop but its operations were opaque to outsiders. Since the advent of the boatmasters' license, the continuing challenge for the Company is to re-position itself with the PLA, looking at its role in training, qualifications, education, and examination.

'The Company is seen as a place of huge relevance by the PLA, City Hall, Transport for London and people involved in the river. It's a centre of expertise, or certainly of opinion, where you get a spread of ideas and thoughts from a very expert bunch, without being a trade association, a trade union or a closed shop. It's there because it's there, and it's a good network still.'

The frustration of the training programme, particularly a European-driven programme, is that the Company believes that a high level of local knowledge is required on the Thames. 'The Maritime and Coastguard Agency (MCA) took on the mantle, but they are big ship men, not inland waterways people,' Redmond says. 'They are learning the hard way and it is a tiny fraction of their job. There is almost an admission on their part that their tests and required skills are not as good as many of our tests and required skills. They have flattened the playing field, making it more above board, but there are fewer local experts setting the syllabus and doing the marking, so that the test as now applied is not as good as the old Company one. They say local knowledge starts at Putney. We say it starts at Teddington and goes down to the 'Ness', covering all of the tidal river.' Even though, as he points out, the working life of an individual is usually limited to one stretch and to either cargo or passenger boats.

The Company also brings added value. Once you are a freeman, whether a craft-owner or a journeyman, you are amongst your peers. 'That river family is a very important network, and a good comfort factor. It holds you in good stead in moving round other parts of the river and employers. You are carrying a very special *curriculum vitae*. This is a rôle assumed by the river community, not a legal requirement, but accepted by it as a good place to be. It's your reference point. That's very important,' Redmond says.

His view is that this is the cement holding the Company together. 'Much time is spent on training, and it's expensive. The time taken to progress from making tea to skippering a passenger ship is now much shorter than it used to be. Many of the required skills have changed; you need to demonstrate knowledge of meteorology, chart work, basic waterborne skills above and beyond rope handling and steering. We have weight of numbers, and we still have clout. We influence the syllabus, we tier it up through the Maritime Skills Alliance.'

As the Company moves into its sixth century, he concludes: 'we should be key players in the system. We must persuade others to delegate powers down the line. We must rebuild our position by becoming an approved education and examination body and be recognised, financially and politically, for the expertise we can bring to bear on the safe and healthy future of the River Thames. We need recognition for our influence.'

2012 Barge Race (Photograph by Christopher Dodd)

The bottom line, then, is that after five hundred years the Watermen and Lightermen's Company of the River Thames is poised between purpose and perpetuity. Its charities are in order. Its annual barge and sculling races echo its past and bring colour to London's river and, in the case of Doggett's Coat and Badge, added value to the sport of rowing. Its main purpose – to bring skill, knowledge and experience to the working river through its well-tried apprenticeship scheme – is on offer to stakeholders of the Thames and inland waterways. They have a choice – to grasp the Company's values and ethos, its contribution to the 'landscape and memory' of the Tideway, or to squander it.

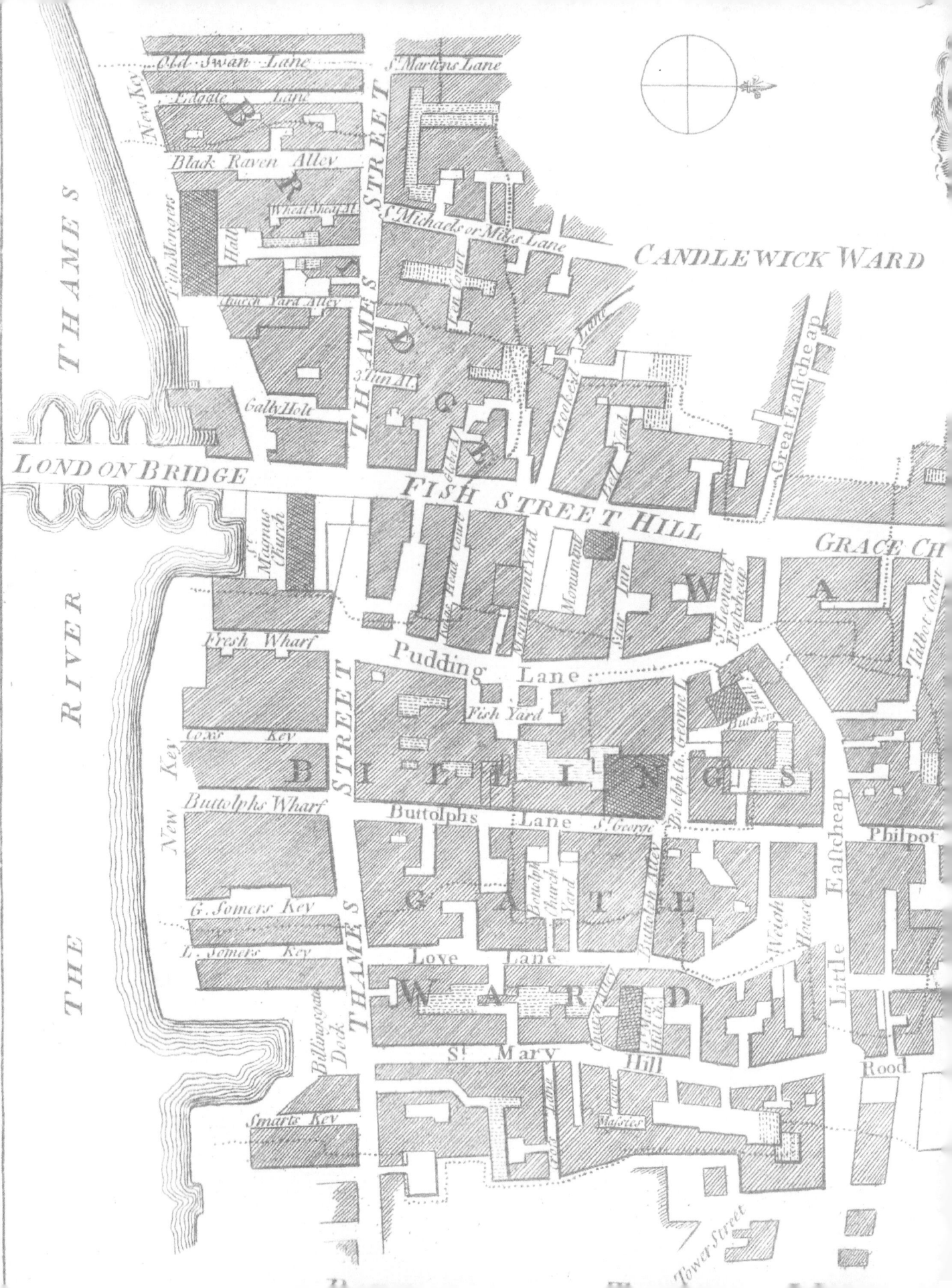

THAMES

Old Swan Lane

St Martins Lane

New Key

Endgate Little

Black Raven Alley

R

Fish Mongers Hall

CANDLE WICK WARD

Wheat Sheaf

St Michaels or Miles Lane

Church Yard Alley

THAMES STREET

3 Tun Al.

Crooked Lane

Galley Holt

G

Fish Hill

LONDON BRIDGE

St Magnus Church

FISH STREET HILL

GRACE CH

GRACE CH

Monument Yard

St Leonard Eastcheap

W

A

Monument

Star Inn

Talbot Court

Great Eastcheap

Fresh Wharf

Pudding Lane

Coxe Key

Fish Yard

B I L L I N G S

Butchers

STREET

New Key

Buttolphs Wharf

Buttolphs Lane

St George

St Buttolph Ch. George

Philpot

Buttolph Church Yard

Buttolph Alley

G. Somers Key

G A T E

Little Eastcheap

Weigh House

L. Somers Key

Love Lane

THAMES

Billingsgate Dock

W A R D

St Mary Hill

Rood

Smarts Key

Maltster

THE RIVER THAMES

Tower Street

A New and Accurate PLAN of
BILLINGSGATE WARD,
and BRIDGE WARD WITHIN,
Divided into Parishes from
a late SURVEY.

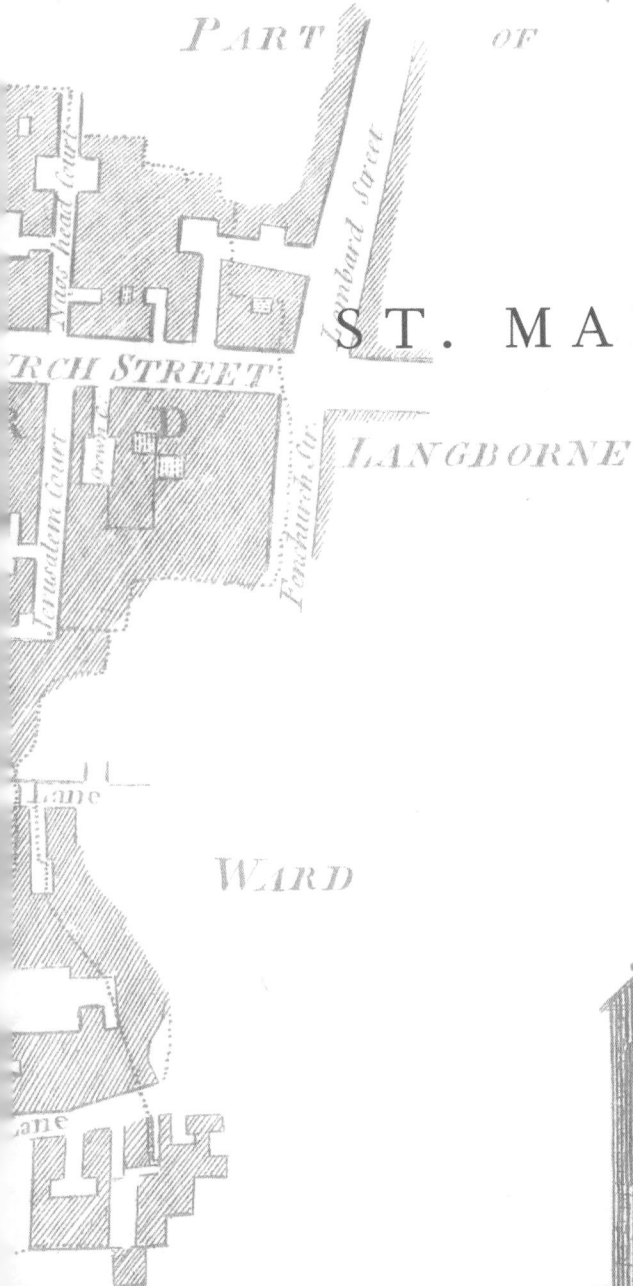

PART OF

32
ST. MARY-AT-HILL

St. Mary at Hill near Billingsgate.

LANGBORNE

WARD

St. Botolph's in Botolph Lane.

The present Hall, drawing by Hanslip Fletcher 1931 (Watermen's Hall Collection)

Mr. Middleton took Thornhill up St-Mary-at-Hill to the Watermen's Hall for his binding. A door led into a draughty passage flagged with worn stone, and here boys waiting to be bound sat on a hard bench, too narrow for a bottom. Cold flagstones froze his feet in their wooden pattens. Mr. Middleton sat puffing beside him from the steep climb up the hill, and Thornhill felt breathless too, with the possibility of a future better than anything he could have hoped. For if he could get through the seven years of the apprenticeship he would be a freeman of the River Thames, and as long as he kept his heath he wouldn't starve.

The stairway was out of a dream, curving upward like a coil of orange peel around a slender rail, towards the radiance pouring down from the fanlight in the roof. At the top, Thornhill hung back, had to be almost pulled by Mr. Middleton into the grand room and

Previous page: 'A New and Accurate Plan of Billingsgate Ward, and Bridge Ward within, Divided into Parishes from A late Survey', engraved for Noorthoucks History of London 1772 (Watermen's Hall Collection)

stand on the Turkey rug under the glitter of the chandelier, feeling the fire blazing away beneath the daunting waterman's skiff, oars and dolphins of the armorial bearings looming above the grate, staring at the dark solemn pictures on the walls. He stood in the lee of Mr. Middleton and faced a vast mahogany table behind which sat half a dozen men in robes. He had a sudden dizzying understanding of the way men were ranged on top of each other, from the Thornhills at the bottom, up to the King, or God, at the top.

The man weighted down with a heavy gilt chain asked, 'Who is this lad, Richard?' and Mr. Middleton answered stiffly, 'This is William Thornhill, Master, and I am here to vouch for him.' Another of them asked, 'Can he handle an oar?' and a little one on the end chimed in, 'Has he got his river hands?'

Mr. Middleton's voice was happier now, on solid ground as he answered, 'Yes, Mr. Piper, I had him row from Hay's Wharf to the Sufferance Dock and from Wapping Old Stairs to Fresh Wharf for this past week gone.' The man with the chain cried, 'Good man!' as much to Thornhill as to Middleton, and then another said, straight to Thornhill, 'Blisters healed yet, sonny?'

Thornhill did not know whether to say yes or no. His palms were still puffed up from all the heavy rowing Mr. Middleton had been making him do, but they were no longer bleeding. He held them out without speaking, and there was a general laugh.

The questioner said, 'Good lad, they have the look of a waterman's hands already, eh gentlemen? Licence granted, I would say,' and it was done.

Thornhill's account of being bound at Watermen's Hall in the eighteenth century is paraphrased from Kate Grenville's novel The Secret River. All that has changed substantially is that, today, Thornhill would be older and face fewer years as an apprentice. He would still walk the cobbles up St. Mary-at-Hill to the imposing door of the only surviving Georgian hall in London. He would still enter a gloomy passage to wait on a narrow bench – the present one dating from 1820 - to stare at the wherry backboards and priceless prints of the London River before being summoned to mount the stone coil of orange peel under a lantern of natural light. Very likely he would take in a gulp of breath as he is called forth into the court room, with its blazing chandelier, its Wedgewood-esque high ceiling, its imposing fireplace and its grave portraits of benefactors, its Company arms bearing the motto 'At command of our superiors', to face the robed members of the court arrayed before him, with the Master perched between griffins on his high chair.

A modern-day Thornhill likely had neither opportunity nor inclination to view the treasures of the hall at his binding. He would not notice the 1695 barometer presented by the White family in memory of Thomas White, a ruler of the Company at the time. He would have missed Peter Monamy's oily-black contemporary portrait that allegedly depicts the unnamed winner of the first Doggett's Coat and Badge wager, although it turns out that the painter was away from London at the time of the race. Robert Cottrell has identified the first winner as John Opey. Thornhill would pay scant attention to the three imposing portraits on the north wall - Francis Theodore Hay, barge-builder and first master in 1827 by George Patten RA; or academician John Prescott Knight's pictures of John Dudin Brown, promoter and president of the Company's asylum and donor of land at Penge on which to build it, and Matthias Prime Lucas, Lord Mayor in 1827 and initiator of the poor's fund, an annual pension for aged watermen (known now as Lucas-aid).

On his way out, the 21st century Thornhill would pass a large, exquisite model of a 104-gun ship of the line, built of whalebone in about 1825 in a case made partly of timber from the Fighting *Temeraire*. Nearby is the Company's oldest prize wherry backboard, won on 26 August 1847 and bearing a quotation attributed to 'Shakspere' [sic]: 'There is a tide in the affairs of men which taken at the Flood, leads on to fortune.' At the foot of the stairs he will have a glimpse of the parlour, should the door be open, furnished in dark mahogany with a stained glass window to the street and displaying more treasures concerned with the Company's history and purpose. There is a rack of wooden truncheons carried by beadles and a beadle's black topper sporting the Company's badge of an arm holding an oar, beadles being the Company policemen charged with checking wherrymen's licences and routing out 'tickling' or shaving wood from boats to lighten them beyond lawful dimensions. Amongst the prints on the walls is one of a frost fair in 1811 showing watermen's oars serving as tent poles. There is a Monamy painting of the capture of Porto Bello by Admiral Vernon in 1739 and the keys of the city presented to the Company by waterman 'Pug' Mason who took part in the raid on the isthmus of Panama. Cabinets house a variety of silver badges from regattas and races.

Out in St. Mary-at-Hill and released from his first audience with the fellowship that he is in the process of joining, we will leave young Thornhill glancing at the shimmering tower of the Shard rising behind the classical façade of old Billingsgate market on the river side of Lower Thames Street as his master steers him towards the Walrus and

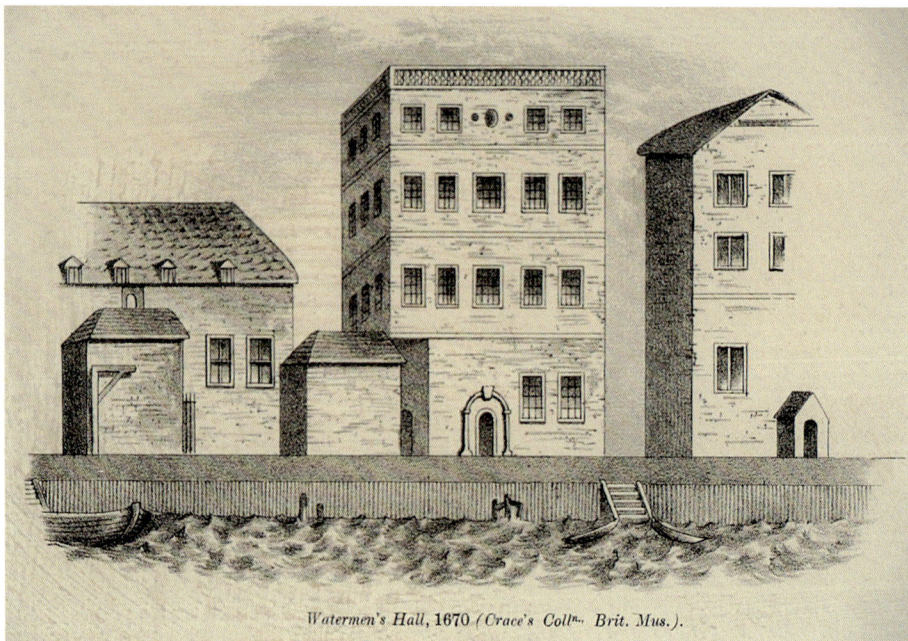

Watermen's Hall, 1670 (Crace's Collⁿ. Brit. Mus.).

Watermen's Hall 1670 (Watermen's Hall Collection)

Carpenter for refreshment. His brush with the hall has, thus far, only involved the oldest, Georgian rooms and a handful of the *objets* therein.

The building was designed by William Blackburn of Southwark early in 1776, built by Thomas Barnes for £1,139 and opened for business in April 1780. Blackburn's plans do not survive, but T. H. Shepherd's 1830 depiction of the exterior suggests that the Hall hardly changed in its first fifty years. The Company's conservation survey of 2004 describes the front as faced with Portland stone, rusticated on the ground floor, with a central, round-headed window flanked by square-headed openings with bold keystones, the left being a dummy and the right the main entrance. Both have rectangular plaques with tritons set above them. The upper façade has pairs of giant ionic pilasters supporting a frieze and a plain pediment. They frame a tripartite window with Doric columns for mullions, with a huge lunette window above. Festoons in the frieze and the ground floor plaques are of Coade stone. The inside was much as it is today, with the ground floor entrance passage and Beadle's room, the present parlour and the stairway to the courtroom.

Watermen's Hall 1749 (Watermen's Hall Collection)

The present hall was not the first. The first written reference to a hall is in the 1603 act of parliament requiring eight overseers or rulers to hold court there twice a year to police offences. Henry Humpherus, the Company's first historian, writing in the middle of the nineteenth century, believed the original to be Cold Harbour Mansion in Upper Thames

Ward map showing old Watermen's Hall 1756 (Watermen's Hall Collection)

The Parish Church of
S.t Stephen in Walbrook?

PART OF CHEAP WARD

PART OF CORDWAINERS WARD

PART OF

PART OF LANG-BORN WARD

WALBROOK

B ROOK

The Parish
S.t Michael
College

Church of
Royal
Hill?

WALBROOK WARD
AND
DOWGATE WARD
with their Divisions into
PARISHES
according to a New
SURVEY.

B. Cole sculp.t

in 1756. And to S.r Richard Glyn Kn.t &. Alderman of Dowgate Ward. 1755.

Cold Harbour c1550
afterwards Watermen's Hall
(Watermen's Hall Collection)

Street, just upstream of London Bridge. The conservation survey describes Cold Harbour as a substantial building, 'three stories high with a five-gabled and many windowed elevation to the river and a grand arched opening in the centre of the river front leading to the main river stairs'. Humpherus acknowledges that his information is shrouded in mist, and admits that the buildings cannot be identified without question in Raph Agas's 1633 survey map of the City. His belief seems to have been based on an engraving entitled Watermen's Hall, Cold Harbour 1650-1780 by nineteenth-century artist George Shepherd, allegedly derived from Wenceslas Hollar's map of 1647. Hollar clearly shows Watermen's Hall at Cold Harbour in Upper Thames Street.

According to C. O'Riordan in Wikipedia, the first hall was a building leased from the Merchant Taylors' in about 1565 at the southeast corner of Broad Lane, directly south of the Guildhall and fronting onto Three Cranes Wharf. Three Cranes was so named after its hoisting gear, and was the point of embarkation for mayoral processions. The lease was renewable at 21-year intervals (£66 for the lease plus yearly fee of £8).

The Company struggled to keep up the payments, and in the 1640s the lease was mortgaged. It was renewed in 1653, but was assigned to William Fellowes, a woodmonger, suggesting that the premises were no longer used as a hall. O'Riordan speculates that, as Fellowes was a member of a consortium whose names appear as property holders in Cold Harbour, an interest in the substantial mansion could have been exchanged with the Company for the Three Cranes building some time before the event which precipitated the next development.

Model of the Thames Barge *Daphne* (Watermen's Hall Collection)

The destruction of the Three Cranes hall in the Great Fire of 1666, together with the Company's records, led to the construction of a new hall on the site of Cold Harbour mansion in 1670. An engraving at the Crace collection at the Guildhall shows a plain rectangular four-storey building with a five-bay river frontage.

The Company was either not happy with the hall or in difficulties with the lease, because various attempts were made to find an alternative. In 1697 it purchased several houses, yards and passages with a view to erecting a hall and a school adjoining Marigold stairs in Southwark, in the manor of St Mary Overy's and Old St Saviour's. This led to several years of wrangle with the City corporation because such a move would take the watermen beyond the City's jurisdiction. The City eventually succeeded in frustrating the scheme.

Master's chair

A committee charged with finding a new hall in 1718 failed, and the lease of the Cold Harbour property was renewed for 61 years from Lady Day 1719. It was immediately pulled down, and replaced three years later by a building showing 'architectural pretension but a little clumsy in detail', according to the conservation report's view of a T. H. Shepherd sketch. 'The main front to the river was three stories high and four bays wide with a doorway in the right-hand bay. The two central bays... were topped with a cramped pediment bearing royal arms. The two outer bays had balustrade parapets... on the first floor... the windows were enriched with bold keystones and impost blocks characteristic of English Baroque.' Architect and builder are unknown. Messrs S. & W. Buck depicted the new building in a drawing in 1749.

In 1744 a severe fire in Upper Thames Street destroyed part of Sir William Calvert's brewery next door to the hall, but the latter escaped damage. Next year there were estimates for preventing recurring tidal inroads, but these were not followed through. Another thirty years passed until the brewery, which was the Company's landlord, gave notice that it would require the premises when the lease ran out five years' hence. A committee was consequently formed to seek a new hall. The present premises began its life on 1 March 1776 at the Punch-bowl and Magpye in Fenchurch Street when the clerk agreed to purchase Mr. Brett's estate, comprising numbers 18 and 19 St. Mary-at-Hill, for £800. Conveyance of the site, formerly occupied by a tavern, a coffee house and a further building, was completed on 29 May. Number 19 was leased to Mr. Le Hey for 21 years from 1765.

St. Mary-at-Hill, the name of the narrow passage connecting Eastcheap with the Roman thoroughfare of Lower Thames Street, was first registered in 1275, and is associated with the church on the west side. The Abbot of Waltham's Inn occupied a substantial plot in the Middle Ages, and there was settlement in the vicinity from the First Century AD. At the time that the Company moved to St. Mary-at-Hill, Billingsgate Dock did a roaring trade in fish and coal at the foot of it, and a new coal exchange was erected in Lower Thames Street contemporaneously with the hall. In 1849 this was replaced by another splendid building by John Bunstone Brunning on the corner of Lower Thames Street and St. Mary-at-Hill, opposite Watermen's Hall. It was opened by Prince Albert amongst much pomp and ceremony and demolished amongst much bluster and controversy in 1962.

The new hall took two years to build, and William Blackburn, the architect, went on to become surveyor to St. Thomas's and Guy's hospitals as well as to the Company before finding fame as the country's leading prison architect (parts of his gaols at Chester, Dorchester, Gloucester, Stafford and Oxford survive). His cramped Watermen's Hall remained substantially unaltered during the nineteenth century, although it was saved by prompt action of firemen and their engine in 1836 when fire broke out in the back cellar. Books and papers were lost, and a new strong room was built as a consequence. The hall survived the practice of illuminating it to honour special occasions, such as Admiral Hood's defeat of the French fleet in 1794 and peace with France in 1801.

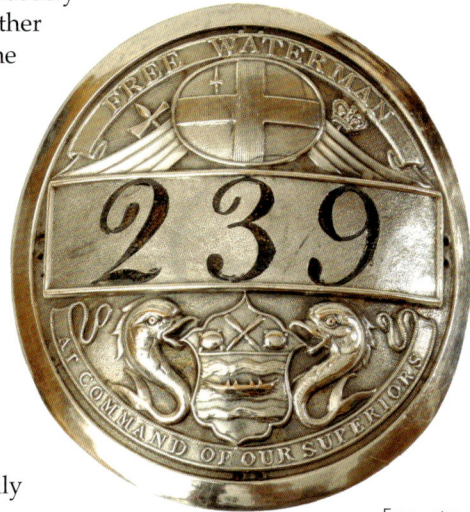

Free waterman's licence badge No. 239

Maintenance was carried out from time to time. A new crystal chandelier was purchased from Rothschilds for the courtroom in 1842. A surveyor's inventory of work in 1822 listed the rooms – committee and beadle's rooms on the ground floor, court room and kitchen on the first floor and four rooms reached by the back stair on the second floor. In 1856 the Company, still in possession of 19 St. Mary-at-Hill, acquired number 16. In 1894 it bought number 17, the premises formerly occupied by the now defunct corn and salt porters' association of Billingsgate, known variously as a fellowship, company or society. Harmer & Pocock, fishmongers, had a valid lease for those premises until 1908. Meanwhile, 19 St. Mary-at-Hill had been disposed of by 1888 when the building was demolished and replaced by a new one for the Billingsgate Christian Mission, designed by architect George Baines. Thus before the century closed the hall's frontage was increased considerably, and the way was open to unify numbers 16, 17 and 18.

Beadle's hat

However, no major works were undertaken until the 1960s. Bomb damage inflicted during the Second World War was repaired in 1951, and in 1961 the parlour was overhauled and given a lower, decorated ceiling and a new chimneypiece by architects Gordon & Gordon. At the same time the chimneypiece in the courtroom was enlarged, and the paint was stripped from the room's dado and corner pilasters. Redevelopment schemes by Gordon & Gordon and the Moxley Jenner Partnership came to nought, but in 1980 the Company adopted a scheme by Cluttons architect Peter Hubbard to rebuild the front of 16 and retain the façade of 17 to return them to something like their appearance in 1830 while re-fettling the spaces behind them. Thus came about works in 1984 that created the present configuration of a large freemen's room for entertaining, and improved kitchens, cloakrooms and offices.

So now, when a modern-day Thornhill returns to the hall to be awarded his freedom, or perhaps as a Doggett's winner, he will enjoy a bigger and better place than the one his ancestor visited. Honours boards of masters and clerks confront him in the elegant panelled silver room that he will pass through if he enters via the front office. Glass fronted shelves house volumes about the Thames and the lives of watermen and lightermen. There is a superb model of the *Lady Daphne*, a Thames sailing barge still extant; another of a Thames wherry made in 2010 by Anthony Smith from drawings in Fredrik Henrik af Chapman's Architectura Navalis Mercatoria, published in 1768. There is a model of the Alexandra Ship Towage Company's *Sun Surrey*, built by Richards shipbuilders in 1992. An earlier motor tug, the steel screw *Sir John* of the Humphrey & Grey lighterage company, is on show in the basement, the model made by Robert A Brown. In the parlour is another first class wherry model, this one by Bob Crouch, the only freeman thus far to have served as clerk to the Company, master of the Company, and Queen's bargemaster.

The Jack Stratford Memorial Rose Bowl given 9 January 2013 by Craft Owning Freeman John M. Stratford in memory of his father, Past Master Jack Stratford 1958 and his grandfather, Past Master John T. Stratford 1919

The Batchalors Bowle made by George Garthorne 1695

Some of the vessels that represent the interests of the Company and its members also feature in the freemen's room. There is a silver wherry, a silver shallop and a small silver version of the tug *Sun Surrey*. The select silver collection includes the Bachelors Bowl of 1695. Until 1835 this was used at the court of admissions to freedom, where a widow offered each young freeman a draught of ale from the bowl in return for a shilling. There is also a modern rose bowl depicting various coats of arms and scenes of ships and docks presented by John Stratford in memory of his father Jack, a past master.

Some of the Company's coats and badges are on view, examples being from the 1870 Victoria and West Ham Apprentices regatta won by William Robert Young of Rotherhithe, and the 1929 Royal Borough of Kingston-upon-Thames Coat & Badge won by George Henry Arlett. There is also a plastron, or cloth breastplate, from the livery of the Queen's barge master, and a selection of prize silver arm badges. The coats and badges illustrate the diversity and extent of events and competitions once on offer from Gravesend to the top of the Tideway, a reminder that over the centuries Doggett's was by no means a race alone. Examples from the badge collection are St. Mary's Rotherhithe 1832, Thames Regatta 1844, All Saints Poplar Blackwall 1867, Westminster 1868, Lock's 1877, Woolwich and Charlton Watermen's Apprentice Grand Annual Regatta 1882, City of London and St John's Surrey 1883, City of London, Southwark and Lambeth 1886, Tower Bridge 1894, London Rowing Club, 1903, Richmond Watermen's 1909, Kingston 1912 and Seamen's Hospital Society 1913. And a curiosity: a badge presented to Alfred George Chapman 'by a number of friends for the manly way in which he rowed for the City of London Coat and Badge on Monday 31 August 1874'.

As he makes his way about among the family silver and the artefacts that bind the Company history together, Thornhill will encounter portraits and pictures that are the tip of the iceberg of the hall's image collections. John Taylor, the combative journalist and water poet, is on the wall. John Broughton, Doggett's winner and pugilist, is on the wall. Thomas Doggett, Whig and wag, is on the wall attired as Nincompoop in Thomas

Silver model of a Thames Wherry

D'Urfey's Love for Money. Thomas Mann, the Stakhanovite 'Honest Waterman', is on the wall, very old and as miserable as sin. William Wyllie's painting of a sailing barge match and Charles John Lacy's equally superb 'Inward Bound' are hung. Francis Moltino's riverscape of the Pool of London features a 'stackie' sailing barge piled with hay amongst a forest of masts and a hazy dome of St. Paul's, manned, as it should be, by sailorman, boy and small dog. In the entrance passage are London river landscapes selected from the comprehensive collection of prints given to the Company by Reginald Francis. And in every room are clocks, marking the tides in the affairs of men.

Rack of beadles' truncheons

So, as the Company of Watermen and Lightermen of the River Thames approaches its sixth century, it presides over the activity of its members and protects their interests from an eighteenth century listed grade II ancient monument within sniffing distance of London's River and in a conservation area in the heart of the City. This control of activity, carried out by rulers first appointed by parliament in 1555 and by its own court and master since 1827, when the Company was formally incorporated by act of parliament, is one function that distinguishes it from the City livery companies among whom it sits. The second distinction is that the Watermen's see - the tidal Thames - extends beyond the confines of the City, and always did so. And its charitable work is as relevant today as when Henry VIII provided alms houses for deserving watermen.

For five hundred years, the Company has played a notable role in the complex world of City trades. The history of water transport is embedded in it; it is a national asset that harbours significant collections of pictures, books and artefacts relevant to the Thames, its port and its past as the emporium of an empire.

But the Company is only sitting pretty in the literal sense. The trade and commerce in which its members engage has contracted extraordinarily on the Thames in the last fifty years, and the stakeholders in the river have shifted in powers and responsibilities. As we have seen in the third section of this book, the Company's ability to continue and enhance its educational role in the life of the river is fundamental to its future. It is the archive, the waterscape and the collective memory of local knowledge, a required ingredient of navigating the Tideway, just as 'the knowledge' is essential for the London cab drivers that watermen begat.

A key element of this is a good grasp of watermanship delivered by the Company's time-honoured apprenticeships, capped for some by the feel for ebbs, flows, eddies and obstacles gained from proximity to the water in the seat of a sculling boat. Doggett's Coat and Badge is much more than a historical anachronism, and working at oars much more than a footnote in maritime lore. The race is a valid test of watermanship as well as a link with a modern sport that was born in port communities for people whose working lives will be spent on the river.

Backboard commissioned by the Company to commemorate the visit of HM The Queen and HRH The Duke of Edinburgh on 27 March 2014

In the twenty-first century the pilots of the Tideway have the use of the global positioning system (GPS), navigation by satellite that has transformed safety on water worldwide. Global positioning is not, however, a panacea to supplant watermanship. As it enters its sixth century, the Company's message is, surely, that neither watermen nor lightermen on London's tidal river can live – nor should be expected to live – by satnav alone.

The Company of Watermen & Lightermen of the River Thames 1514 - 2014

of H. M. Queen Elizabeth II - 27th March 2014

Robert A. Prentice - Master

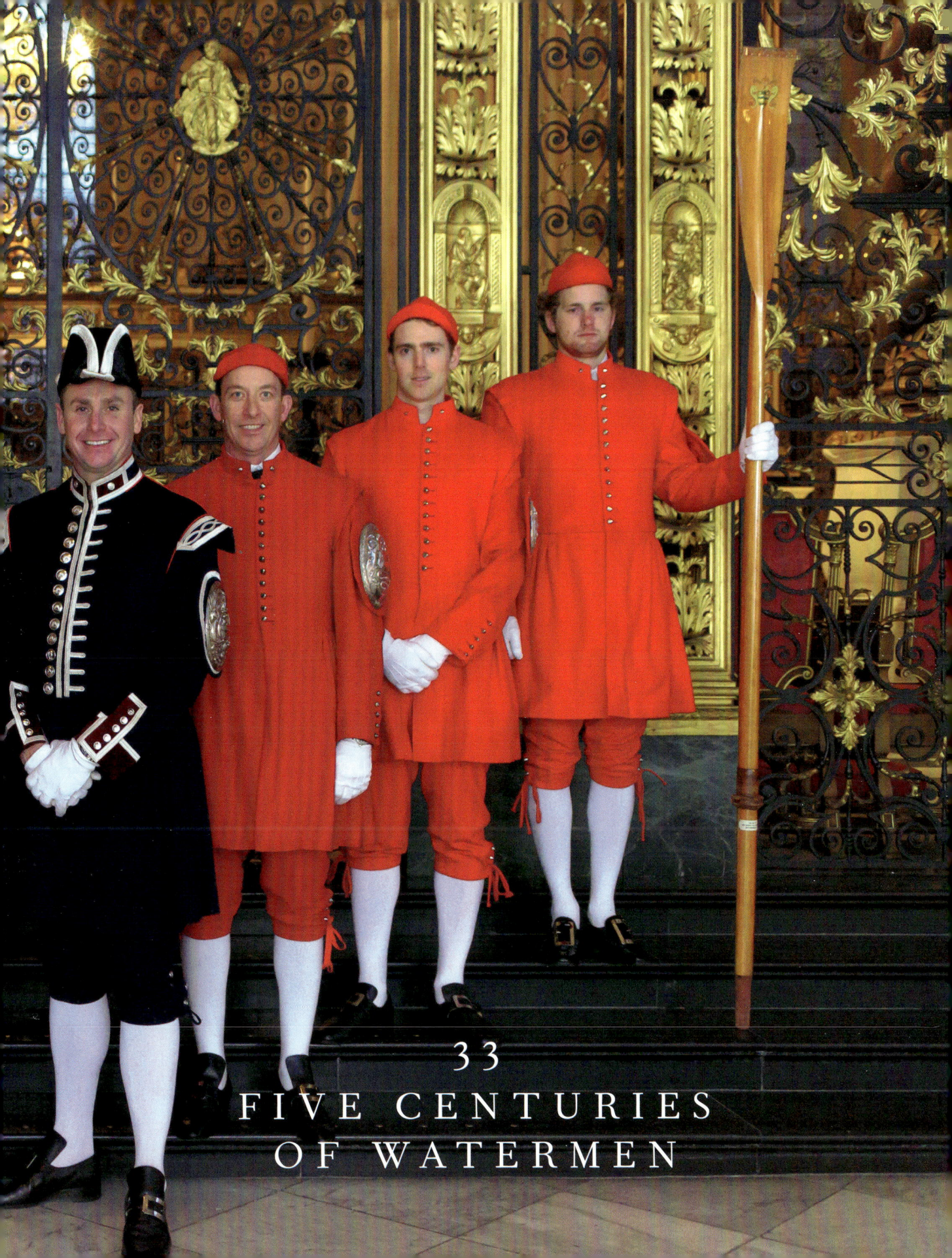

33

FIVE CENTURIES
OF WATERMEN

Watermen's Company 500th Anniversary Gala Dinner on board Silver Sturgeon, held on 11 November 2014.
The Master, Jeremy Randall, second from left, with the guard of honour, Mark Hunter MBE (Millennium Coat & Badge),
Company Bargemaster Scott Neicho, Alfie Anderson (500th Anniversary Coat & Badge), Harry McCarthy (2014 Doggett's
Coat & Badge) and Christopher Anness (Diamond Jubilee Coat & Badge) There is unlikely to be another occasion when
all of these uniforms will be present in the one place, an event worth saving for posterity (Photograph by Susan Fenwick)

In 2014 the Company of Watermen and Lightermen of the River Thames celebrated 500 years of working the tidal river since Henry VIII's regulatory Act came into force.

The first celebration was a choral evensong at St. Paul's Cathedral in the City in the presence of the Lord Mayor and Sheriff and almost a hundred masters and prime wardens of City livery companies. The sermon was given by the Reverend Bertrand Olivier, the Company's honorary chaplain.

The annual dinner at Fishmongers' Hall was attended by HRH the Princess Royal who spoke glowingly in proposing the toast to the Company.

HM The Queen and HRH Prince Philip visited the hall on 27 March to be greeted by the Royal Watermen who can claim a history of at least 800 years to the time before Magna Carta. The royal couple met members of the Company's court, Doggett's winners and hall staff.

Previous page: Company 500th Anniversary Evensong at St. Pauls held on 5th February 2014 – photo Graham Lacdao
Photo: Doggett's winners, from left, Nathaniel Brice 2013, Robert Dwan 2004, Alex Collins 1965, the Master Robert Prentice 1973 (and still the record holder), the Bargemaster Scott Neicho 1995, Robert Coleman 1996, Jude McGrane 2007 and Merlin Dwan 2012 at the Company's Evensong Service

The final event of the Company's 500th anniversary celebrations was the unveiling of a plaque on the Thames Path to mark the approximate location of the first Watermen's Hall by the Chief Commoner of the City of London, John Bennett on 19 November 2014. Mr. Bennett is pictured with the Master, Jeremy Randall and Doggett's Winners Nick Beasley and Robbie Coleman (Photograph by Ron Collyer)

Start of the Watermen's Company 500th Anniversary Coat and Badge Wager held on 11 September 2014 (Photograph by Jeremy Dale)

A garden party at Watermen's Close, the charity's almshouses, raised £2,000 that was shared by St. Michael's Hospice in Hastings and the Company's charities. A fine day on the Kent coast brought pensioners, apprentices, journeymen and craft owning freemen together.

A 500th anniversary Coat and Badge race open to all journeymen freemen and apprentices was held from London Dock to London Bridge on 11 September. Apprentice Alfie Anderson was the winner.

The lasting legacy of the anniversary is the unveiling of a new street sign, 'Old Watermen's Walk', for an ancient lane linking the Thames Path with Lower Thames Street. A plaque on the Thames Path sunk into the pavement downstream of Cannon Street railway bridge marks the approximate location of the first Watermen's Hall that was destroyed in the Great Fire of 1666. As the Company's anniversary year draws to an end, there is a proposal to erect a statue of a waterman at the foot of St-Mary-at-Hill, hard by the present hall.

The 500 years celebrations concluded with a cruise aboard the Silver Sturgeon on 11 November on the waters first regulated by the Company in 1514.

As part of the Company's 500th celebrations, the Corporation of London named a section of path leading to the Thames to be named 'Old Watermen's Walk'. It runs between the Northern and Shell building next to old Billingsgate Market and the Clarkson building on Thames Street near to the Hall in St. Mary-at-Hill. The Walk was opened by Sheriff Adrian Waddingham on 12 May 2014 in the presence of the Master, Wardens, Court and members of the 500 Club – (Photograph by Martin Laws)

Taken on the occasion of the visit of HM The Queen and HRH The Duke of Edinburgh on 27th March 2014 to mark the 500th Anniversary of the Watermen's Company and the 800th Anniversary of the Royal Watermen.
Back Row: Don Rowland, James Howard, James Clifford, Robert Coleman, John Turk, Simon McCarthy, Paul Bryant, Tim Keech, David Eldridge, Jeremy McCarthy, Alan Woods, Martin Spencer
Middle Row: Edward Barlow, George Saunders, John Salter, Gary Anness, Paul Prentice, Lou Lewis, Len Saunders, Chris Livett, John Dwan, Fred Burwood, Tony Hobbs
Front Row: Michael Turk, Robert Crouch MVO, Colin Hinton, Robert Lupton, Paul Ludwig, Her Majesty, The Duke of Edinburgh, Robert Prentice, Paul Wilson, Edwin Hunt MVO, George Green

GLOSSARY

Admiralty cutters – four or six oared open boats for navy officials, excise men etc.

Baulk uncompleted job

Bum boats – suppliers of provisions and services for ships in the Thames.

Burthen athwartships

Canting slanting the blade of an oar

Cotchel small quantity of cargo

Doggett's sculling race for watermen and lightermen in first year of freedom

Driving drifting broadside

Foist – slight boat managed by oars or sail, C16.

Gallet - – slight boat managed by oars or sail, C16.

Gill proceed while dragging knotted anchor chain to keep barge head up

Gunwhale barge's deck ???

Hoveller bridge pilot for sailing barges (pronounced 'huffler')

Lee shore towards which wind in blowing

Lighter

Livery barge – elaborate barges of London livery companies, up to 18 oars.

Long ferry ferry from London Bridge to Gravesend that ran with the tide

Pepperers grocers (medieval)

Randan 3-oar with stroke and bow rowing one oar each, and centre man rowing a pair

Roads buoyed moorings for lighters

Royal barge – eight-oared barge for monarch, powered by royal watermen.

Screw gimlet

Shallop – four, six or eight-oared private or company boat.

Side-winder hitting a bridge buttress side on

Sixes and sevens – see Crouch boat notes

Skiff – similar passenger ferry to wherry but with flat transom.

Spelled to give someone a break

Spiled plugging a hole in a cask

Square meal – see navy chapter

Starlings wooden piers supporting old London bridge (wooden protectors for stone piers?)

Thwart seat

Tiers buoyed ship moorings

Tow rags – men who towed western barg,njTurn and turn about -see Crouch boat notes

Wafter – slight boat managed by oars or sail, C16..

Western barge – large inland barges operating between London Bridge and Oxford.

Wherry – double ended passenger boat with one or two watermen.

Windward shore from which wind in blowing

BIBLIOGRAPHY

History of the Origin and Progress of the Company of Watermen and Lightermen of the River Thames 1514 to 1924 in five volumes.

I – 1514-1699 by Henry Humpherus.

II – 1700-1799 by Henry Humpherus.

III – 1800-1849 by Henry Humpherus.

IV – 1850-1882 by Henry Humpherus.

V – 1883-1920 by Jon Temple.

Anon — The Life and Character of Thomas Mann, honest waterman of St. Katharine-by-the-Tower, 1825.

Clive Birch — Carr and Carman, the Fellowship of St. Katherine the Virgin and Martyr of Carters, Baron, 1999.

Frank C. Bowen — Sailing Ships of the London River, Sampson Low Marston, 1939.

Thomas Burke – Out and About, a note-book of London in wartime, George Allen & Unwin, 1919.

Paul Cohen-Portheim — The Spirit of London, Batsford, 1935.

Joseph Conrad — The Faithful River, The World's Work and Play, 1904 (from The Mirror of the Sea).

Theodore Andrea Cook and Guy Nickalls — Thomas Doggett, Deceased, a famous comedian, Constable, 1908.

P. L. Cottrell and D. H. Aldcroft (Eds.) — Shipping Trade and Commerce, essays in memory of Ralph Davis, Leicester University Press, 1981.

Robert John Cottrell — Thomas Doggett Coat & Badge, the 'Hanover Prize' 1715-2009, Cottrell, 2009.

Thomas Dibdin — Dibdin's Songs, London, 1841.

Charles Dickens — Our Mutual Friend, 1864-65.

Frank L. Dix – Royal River Highway, David & Charles, Newton Abbot, 1985.

Aytoun Ellis — Three Hundred Years on London River, the Hay's Wharf Story 1651-1951, Hay's Wharf, 1951.

Chris Ellmers and Alex Werner — Dockland Life, a pictorial history of London's docks 1860-1970, Museum of London, 1991.

Dick Fagan and Eric Burgess — Men of the Tideway, Robert Hale, 1966.

Michael Foley — Disasters on the Thames, History Press, 2011.

Elspet Fraser-Stephen — Two Centuries in the London Coal Trade, the story of Charringtons, privately printed, 1952.

Jack Gaster — The Life of a Thames Waterman, Amberley, 2010.

Harry Gosling — Up and Down Stream, Methuen, 1927.

L. Grenard – The Singularities of London, 1578, London Topographical Society, 2014.

Kate Grenville – The Secret River, Canongate, 2005.

Kate Grenville – Searching for The Secret River, Canongate, 2006.

Harry Harris — Under Oars, reminiscences of a Thames lighterman 1894-1909, illustrated by Albert Rolles, Centerprise Trust, 1978.

Arthur Herman — To Rule the Waves, how the British Navy shaped the modern world, Harper Perennial, 2004.

Stephen Inwood — A History of London, Macmillan, 1998.

David Kynaston — The City of London, Vol 1: A world of its own, Chatto & Windus, 1994.

Michael Leapman – London's River, a history of the Thames, Pavilion and Olympia & York, 1991.

Walter Leon — Thomas Doggett Pictur'd, Company of Watermen & Lightermen, 1980.

A. G. Linney — Peepshow of the Port of London, Sampson Low, Marston, 1929.

H. J. Massingham — London Scene, Cobden-Sanderson, 1933.

H. V. Morton — The Heart of London, Methuen, 1928.

Andrew Motion – Salt Water, Faber, 1997.

Anthony Osler — Whe're Yer For?, the recollections of Capt. Harold Smy, sailing bargemaster, Chaffcutter Books, 2006.

D. J. Owen – The Port of London Yesterday and Today, PLA, 1927.

Vladimir Peniakoff – Popski's Private Army, Bantam, 1980.

Maurice Phelps — The Phelps Dynasty, a story of a riverside family, Words by Design, 2012.

David Ramzan — Maritime Greenwich, The History Press, 2009.

Chris Roberts — Cross River Traffic, a history of London's Bridges, Granta, 2005

Simon Schama — Landscape and Memory, Harper Collins, 1995.

Robert Simper – Thames Tideway, Creekside Publishing, 1997.

Raymond Smith — Sea Coal for London, Longmans, 1961.

David Starkey and Susan Doran — Royal River, power, pageantry and the Thames, Royal Museums Greenwich, 2012.

Gavin Thurston — The Great Thames Disaster, George Allen & Unwin, 1965.

Gillian Tindell — The House by the Thames and the people who lived there, Chatto & Windus, 2006

H. M. Tomlinson — London River, Garden City Publishing, 1921.

Rosalind Vallance — Dickens' London, selected essays, Folio Society, 1966.

Philip Warren — The History of the London Cab Trade, Taxi Trade Promotions, 1995.

Nigel Watson — A Century of Service, the Port of London Authority 1909-2009, PLA, 2009.

Peter Whitfield — London, a Life in Maps, The British Library, 2006.

Geoffrey Lee Williams – A Couple of Duffers go to War, Amberley, 2011.

The Earl of Wilton — Sports and Pursuits of the English, Harrison, 1869.

JOURNALS, CORRESPONDENCE AND PAPERS

Age Exchange – On the River, memories of a working river, 1989.

James Bone – Doggett's Coat and Badge 1910, Manchester Guardian.

Able Seaman M. F. Callen – D-Day on HMS Eglinton.

J. H. Campbell – cuttings (royal watermen, Doggett's, Wingfields, rowing matches, death of Queen Victoria, Crimea veterans) c1900, Watermen's Hall.

Company of Watermen and Lightermen — Collection of Uniforms, Coats & Badges, Library and Heritage Committee, 2012.

Tom Gillam – Rivermen.

Major Edwin 'Ted' Hunt – Sapper Lightermen, Rhino Ferries and Landing Ships.

Sue Jones – letter on frost fairs and watermen, London Review of Books, 6 June 2013.

C. O'Riordan – Watermen's Hall, Wikipedia.

Alan Spong obituary – The Times, 24 September 2014.

Enid Stokes – letter to John Dodd on student visit to East India Dock, April 1924.

Lieutenant Brian Thomas – Popski's Private Navy.

Richard Williams – In praise of watermen and race with a history twice as long as Ashes, The Guardian, 13 July 2013.

Conservation statement for Watermen's Hall, 2004.

APPENDIX A - MASTERS OF THE COMPANY

1827	Francis T HAY		1863	Francis SALES
1828	John DRINKALD		1864	John DOWNEY
1829	Anthony LYON		1865	William TOMLIN
1830	Robert THOMPSON		1866	Thomas PILLOW
1831	Joseph TURNLEY		1867	John R BERRY
1832	Thomas EAST		1868	William BROMLEY
1833	Robert BANYON		1869	William WINN
1834	William EASTON		1870	William WINN re-elected
1835	William RANDALL		1871	William S PAGE
1836	Charles HAY		1872	Joseph LUCEY
1837	Charles J WHITE		1873	William T BOND
1838	John DREW		1874	Samuel WILLIAMS
1839	James J THOMPSON		1875	John D LEE
1840	John RAYMOND		1876	Richard CORY
1841	Thomas YOUNG		1877	John GAYWOOD
1842	William H HOBBS		1878	Thomas W ELLIOTT
1843	Francis FLOWER		1879	George WARD
1844	John ADDIS		1880	Richard PHILLIPPS
1845	John D BROWN		1881	William S HINTON
1846	Thomas GROVES		1882	Joseph J SMITH
1847	Richard ROBBINS		1883	Thomas R HUNTLEY
1848	William W LANDELL		1884	Thomas F WOOD
1849	Samuel POCOCK		1885	Thomas GARDNER
1850	Webster FLOCKTON		1886	John P DORMAY
1851	John NEWELL		1887	Robert GREY
1852	Clement PEACHE		1888	Robert GREY
1853	George COOPER		1889	Robert GAMMAN
1854	Charles LUCEY		1890	John R BERRY
1855	Henry GREY		1891	William BROMLEY
1856	Joseph TURNLEY		1892	Joseph LUCEY
1857	William A JOYCE		1893	Benjamin J JACOB
1858	Charles H THOMPSON		1894	Thomas JONES / Benjamin J JACOB
1859	William C RAYMOND		1895	Frederick C COLE
1860	William DOWNING		1896	Edward J GOLDSMITH
1861	Thomas WHITE		1897	Richard BRIDGE
1862	Thomas PILLOW		1898	William FLETCHER

1899	Arthur SALES	1938	Reginald R FRANCIS
1900	Arthur SALES	1939	Leonard J P BROWN
1901	Arthur SALES	1940	Harry ROGERS
1902	Harry KEEP	1941	Charles D ETHEREDGE
1903	Harry KEEP	1942	Charles D ETHEREDGE
1904	Richard DEERING	1943	Charles T BRAITHWAITE
1905	W Varco WILLIAMS	1944	Charles T BRAITHWAITE
1906	W Varco WILLIAMS	1945	Henry L COLLARD
1907	Sidney G MURRAY	1946	Henry L COLLARD
1908	Richard W EAST	1947	Edward J K GOLDSMITH
1909	Frederick PHILP	1948	Robert G WRIGHT
1910	Frederick PHILP	1949	Walter J B LINES
1911	Gilbert ALDER	1950	Sydney G WHITEHAIR
1912	Thomas W JACOBS	1951	Richard G ODELL
1913	James CLEMENTS	1952	Harry D HARDEE
1914	Edward A SPICER	1953	John B TAYLOR
1915	Gilbert ALDER	1954	Geoffrey A BROWN
1916	Edwin W TAYLOR	1955	Frank B LOCKET
1917	James CLEMENTS	1956	A Lawrence WILLIAMS
1918	Edward A SPICER	1957	Ian E PHILP
1919	John T STRATFORD	1958	Jack STRATFORD
1920	Edward J GOLDSMITH	1959	Sir Ralph METCALFE
1921	Leonard J P BROWN	1960	Frederick A SUDBURY
1922	Reginald JACOB	1961	Frederick A SUDBURY
1923	John T SCOULDING	1962	Frank B LOCKET
1924	William PEARCE	1963	H Percival ROBOTTOM
1925	Forrester CLAYTON	1964	Sir David H BURNETT
1926	Harry B HIGGS	1965	William H MARRIOTT
1927	Harry Jacob CATT	1966	A John PAGE
1928	William P BAILEY	1967	Alderman Sir Lionel DENNY
1929	Robert M BRYAN	1968	C P SHELBOURNE
1930	F Ainslie WILLIAMS	1969	Auriol S GASELEE
1931	Frank GARDNER	1970	H J GILMAN
1932	William L WRIGHTSON	1971	Robert M SARGENT
1933	Charles T PERFECT	1972	David S CLARABUT
1934	William COULTON	1973	K N WOODWARD-FISHER
1935	William C SCANLAN	1974	Geoffrey L COLLARD
1936	Reginald E PHILP	1975	Geoffrey E GARRETT
1937	Reginald R FRANCIS	1976	Malcolm R FRANCIS

1977	Ryan A CUNIS
1978	John CONSTANT
1979	T J Tertius METCALF
1980	S E Alan SPONG
1981	C P BRAITHWAITE
1982	Alderman Christopher RAWSON
1983	Alderman Christopher RAWSON
1984	Alec C CLARK-KENNEDY
1985	D J (Peter) PIPER
1986	Sir Geoffrey PEACOCK
1987	Robert G CROUCH
1988	Michael J TURK
1989	John G ADAMS
1990	H Graham MACK
1991	James G P CROWDEN
1992	Alan T WOODS
1993	Peter D T ROBERTS
1994	Julian K BADCOCK
1995	David ALLEN
1996	Captain Sir Malcolm EDGE
1997	Jeffrey JENKINSON MVO
1998	Christopher J LIVETT
1999	James G JOHNSON
2000	Lionel G BARROW
2001	Chas G NEWENS
2002	John S ALLAN
2003	Robert E LUPTON
2004	Sir Christopher BENSON
2005	Andrew HOWARD
2006	Brian WHEELER
2007	Kenneth V DWAN
2008	Richard S GODDARD
2009	David GORDON
2010	Duncan CLEGG
2011	Paul LUDWIG HMB
2012	John M REDMOND
2013	Robert A PRENTICE
2014	Jeremy D RANDALL

APPENDIX B – WINNERS OF DOGGETT'S COAT AND BADGE WAGER

YEAR	NAME	DISTRICT	YEAR	NAME	DISTRICT
1715	Opey John	Saviours Mill	1751	Earle J	Irongate
1716	Gullyford Edward	Westminster	1752	Hogden J	
1717	Church William	Saviours	1753	Sandiford N	Masons Stair
1718	Not known		1754	Marshall A	St. Saviours
1719	Dolby J	Rotherhithe	1755	Gill C	Old Swan
1720	Not known		1756	Not known	
1721	Gurney C	Foxhall	1757	White J	Putney
1722	Morris W	Rotherhithe	1758	Danby J	Christ Church
1723	Howard E	Capers or Cupids Bridge	1759	Clarke J	Blackfryers
			1760	Wood E	
1724	Not known		1761	Penner W	
1725	Not known		1762	Wood W	
1726	Barrow T	Sunbury	1763	Egglestone S	Pauls
1727	Not known		1764	Morris J	Horseferry
1728	Gibbs J	St. Mary Overy	1765	Egglestone R	St. Catherines
1729	Bean J	Steel Yard	1766	Not known	
1730	Broughton J	Hungerford	1767	Not known	
1731	Aliss J	Battersea	1768	Watson W	Westminster
1732	Adams R	Masons	1769	Not known	
1733	Swabey W	Whitehall	1770	Goddard T	Greenwich
1734	Bellows J	Black Lion	1771	Badman A	Queenhithe
1735	Watford H	Temple	1772	Briggs H	Somerset
1736	Hilliard W	Westminster	1773	Frogley J	Marigold
1737	Heaver J	Battersea	1774	Not known	
1738	Oakes J	King's Arms	1775	Not known	
1739	Harrington G	St. Saviours	1776	Price W	Mills
1740	Winch J	Whitefryers	1777	Pickering J	Greenhithe
1741	Roberts D	St. Mary Overy	1778	Pearson H J B	Lambeth
1742	Not known		1779	Boadington W	Brickwell Point
1743	Wood A		1780	Bradshaw J J	Pickle Herring
1744	Polton J	Marigold	1781	Reeves E	
1745	Blazdell J		1782	Truckle	Tower
1746	White J		1783	Bowler J	
1747	Joyner J	Beer Quay	1784	Davis J	Greenhithe
1748	Wagdon T	Whitefryers	1785	Not known	
1749	Hilden H	Mills Stairs	1786	Nash J	King's Stairs, Horseleydown
1750	Duncombe J	Blackfryers			

YEAR	NAME	DISTRICT	YEAR	NAME	DISTRICT
1787	Rawlinson B	Bankside	1825	Staple G	Battle-Bridge
1788	Radbourn T	Wandsworth	1826	Poett J	Bankside
1789	Curtis J		1827	Voss J	Fountain Stairs
1790	Byers		1828	Mallet A	Lambeth Stairs
1791	Easton T	Old Swan	1829	Stubbs S	Old Barge House
1792	Kettley J	Westminster	1830	Butler W	Vauxhall
1793	Haley A	Horsleydown	1831	Oliver R	Deptford
1794	Franklin J	Putney	1832	Waight R	Bankside
1795	Parry W	Hungerford	1833	Maynard G	Lambeth
1796	Thompson J	Wapping Old Stairs	1834	Tomlinson W	Whitehall
1797	Hill J	Bankside	1835	Dryson W	Kidney Stairs
1798	Williams T	Ratcliffe Cross	1836	Morris J	Horsleydown
1799	Dixon J	Paddington St.	1837	Harrison T	Bankside
1800	Burgoyne J	Blackfriars	1838	Bridge S	Kidney Stairs
1801	Curtis J	Queenhithe	1839	Goodrum T	Vauxhall Stairs
1802	Burne W	Limehouse	1840	Hawkins W	Kidney Stairs
1803	Flower J	Hungerford	1841	Moore R	Surrey Canal
1804	Gingle C	Temple	1842	Liddey J	Wandsworth
1805	Johnson T	Vauxhall	1843	Fry J	Kidney Stairs
1806	Goodwin J	Ratcliffe Cross	1844	Lett F	Lambeth
1807	Evans J A	Mill Stairs	1845	Cobb F	Greenwich
1808	Newell C	Battle-Bridge	1846	Wing J	Pimlico
1809	Jury F	Hermitage	1847	Ellis W	Westminster
1810	Smart J	Strand	1848	Ash J	Rotherhithe
1811	Thornton W	Hungerford	1849	Cole T Jnr	Chelsea
1812	May R	Westminster	1850	Campbell W	Westminster
1813	Farson R	Bankside	1851	Wigget G	Somer's Quay
1814	Harris R	Bankside	1852	Constable C	Lambeth
1815	Scott J	Bankside	1853	Finnis J R	Tower
1816	Senham T	Blackfriars	1854	Hemmings D	Bankside
1817	Robson J	Wapping Old Stairs	1855	White H J	Mill Stairs
1818	Nicholls W	Greenwich	1856	Everson G W	Greenwich
1819	Emery W	Hungerford	1857	White T C	Mill Stairs
1820	Hartley J	Strand	1858	Turner C J	Rotherhithe
1821	Cole T Snr	Chelsea	1859	Farrow C S	Mill Stairs
1822	Noulton W	Lambeth	1860	Phelps H J M	Fulham
1823	Butcher G T	Hungerford	1861	Short S	Bermondsey
1824	Fogo G	Battle-Bridge	1862	Messenger J	Cherry Garden Stairs

YEAR	NAME	DISTRICT	YEAR	NAME	DISTRICT
1863	Young T	Rotherhithe	1902	Odell R G	Lambeth
1864	Coombes D	Horsleydown	1903	Barry E	Brentford
1865	Wood J W	Mill Stairs	1904	Pizzey W A	Lambeth
1866	Iles A	Kew	1905	Silvester H	Hammersmith
1867	Maxwell H M	Custom House	1906	Brewer E L	Putney
1868	Egalton A	Blackwall	1907	Cook A T	Hammersmith
1869	Wright G	Bermondsey	1908	Graham J	Erith
1870	Harding R	Blackwall	1909	Luck G R	Erith
1871	Mackinney T J	Richmond	1910	Pocock R J	Eton
1872	Green T G	Hammersmith	1911	Woodward Fisher W J	Millwall
1873	Messum H G	Richmond	1912	Francis L E	Kingston
1874	Burwood R W	Wapping	1913	Gobbet G H J	Greenwich
1875	Phelps W	Putney	1914	Mason S G	Charlton
1876	Bullman C T	Shadwell	1915	West L P J	Wapping
1877	Tarryer J	Rotherhithe	1916	Pearce F W	Hammersmith
1878	Taylor T E	Hermitage Stairs	1917	Blackman J H	Gravesend
1879	Cordery H	Putney	1918	Gibbs A	Richmond
1880	Cobb W J	Putney	1919	Phelps H T	Putney
1881	Claridge G	Richmond	1920	Hayes H	Deptford
1882	Audsley H A	Waterloo	1921	Briggs A E	Ratcliffe Cross
1883	Lloyd J	Chelsea	1922	Phelps T J	Putney
1884	Phelps C	Putney	1923	Phelps R W	Putney
1885	Mackinney J	Richmond	1924	Green H C	Poplar
1886	Cole H	Deptford	1925	Barry H A	Barnes Bridge
1887	East W G	Isleworth	1926	Green T G M	Mortlake
1888	Harding C R	Chelsea	1927	Barry L B	Barnes
1889	Green G M	Barnes	1928	Phelps J L	Putney
1890	Sanson J T	Strand-on-the-Green	1929	Taylor C F	Blackwall
1891	Barry W A	Victoria Docks	1930	Phelps E A	Putney
1892	Webb G	Gravesend	1931	Harding T J	Putney
1893	Harding J Jnr	Chelsea	1932	Silvester H T	Hammersmith
1894	Pearce F	Hammersmith	1933	Phelps E L	Putney
1895	Gibson J H	Putney	1934	Smith H J	Gravesend
1896	Carter R J	Greenwich	1935	Gobbett A E	Blackwall
1897	Bullman T	Shadwell	1936	Taylor J A	Gravesend
1898	Carter A J	Greenwich	1937	Silvester W F	Hammersmith
1899	See J	Hammersmith	1938	Phelps E H	Putney
1900	Turffrey J J	Bankside	1939	Thomas D E	Dagenham
1901	Brewer A H	Putney	1940	Lupton E G	Northfleet

YEAR	NAME	DISTRICT	YEAR	NAME	DISTRICT
1941	Bowles G D	Isleworth	1980	Woodward-Fisher W R	Battersea
1942	Dott F	Erith	1981	Hickman W D	Poplar
1943	McGuinness E F	Greenwich	1982	Anness G B	Stratford
1944	Ambler F E	Twickenham	1983	Hickman P J	Charlton
1945	Thomas S	Dagenham	1984	McCarthy S J	Blackheath
1946	Amson J D	Northfleet	1985	Spencer R B	Rainham
1947	Palmer J V	Gravesend	1986	Woodward-Fisher C J	Battersea
1948	Clark H F	Ilford	1987	Spencer C	Rainham
1949	Dymott A H	Gravesend	1988	Hayes G A	Mottingham
1950	Palmer G J	Gravesend	1989	Humphrey R A	Greenwich
1951	Martin M A J	Upminster	1990	Collins S C	Bromley
1952	Green G E	Putney	1991	Neicho L C	Sevenoaks
1953	Bowles R E	Brentford	1992	McCarthy J J	Blackheath
1954	Everest K C	Hornchurch	1993	Clifford J D	Gravesend
1955	Goulding J T	Deptford	1994	Bullas C G	Gravesend
1956	Williams C	Deptford	1995	Neicho S M	Isle of Dogs
1957	Collins K C	Bermondsey	1996	Coleman R G	Ladywell
1958	Crouch R G	East Greenwich	1997	Russell M J	Gravesend
1959	Saunders G L	Erith	1998	Bushnell D J	Wargrave
1960	Easterling R W	Lee	1999	Woods T W	Wapping
1961	Usher K R	Limehouse	2000	Rickner B	Greenwich
1962	Dearsley C A	North Woolwich	2001	Beasley N T	Barking
1963	Allen D	Erith	2002	Dwan N R	Swanley
1964	Walker F F	Eltham	2003	Cairns L M G	Greenwich
1965	Collins A G	Bromley	2004	Dwan R E	Swanley
1966	Stent D	Eltham	2005	Dean J	A Dartford
1967	Briggs C M	East Ham	2006	Hunter R T	Stepney
1968	Lupton J E	Gravesend	2007	McGrane J F	Greenwich
1969	Grieves L E	Mile End	2008	Enever T J	Poplar
1970	Spencer M S	Greenwich	2009	Metcalf T	Royal Docks
1971	Dwan K V	Gravesend	2010	Arnold D J	Bromley
1972	Wilson P	Catford	2011	Anness C G	Whitechapel
1973	Prentice R A	Wapping	2012	Dwan M J	Stepney
1974	Lupton R E	Gravesend	2013	Brice N E	Greenwich
1975	Drury C M	Battersea	2014	McCarthy H J	Greenwich
1976	Prentice P	Wapping			
1977	Dwan J	Dartford			
1978	Macpherson A L	Poplar			
1979	Burwood F J	Plaistow			

Geoff C Adams

John S Allan

David Allen

Donald G Anderson

John S Anderson TD

Monsignor John J Armitage

Paul Baldwin

Graham I Barnard

Nicholas T Beasley

Sir Christopher Benson

Gina A Blair

Cliff J Blakeway

Mark Blandford Baker

Tony Braithwaite

Stephen W Burgess

L W L William Collard

Sean C Collins

Ronald M Collyer

Robert G Crouch MVO

Paul Deverell

John F Doble OBE

Kenneth V Dwan

Nicholas R Dwan

Capt Sir Malcolm Edge KCVO FNI

William D Everard

C A R Andrew Fenemore-Jones

Fabian J A Finlay

Richard G Fletcher

R T G George Franklin

John F Furlonger

Richard S Goddard

E L (Ted) Gradosielski

Greg Gregory-Jones

George Hammond

Sinéad Hayes

John Hedger

Ian D Henderson

Jonathan R B Hobbs

Robin A Hulf

Major Edwin Hunt MVO

David C P Hurley

E A (Ted) Jackson

Darren J A Knight

Brian S Lamden

Christopher J Livett

Paul R Ludwig HMB

Anthony J Lunch

Alderman Professor Michael Mainelli

Alan R W Marsh

Chris G Martin

A (Tony) Maynard

Benjamin R A McCann

Gordon P McCann

Simon J McCarthy

Dean J McGlinchey

Charlotte E Thompson-McGlinchey

Robert A Moore

Peter R Moulden

Richard Nemeth

Grp Capt David Packman RAF Rtd

The Late Raymond Painter

The Late Andrew Paterson

John R Potter

David U Powell

Ivan Pratt

Robert A Prentice

Jeremy D Randall

John M Redmond

John Redwood

Dr Iain Reid

Peter D T Roberts

W T (Bill) Robinson

John S E Salter HMW

Eric F Shawyer CBE FICS

The Late Nigel Smith

Dr Noel J C Snell

Richard Springford

N C (Nick) Stahl

John M Stratford

David E Thomas

W C (Tommy) Thomson

Richard George Turk

George W T Tutt

Giles E Vardey MA FSI

Major the Hon Andrew Wigram MVO

Michael A Woolf FRICS

Charles A Woollacott

Stephen Charles Woollacott

John Adams

Chris Aistrop

Peter L Albery

Simon Allen

Philip F Anschutz

Michael Baldwin

John D Barrett

Lionel G Barrow

Doug Benjafield

Andrew C Bourcier

John V Bartlett

Michael Braithwaite

Robert Braithwaite

Rosemary Braithwaite

Chris W Bright

Thomas William Carlaw

Mrs M P Churcher

Derek Coffey

Robert G Coleman

Daniel J Coleman

Martin S Spencer

William J W Courtney CBE

Paul Coxon MVO

Pete Crispin

Peter Crowley

William M Curtis

Michael Cutterham

Peter D S Dale

Bob Davis

Maldwin Drummond

J R R Ebsworth

London Rowing Club

M B D Helm

D V Melvin

Kenny Everest

Roger K Falconer

Len (Jack) Faram MBE

David Farnham

Peter Finch - River Thames Society

Lynne Ennis-Goatham

Alan Goatham

Daniel Goatham

Paul Goatham

Roy Goatham

Simon Alan Goodey

Ernest Edwin Harries

Ronald Edwin Harries

Keith Albert Harris

Peter Geoffrey Hill

Susan Rebecca Hort

John A Jupp

D C F Latham OBE

John Ledger

Jamie Locke

Jonathan Lynn

Paul E Mainds BEM

Colin C Middlemiss

David A Newcomb

Paddy Nicol

Richard Phelps

Annamarie Phelps

Maurice A Phelps

R C J Prentice

Robert Rakison

Lee Marriner

Carol Ratcliffe

Brian L Richardson

Hugh Richardson

Michael John Roche

Christopher Rodrigues CBE

Donald Rogers

George Saunders

David Suchet CBE

Mark Telfer

Mark Thomson

T C Upperdine

Peter James Weekes

Professor Alan Lee Williams OBE

Michael Williams

G J Wingfield

Thomas William Woods

Steve Wright

RIVER THAMES WHARF CHART No. 2. SHOWING

TOWER BRIDGE TO BLACKFRIARS

Half Nautical Mile

BLACKFRIARS TO VAUXHALL BRIDGE

Half Nautical Mile

Published by Imray, Laurie, Norie